The Independent Filmmaker's Guide to
Writing a Business Plan for Investors

The Independent Filmmaker's Guide to Writing a Business Plan for Investors

Gabriel Campisi

foreword by Fred Olen Ray

McFarland & Company, Inc., Publishers

Jefferson, North Carolina, and London

39.95

LIBRARY OF CONGRESS CATALOGUING-IN-PUBLICATION DATA

Campisi, Gabriel, 1968–
The independent filmmaker's guide to writing a
business plan for investors / Gabriel Campisi ;
foreword by Fred Olen Ray.
p.   cm.
Includes bibliographical references and index.

ISBN 0-7864-1682-3 (softcover : 50# alkaline paper)

1. Motion picture industry — Finance.   2. Independent filmmakers.
3. Business planning.   I. Title.
PN1993.5.A1C334   2004   384'.83 — dc22   2003023321

British Library cataloguing data are available

Cover image: ©2003 Comstock

Manufactured in the United States of America

*McFarland & Company, Inc., Publishers
Box 611, Jefferson, North Carolina 28640
www.mcfarlandpub.com*

Disclaimer

 skeletal format and basic content of any commercial business plan is for the
 rt universal. As with employment resumes, there are only a handful of accepted
 regardless of their individual content. As a result, the reader may sometimes
 ilarities between this book and others when it comes to certain examples and
 ns. Any such similarities are purely coincidental and unavoidable.
 present the theories behind a filmmaker's business plan, fictitious names of
 ers, production companies and motion pictures have been utilized in the sam-
 ess plan (Appendix A). Any resemblance to the names of actual persons, com-
 films is purely accidental and coincidental.
 e interviewees in Chapter 9 are, of course, real filmmakers, and the artwork scat-
 oughout chapters 2 through 8 represents actual films they have made.)
 iness plans are not legal and binding documents, and should not be construed
 In all instances of negotiating a financial deal with investors of any kind, an
 with experience in corporate, finance and entertainment matters should be
 d to further guide you in pursuit of attaining capital.
 Federal Securities and Exchange Commission (S.E.C.) has specific rules and reg-
 egarding matters of finance and of approaching investors. Readers should famil-
 mselves with these rules before initiating contact with potential investors.
 more information, contact the S.E.C. at:

S.E.C. Headquarters
450 Fifth Street, NW
Washington, DC 20549
(202) 942-7040
E-mail: help@sec.gov
Internet: http://www.sec.gov/

 uthor and publisher are not in the business of providing legal advice and assume
 y for incidental or consequential damages in connection with or arising out of
 the information contained within this book. Readers should not rely on this
 legal instrument or for professional legal counsel.

For Iliana, Aaron and

Th
most p
format
find sir
discuss
To
filmma
ple busi
panies o
(Th
tered th
Bu
as such.
attorne
employ
The
ulations
iarize th
For

The
no liabili
the use o
book as a

Contents

Acknowledgments

I must acknowledge a very special "thank you" to my dear friend and fellow filmmaker, Ron Ford, for suggesting I write this book — based on business plans I have used over the years to attract funding for client pictures — in the first place. If it were not for him, this book would not exist today.

Thank you to Kevin J. Lindenmuth, another fellow filmmaker and author, for paving the way with his own books and making me believe it could be done.

A special thank you to my dear friend and Hollywood agent-manager Sherry Robb for her constant blessings, insight and companionship. *Keep the light shining, Sherry!*

To my family in this crazy industry — Paul Fleck, Fritz Lieber, Pam L. Van Nest, Jeff Forsyth, Mike Strain, Sean Strebin, Eddie Aguglia, Victoria Hutchins, Brian McNeal, Paul Duran, Alex Aragonez, Julio Espinoza, Sam Osman, Jeff Rivera, Juan Juarez, Robert Escobar, Steven Silvas, Billy Karl, Willie Beauford, Brian Packer, Johnny Strader, Marvin Acuna and especially indie filmmakers Pat Kerby and Jay Nemeth — thank you for always believing in me and my career, and for inspiring me to do my best by perpetual example.

A special thank you to Lawrence Buck for being my soul-brother and guiding light in this business, and for all the late night brainstorming sessions at "CJ's."

Thank you to Jeffrey Hardy for allowing me to include printouts from his proprietary software in this book; to Mark Pacella for his wonderful artwork; to Fred Olen Ray for writing the foreword; to all the interviewees who appear in this book for enlightening and reminding me that we are constantly learning and digesting new information.

Thank you to Art Bell for keeping me company so often on the radio as I typed away deep into the abyss of many endless nights. *You will be missed, dear sir!*

And finally a blessed thank you to my beloved wife, Anje, for her undaunted support as I pursue my half-crazed dreams. There's no way I could do anything in this world without her by my side. Thank you to our wonderful children, Iliana and Aaron, for reminding me that every day is a good day — and a day to smile and laugh; to my brother Jim, for his constant patience and understanding; to my mother, for always being the realist that she is, providing strict guidance and making sure I keep both feet on the ground.

To God, *thank you for all your blessings.*

And lastly, I must say thank you to my father who is reading this from above. He always believed in my dreams and pushed me to reach for the heavens. All of my successes today I accomplish standing on his mighty shoulders. He always reminded me that we never fail until we quit trying. *Thank you, pops!*

Foreword
by Fred Olen Ray

I have always said that the two most difficult aspects of independent filmmaking were getting the money to make the film, and then getting the money back afterwards.

Making the movie is the easy part.

It's frustrating to approach people with the idea that they will place into your hands their hard-earned cash to make something as vaporous as a motion picture. What do you say when they ask you how much they can expect to earn for their investment? Or how long will it take to get their money back? Worse yet — how many other *successful* movies have you already made?

Well, you have to be honest and tell them that there are no guarantees and even if you get lucky, it could easily be two years from the time you start until you break even. They might also expect to earn a big zero return on their dollar.

Not very promising? You bet. Films do get made and do get distributed and some do make money, but given the odds, why in the world would anybody in their right mind trust you with their savings? Usually it's because they like you, or they have faith in you and want you to succeed. Some-

Fred Olen Ray, Retromedia Entertainment.

1

times the amount of money you are asking for is pretty small and people might be willing to take a risk in order to be involved in the movie business.

Business? That's right!

Regardless of how low your budget is you'd better treat it like what it really is—a bona fide business venture. If you don't, why should you expect anyone else to?

If you're hoping to interest investors in your project you must be prepared to show them that you have your financial act together. Forget whether you can make the world's greatest independent zombie-vampire-cheerleader film. What they really want to know is that you can handle the business end of things, and trust me—this is one area where almost every potential Roger Corman is weak. (Roger himself, however, has an amazing ability to mix business with art. That's why he's so wealthy. One eye is always on the checkbook.)

Using Gabriel's book to help you put forth a defined plan of attack is not only a wise move, but you'd be crazy not to take advantage of this concise guide.

You could quickly spend a great portion of your valuable time, not to mention copious attorney's fees, in preparing such a business plan from scratch when actually all you really want to do is start filming naked girls taking a shower together.

Follow this guide, create a sound business plan, secure that all-important venture capital, and then pretend you know what you're doing. Should work like a charm! And besides, who wouldn't want to see a movie about two girls taking a shower?

Fred Olen Ray is an independent filmmaker, having shot over 50 studio-independent films to date. He is the director of such classics as Stranded, Submerged, Critical Mass *and* Venomous.

Introduction

With money, you can call the very gods to help.
Without it, not a single man.

— Chinese Proverb

Banks, financiers and private investors did not get rich and powerful by giving their money away. It is no wonder, then, that independent filmmakers will almost unanimously agree the corporate and economics arena of financing and investments is by far the most challenging aspect in their pursuit of producing higher-budget, entertaining motion pictures.

Independent — or "indie"—filmmakers, by their very nature, are a creative bunch of individuals whose primary work-tools are their own imaginations and ingenuity. They are cinematic storytellers. As such, many of them consciously bypass the traditional route of approaching and negotiating with mainstream studios and television networks who can otherwise fully finance their creative endeavors. Most do not have the patience to put up with all the bureaucracy involved. They want to make their movies *now*. Others simply prefer to have more control over their projects.

Whatever reason they profess for making films on their own, all indie filmmakers, regardless of the movie's budget or the format they shoot it on, ultimately require the same bottom line: proper financing for the realization of their motion pictures. Without money, a movie can not possibly be produced, period. Cameras, lights, film or video stock, tripods and dollies, grip gear, food for the crew, fuel and transportation, wardrobe, scripts, props, sets, etc.— all things indigenous to the production of any motion picture — cost money. Now if you, as an indie filmmaker, have all the financing you require readily available, this book is not for you. You are well ahead of the rat race. Take your money and produce your picture. On the other hand, if you are an indie filmmaker or entrepreneur that is seeking capital to finance your project, read on.

In order for you as an indie filmmaker to merge your cinematic vision with a financial source to cover the cost of producing the project, you must make a leap from the world of imagination and storytelling to the arena of economics and investors. The world of finance normally consists of numbers, banks, loans, grants, equity investments, financiers, private investors, public investors, investor groups, investor angels, figures, projections and statistics, holding companies, contracts, attorneys, escrow accounts, strategy, market and industry analysis, and more often than not, the Federal Securities and Exchange Commission.

3

Gabriel Campisi, Starlight Pictures.

A far cry from the world of imagination and story-telling.

As an indie filmmaker, it becomes your job to effectively bridge the gap between these two very different worlds if you are to realize the production of your project. You must succeed in the world of finance if you are to obtain the necessary capital for producing your motion picture or pictures.

So how exactly does one go about doing this?

If you are looking for a few thousand dollars, you might get away with begging friends and family for donations. If you are seeking $10,000, $100,000, $1 million or perhaps even more — and you don't have a rich uncle in the oil business — you will ultimately be required to present yourself, your project and your investment plans to third-party financiers in a professional, accurate and meticulously concise manner for them to consider funding your movies. In essence, you will be presenting to them your *business plan*.

A business plan is like a road map that clearly shows your destination and what you must do to get there. It is like a blue print to building a house. It shows what the end-product should be, and it lays out specifically how to go about attaining it. Furthermore, it shows a common vision — one employed by all entities presently involved or to become involved in the realization of your motion picture. Keep in mind that a film does not get made by a single person. Rather, it gets made by a team of professionals, all working in unison like a well-oiled machine to reach a specific and common goal.

Imagine for one second a construction crew trying to build one house using ten different blueprints. Imagine a group of horses harnessed to a carriage, all fighting to go off in different directions. Imagine a football team in which every player was a wide receiver. These analogies might sound silly, but they are exactly the kind of scenarios that will develop if you try to garner financing, pull a team together and assemble a motion picture without a clear and concise strategy in place.

A business plan, if written and assembled properly, should answer every question a financier could conceivably ask in consideration of funding your project. *Who, what, when, where, why* and *how* — the answers to these questions are what will influence and contribute to the financier's decision on whether or not to take a chance with you and your film project. It is the answers to these same questions that will make up the entirety of your business plan. The concept behind writing a business plan is that simple. Answering the questions and committing them to a formal document in a professional and presentable manner, however, is not quite so easy.

Try, for example, to answer (convincingly!) some of these questions you may be faced with if and when given the chance to sit in the hot seat:

Who exactly are you? Why should I sit here and waste my time listening to anything you have to say?

Why should I invest in your motion picture project, when I can just as easily invest my money in that other filmmaker's project?

What is so special about your project and story? How is it any different from that other filmmaker's?

What kind of experience do you have? And how does that experience translate into anything viable for me to consider in taking a risk with you?

How do you plan on getting my money back, and ultimately making some money on top of the initial investment? Are you a banker? Are you an investment specialist? Then how do you profess to "know" what the results will be, and how can I even begin to trust you?

Tell me about the market for the film you propose. How exactly are you going to compete with all these other motion pictures, studios and distributors?

What kind of return do you expect, and how can you guarantee my stake in it?

Who will ultimately be held responsible for my money?

If you cannot answer these questions effectively, you can imagine what your chances of getting funding will be. If you can bat the answers back as quickly as the potential financier can pitch the questions, however, you may stand a chance of being seriously considered by the investor.

Now, in order to answer these very real questions demanded of indie filmmakers, one must take the time to do a lot of research, carefully consider and construct the appropriate answers, and then take the time to present them accurately and professionally so as to garner the trust and comradery of the financier. The purpose of this book is to guide you, in a very clear and concise manner, in answering these questions, and then show you how to go about assembling them in your own individual business plan suited to your own unique projects. This book will describe the theory behind every part of an independent filmmaker's business plan, and will feature a fictitious plan in the appendix for your perusal.

While eventually you will require formal contracts and documentation written by entertainment attorneys to enter into any kind of motion picture financial deal, a business plan is the first step you will require to get someone interested in your ventures and projects in order to proceed to the next level. In other words, a business plan will get the ball rolling. This goes for filmmakers just starting out as well as those already established. Investors want to know what your plans are, period. They want to see what you have in mind from a creative as well as a financial perspective.

You might ask one interesting question at this stage:

What if I am an established indie filmmaker and have already written, directed or produced another project that governed a lot of attention? Wouldn't that be enough to convince an investor to finance my next project?

It is possible, depending on the financier. More than likely, however, the answer is no. If you have produced an exciting prior film, it is a definite plus, will certainly contribute to your overall presentation and will augment the business plan greatly. All you have done, however, is proven you can make a movie. You have not proven you can invest someone else's money properly, manipulate it accordingly, recoup the investor's capital and turn a profit in today's aggressive motion picture marketplace.

An interesting thing to point out at this time is the change Hollywood is going through at this moment. The entire motion picture industry is changing before our very eyes with the saturation of cable and satellite television across the planet, creating so many potential outlets for so many projects.

The last decade in particular saw an unprecedented revolution in Hollywood as a whole. Major studios and networks accepted a new breed of product suppliers entering the mainstream arena and began doing business with them. These suppliers tended to be independent and unknown filmmakers and producers who offered cheaper but often more creative films financed by entities and sources outside the Hollywood system. Many production companies began to dedicate their resources to acquiring outside properties for distribution as opposed to producing their own fare.

So what began as a rare and unorthodox means of creating motion pictures has become part of the norm. From movie theaters and network television to video shelves and even cable and satellite entertainment, indie filmmakers and their movies are popping up everywhere. Independent films and their respective filmmakers are indeed becoming major players, and they are here to stay.

For indie filmmakers hoping to attract financiers to their projects, the timing could not be better. Investors have seen what independent filmmakers and production companies can do, and they are dumping millions and millions of dollars every year into the creation of these independent projects. It is my solid impression that motion picture investing is one of the best kept secrets in the world for those who have the money to do a little gambling. Where else could you potentially turn a half million dollar investment into several million dollars in returns in just a year or two?

Certainly there are those who will argue that no one can predict which movies will or will not be hits at the box office. I agree and disagree, however, because you do not necessarily need a runaway hit to have a successful project. Even a movie with mediocre box-office can return your investor's money many times over if the project's planned and executed properly. Not even Vegas offers such fabulous odds or the potential to score so big.

This book was written for those independent story-tellers and dreamers who have stayed up late into the wee hours of the morning, writing, shooting, editing, plotting and honing their craft with (alas) more ingenuity than cash — daring to take a chance with their projects and seek out their own financing to put their visions before the world. This book was written for the rule-breakers, the ones who refuse to take "no" for an answer. This book was written with great respect and admiration for the independent filmmaker.

1

Taking the Next Step

"Hooray for Hollywood!"
— Johnny Mercer (1909–1976)

DREAMS AND PLANS OF ACTION

Independent movies are as much a part of today's filmgoing experience as drive-ins were to the 1950s and '60s. Not all indie films, however, achieve the same level of success as others. With varying themes and budgets, many independent productions acquire little more status than that of an elaborate home movie.

But what about those movies that take film festivals by storm, acquire distribution deals, make sales to video outlets and cable television domestically and abroad? What about those indie filmmakers who move onto bigger projects and notoriety? Certainly luck and timing plays a role in most success stories, but many independent moviemakers have consciously taken the next step in pursuit of their dreams. They have carved out a clear cut plan of action or business plan for their projects and careers, analyzing and approaching them for what they truly are — a business.

The ensuing chapters will look at the business of filmmaking and present the theories behind underlying concepts that dictate which movies get made and which do not — and *why*. This book may not be an easy read, but it will spell out the prerequisites for you as an independent filmmaker to assemble before approaching a potential investor — saving his time as well as yours. Remember, in this business, first impressions are usually the last impressions. This means that you don't always get a second chance in Hollywood. So when you take a crack at something in this industry, it had better be a well-timed and educated move.

Chapters 2 through 8 of this book follow the outline of the fictitious business plan at the end of this book, each chapter covering one section of the plan. As you read through the book, you can flip to the business plan (Appendix A) to see how the ideas presented in each chapter are translated into the plan; conversely, when you're writing your own plan, you can flip back to the appropriate chapters anytime you need some help. Each of these chapters (2–8) offers general information on one section of the business plan, as well as more specific instructions under the heading "A Practical Guide."

As you read this book, you will also notice that at times some information may appear redundant. One chapter might speak at length about a particular element of the motion picture industry; then, in another chapter, the same topic might be brought up again. In most business plans the information in the various sections tends to overlap to some degree. You must keep in mind that almost all of the data and information in each segment of a business plan is interdependent with every other section. For example, all manners of marketing are indigenous to the industry of motion pictures, and they are also tied directly to distribution. Because of this, similar elements may be looked at more than once in subsequent chapters, but the information *is always scrutinized from distinct angles*— presenting seminal perspectives and theories that are necessary to comprehend the complexity of this elaborate enterprise.

One last thing to keep in mind as you read this book is the reference to investors and financiers. When I speak of persons that possess the potential to finance your projects, I am not talking about your rich uncle who owns a successful chain of pizza parlors across the country or a cousin who inherited millions from a dead relative in the perfume industry. I am talking about *complete strangers*— third parties with whom you have had little to no prior relationship. At best, your candidate is an acquaintance, such as your dentist or real estate agent.

But be cautious here. The word "stranger" is used liberally. Depending on the specific circumstances, you must be very careful about approaching a person that is entirely unacquainted with you. The Securities and Exchange Commission (S.E.C.) has very strict guidelines in place that govern this kind of activity, so you are advised to check your status accordingly. To approach a complete stranger might indicate a public offering. And to do so usually means you must register with the S.E.C.— a headache, I can assure you.

As for approaching family and friends for money, this is a specific subject I usually tend to steer away from. It is not my forte. Certainly I feel common sense will suggest you do not require such an elaborate manuscript to solicit money from them, but to be honest, think about it— perhaps a solid business plan is exactly what you need to obtain funds from your kin. Why should you treat people you know with any less respect than a complete stranger you hope will hand you millions?

I personally do not suggest taking money from friends and relatives, but movie producer Philip Cable actually made me stop and rethink this conviction in his enlightening interview in Chapter 9 of this book. His take on soliciting funds from friends and relatives is certainly sound and full of common sense.

POTENTIAL FINANCIAL SOURCES

If friends and relatives are out, and complete strangers are questionable, then who do you approach for financing? Filmmakers and producers ask me all the time to point them in the direction of potential investors. They want to know where the money is, and who exactly to contact.

The fundamental answer is everybody is a potential candidate. What it all comes down to is how you will set up your business and financing, and how much money you will actually require. Some investment deals require a minimum investment of x amount of money to participate in a limited partnership. So you have to ask yourself who can conceivably afford such an investment? Perhaps you only need $50,000 for your picture. You might be able to milk the cash out of your friends and relatives. But what if you require ten times that amount? Let's say, $500,000. You might decide your friends and relatives collectively do not possess that much in liquid assets. So now you have to line up third-party candidates, but you have to think about the best way to approach them — and how exactly you can do so without breaking the law. Perhaps you will find registering with the S.E.C. to solicit public funds is your preference. That is perfectly fine.

You might try approaching people that you have met on occasion, such as doctors or attorneys or real estate brokers and investors— people you feel might possess substantial capital. They in turn may be able to turn you onto other prospects. What I personally suggest you do, however, is approach an investment specialist, preferably one that specializes in motion picture financing. What these entities do is line up prospective investors, persons who have already expressed their willingness and desire to fund motion picture productions. This is probably one of the safest ways to proceed. If you live in a large city, all you have to do is open your phone book and you should find several investment specialists that can help you directly, or point you in the right direction. The Internet is another excellent source for finding potential investors. Go to any major search engine and type the words, "Film Investors." You will be surprised at the results you receive.

The bottom line is that you must put your time in, speak with people, ask questions, and network with all potential parties. I have several groups of private investors I know personally that came about as a result of *years* of networking and doing business together in motion pictures and other commercial ventures. I did not meet these entities overnight, and I did not gain their respect immediately.

Always check with the S.E.C. on who you can approach and who you can not. I can not stress this enough.

LENGTH OF PRESENTATION

Every experienced filmmaker or producer I have ever spoken with — including those I interviewed in Chapter 9 of this book — respectfully disagree on what the proper length of a successful business plan should be. Some will argue a three-page document will suffice, while some will tell you that you need to throw everything in the manuscript including the screenplay, complete budget breakdown, letters of interest and commitment, actor head-shots, distribution agreements, and heck, the kitchen sink and a toaster oven just to be safe.

In the end, it is strictly up to you how long your document will be, and what exactly you will include in it. But for now, let me present to you some common sense:

If your business plan is too short, you will not have included enough information to convince anybody of anything except that you were too lazy to do your research and get them all the proper information. Financial candidates will not gain enough information to make a decision as to whether or not they should take a chance with your project. And this usually means they will turn you down.

On the other hand, if your business plan is too long, you will have over abundant information and you may bore or overwhelm your potential investor with it. This is not a good idea, either, as the investor may gloss right over the really important things and major selling points of your business plan. Investors usually hand such thick documents over to their advisors, attorneys and accountants to make a decision for them. This informality usually results in a pass on your project.

One of the Asylum's most successful projects, *The Source* helped take producers David Michael Latt and David Rimawi into the mainstream.

What you want to accomplish with your business plan, then, is to have it implant the necessary knowledge in a potential investor so that he or she may decide to write you a check for the necessary capital to produce your projects. The only way to impart this kind of knowledge is by presenting information. So you must strike a careful balance to present just enough information to get the job done, but not too much that it drowns or distorts the intended effect.

One last thing to keep in mind with this topic: *you will never satisfy everyone*. You might find some potential investors praise you for a job well done on your to-the-point business plan, and others that will berate you for making them look through so much material.

The bottom line: I suggest your business plan runs between 40 and 60 pages. No more. No less.

COSMETICS AND APPEARANCE

When you've finally compiled all your information for your business plan, you will want to present it in a manner that is pleasing to the eye and professional. You might want to get creative and use color or artwork on your cover, but I do not recommend it. I suggest you simply put the title of your company or project on the cover, with your name and contact information, and perhaps a logo or some other form of minute artwork. The page should be black and white. Plain and simple.

If you decide to get colorful or artistic, that is fine. It is your choice. There is no right or wrong. But just be aware that potential investors will react accordingly to your presentation. If you want to appear professional, a black and white document, spiral bound, will suffice. Depending on the circumstances, who the investor is, and what your project is all about, you might find a colorful unorthodox presentation will work better to get their attention.

I also highly recommend you use photographs (head-shots) of your production team in the Company section of your business plan. When potential investors read your document, they will be inundated with facts and figures and information. All of this makes it very easy for them to forget just exactly who they're dealing with. By including the photographs, you will be instilling a level of humanity into your manuscript and reminding them that they'll actually be taking a chance with human beings as opposed to just a bunch of data.

LET'S GET REAL

I remember taking a lunch meeting in Los Angeles about a year ago with a gentleman who claimed he had a can't-lose project. All he needed was $2 million, and everyone would become rich by the end of the year. I agreed to look at the material, and when I remarked it was a high risk venture like any other motion picture project, the gentleman snapped that he was only interested in someone who could slam dunk his project and get him the $2 million, no questions asked. I explained to him that was impossible. I explained I was not the financier myself, and I could not speak for my contacts. I had no way of knowing if they would choose to pursue his project — if I even allowed it to get that far.

The gentleman angrily went on to explain to me how safe his venture was. He explained there was no way it could lose money. There was no way it could make anything less than $20 million by the end of the year. My response to him was that if his project was so safe, he should take it to a bank to get a loan rather than seek an equity investment as he was doing. Banks go for safe commercial projects, and are eager to get their share of the cash pie. And besides, the gentleman should have no problem paying back $2 million to the bank within a year since, as he stated, he would make no less than $20 million.

It's about one year later as of this writing and I have it on good authority that not one person, not one bank, has financed this individual's safe motion picture project.

I know another indie filmmaker who had a certain mentality when it came to investors. His attitude was, "It's my way or the highway." He repeated it all the time. Guess what? Investors everywhere told him to hit the highway.

And I know yet another oh-so-bright indie filmmaker who called a group of investors considering financing his project and gave them a rather rude and unexpected two-week deadline. The investors who originally took an interest in the project told the filmmaker to promptly retrieve his package. They had no more interest in him or his movies.

Why is it so important for me to relay these encounters to you? Because I want you to realize exactly where you are on the chess board when it comes to playing this game of finance. I want you to realize where you stand in the scheme of things when you step in the lion's arena and ask for someone to hand over their hard-earned cash.

It's okay for you as an indie filmmaker to be passionate about your project and believe it will make millions. In fact, it's a prerequisite — you *must believe* in yourself and your abilities or no one else will. But being confident is not an excuse for you to be self-aggrandizing and ungracious. Confidence is a paramount trait, and it is reassuring to potential financiers. Arrogance, on the other hand, is a slap in the face, and there is just no excuse for it.

The arrogant filmmakers above may someday attain the financing necessary for their projects. In the interim, I assure you they are learning many serious lessons the hard way. Investors must carefully weigh 101 variables when deciding the best way to handle your project, and whether or not it is in their best interest to take a chance with you. Imposing grandiose restrictions or expectations on them will only hamper your best efforts.

So proceed with confidence, but be real. Don't be overconfident and believe investors will throw money at you just because you believe you've got the greatest motion picture project since *Gone with the Wind*. They won't. It's okay to believe your project will make millions, but you have to realize all indie filmmakers believe the same thing. Your convictions are nothing new. It's how you deal with them and present them that counts.

Bottom line: the investors already have the money. They don't need you. Conduct yourself accordingly.

2

The Executive Summary

"The last thing that we discover in writing a book is to know what to put at the beginning."

— Blaise Pascal (1623–1662)

FIRST IMPRESSIONS

You can't judge a book by its cover is a well-worn cliché, and for the most part it is a true statement. Until you immerse yourself in the reading and theme and adventure of a book, you never truly know what it is all about. In the case of a business plan, however, the opposite may be true.

The Executive Summary is the first part of the business plan looked at by interested parties, and it is in many ways like the cover of a book. It is the window to the rest of the manuscript. It is just what the name implies—a summary of what is contained within. It is what will make the potential investor and reader decide whether or not to pick up the book and read the rest of it.

Because of this reason, the Executive Summary is perhaps the most delicate part of the business plan you will have to write. From it, prospective investors will gain their first impressions of you and your team, your projects, your knowledge of the industry and market potential, and of course your financial strategies. In many cases, the Executive Summary is the sole section interested parties will read before deciding whether or not to peruse the rest of your presentation.

As fragile and important as this section is, it is also the shortest in length because it is a summary of the rest of the book. And as short as it is, it is also perhaps the most difficult to write. And although it is the first section of the business plan, it should be written last.

Allow me to explain.

The Executive Summary provides a very brief summary of each section in the business plan. This is no simple task. Each individual section of your business plan will be elaborate and extensive. For the Executive Summary, you must modify each section to fit briefly in just a few paragraphs or sentences. And therein lies the challenge. You must decide which key elements must be mentioned, what can viably be left out, and how to go about making it all sound exciting and interesting enough to warrant further reading.

If you make this section too long, it will make the rest of the business plan appear redundant. If you make it too short, it will appear to lack substance. As you assemble your business plan, you must strike a careful balance between the two opposites. A general rule to keep in mind here is that the Executive Summary should be approximately 15 percent of the rest of the manuscript. If your business plan is 50 or 100 pages in length, your Executive Summary should be no more than 7.5 or 15 pages in length, respectively.

With this in mind, you see why this section must be so short in length and why it must be written last. You can *not* summarize that which you have not yet written. And in this case, it is the entire business plan itself.

What I have done in many cases, however, is write a rough draft or outline of the Executive Summary and utilize it as a guide for what the rest of the plan will contain. If you choose to write the Executive Summary before the rest of the manuscript, keep in mind you will more than likely have to return later to rewrite it to match your completed document.

A Practical Guide

For the rest of this chapter, you are encouraged to follow along with the fictitious indie business plan at the end of this book. This section is written in direct correlation with the business plan, explaining in detail what is written there and why.

Business Philosophy

Ask yourself a simple question. *Why do you wish to make motion pictures,* and better still— *why are you and your group attempting to attain financing?* While at first glance these questions may seem mundane, you have to realize investors expect rhetorical responses to the simplest inquiry. You might think, "Well, gee, it's pretty obvious we're looking for money because we want to make movies and make more money," right? The truth is, so are thousands of other people just like you. So your answer in this case would come across as trivial and command little respect. It does not distinguish you from other indie filmmakers and sounds unprofessional. The part about making money is redundantly implied from the mere fact that any motion picture investment venture exists to ultimately do one thing — make money.

Instead, you should mention what kind of movies you wish to produce and why you think they will fare well at the box- office — and what qualifies you and your group to make them. You should include a unique attribute your group possesses to pique everyone's interest. You might have a well-known film star as part of your group, or an award-winning writer, or a successful cinematographer. Or you might have smaller credentials, but powerful nonetheless: perhaps you have published several short stories in small press magazines, or received awards for writing at the school newspaper. Perhaps you starred in several high school or college plays, and received good reviews from the local media. Mention these facts. They are great selling points, and they are what will distinguish you from the rest of the pack.

Now take your response in its purest form and mold a Vision or Mission Statement around it that third parties can relate to and easily comprehend. This is the very first thing you will include in the Executive Summary. To try to forge an intelligent and inspiring statement here can be deceiving — it is not as simple as it appears. To assist you, you might want to ask yourself further, *Why have you formed your company? What are your long term goals? What is the reason for your group's existence?* Compare the statement in the fictitious indie business plan with your own thoughts. Put together a few sentences that describe what your hopes, plans and goals are, but support your statement with sound financial or business substance. Common sense should apply here. Your comments and words should be professional, ambitious, polished and straightforward.

Keep in mind that everyone's Business Philosophy or Mission Statement is special and should reflect the distinctiveness of the individual group. A major goal when you write your business plan is to set yourself apart from other filmmakers or production companies. Always stress your uniqueness. I can not emphasize this enough.

Overview of the Company

For this header, the legal entity of you or your group should be identified. Is your group a corporation, sole proprietorship, limited liability company or something else? Perhaps you have not yet thought about this or have not yet committed yourself to a formal entity. Whatever you ultimately decide, you will need to make this choice on your own or get advice from legal or accounting counsel. The purpose of this book is not to influence your legal and financial options. Rather, it assumes you have previously thought out your alternatives wisely and intelligently, and will assist you in presenting them within the context of your business plan. Different company setups are preferred by different persons, so there is no right or wrong answer here. It is all a matter of preference and suitability.

Some independent filmmakers leave this option open until financing is in place, or about to be. Investors want to know what they're getting themselves into from the very start, so be straight-forward with them. Leaving this option open is acceptable, as long as you mention it clearly. If they have to guess or are uncertain, they may move on to the next business plan on their desk. Here is an example of what you may want to write in lieu of choosing a business structure at this time:

> *The producers of FireGem Entertainment will set up the company once investors have agreed to put up the capital or financing is in place. The producers are leaving the legal business structure open so that all parties can negotiate the most mutually beneficial form.*

Here you should also state what the function and purpose of your company will be. This is similar to the statement under Business Philosophy above, but it is more simple and straightforward. It is mostly universal for most filmmakers and production companies. "FireGem Entertainment is a film company engaged in the development and production of motion pictures for worldwide theatrical, video and television distribution." Simple enough.

Mention something about the motion picture market and how your company and films will fit in this market. Perhaps you or your company have discovered a niche to fill. Or you will stick with current trends that are proven sellers. Elaborate in one or two sentences.

You should be aware that everything you state here and in the rest of your plan can readily be verified by any potential investor that conducts a simple inquiry. This means you should do plenty of research and never base your business or financial support of your decisions on thoughts of the heart. All material and all claims you make should be derived from factual information. There is an abundance of trade magazines and periodicals that keep tabs on all this data. You can begin your quest by checking the very popular *Hollywood Reporter* and *Variety* newspapers. You can enlist the services of companies like *Baseline* or *Big Horse* (see Resources). Go to the library and ask for books and material on the motion picture industry. Surf the Internet by typing "motion picture industry" in a search engine. You will be surprised at all the industry and market information you can easily obtain.

I will elaborate more on these disparate subjects in their respective chapters.

Lastly, you should specify what type of films and how many you plan on making, in approximately what time frame they will be completed, and with what budget or budgets. This will immediately give potential investors the bottom line on what will be asked of them and over how long a period. You might want to write the business plan for a single film, or you may choose to do it for a set of films as well as your company itself. Some filmmakers leave this option open, as well. Whatever you decide, write it here and include the projected budget or budgets.

The Managers and Executive Staff

This header is pretty straight-forward. Who makes up the managers and supervisors of your group? Who is in charge of what? Begin by naming yourself, followed by the immediate members of your company. If you have attorneys, agents, managers, or other immediate faculty that offer outside support, you should name them here as well.

A company is an entity comprised of living, breathing human beings. Investors want to see who they are entrusting their hard-earned finances to. You can have all the fancy numbers and graphics and dramatic presentations in your business plan that you want, but once all the smoke clears it all comes down to one thing: *people.* Investors want to know who you and your associates are, and they want to know as much about all of you as possible. The details will come later; for the Executive Summary, names and titles will suffice.

If for whatever reason you do not have a team in place, now is the time to get one. In the introduction I mentioned that making movies is a team effort. I cannot think of anyone that would argue this fact with me. And I cannot think of any investment opportunity where the financier would hand a check over to a single person.

There is an abundance of critical and different responsibilities involved when handling a financial investment, dispersing that investment appropriately, creating an entertaining motion picture, and seeing the entire project through to completion, distribution and subsequently a financial return. Specific individuals must be in charge of specific duties, and these individuals had better be prepared to handle the tasks at hand. It is these people that make up your team.

When you have your team assembled, begin the list by stating the strength of the group in general. What do the members have in common beside the common goal of making motion pictures? Are they active businessmen or successful entrepreneurs? Former or active motion picture technicians or executives? Provide the names of the individuals in sequential subordinate order. Be sure to separate your immediate team from your support team and outside contractors.

The Movie Projects

This header directly links your potential investors to the creative end of the business—your movies. Here, you should provide the specific titles of the screenplays you desire to produce, as well as the legal specifics. State who wrote the screenplays, what genre they represent, and which rights you own or plan to obtain—theatrical rights, all rights, option rights, television rights, etc. Perhaps you are presently in the process of polishing the script or you are finalizing a contract with another writer. Whatever status your screenplays hold at this time, here is where you should disclose a quick summary of pertinent information.

For the fictitious indie business plan at the end of this book, I included a collection of screenplays controlled by the fictitious movie company. There is a specific reason for this. If you have just one film project in mind for investors, then by all means highlight that one property only. If you are trying to pitch your company as a whole or more than one movie project, however, it is often a good idea to present a collection of scripts you either own or plan to control. This actually gives interested parties more to get excited about, and in many cases more to base their decisions on. You may even be surprised to find an investor choose a secondary project you had in mind as opposed to the first one you planned on producing. In other words, while you might have planned to produce Script X, the investor might have looked over your collection of scripts and decided to make an investment based on Script Y.

As tempted as you may be to visually pitch your scripts in the Executive Summary, you should refrain from doing so. You will have the opportunity to elaborate on your film projects in their respective section of the business plan, complete with sketches and artwork.

For this section, the most you should state is what genres your projects belong to. Are they family films, dramatic films, perhaps science-fiction or horror? Maybe they are a combination of action and comedy, or westerns. Think about your projects and ask yourself if you feel they would be considered mainstream fare or not. Give a quick comparison of the projects you propose with previously-produced projects. Are they comparable to blockbuster films, sleeper hits, or perhaps critically-acclaimed independent movies?

Lastly, you should try to round out the summary of your film projects by citing a quick reason why you chose your specific projects. The reason should be financially sound, enticing potential investors to want to invest in your projects despite the genre or choice of subject matter. An example of this would be to cite the strength of your type of films at the box office, home video, cable television, or in foreign markets.

As important as the descriptions of your film projects are, investors are always more interested in knowing how well they will perform financially.

The Movie Industry

For this header, you should summarize the bare facts of the industry—and little else. What are the latest box-office grosses, domestic and worldwide, for the motion picture industry? What is the immediate forecast—will the industry rise or fall? How is the industry segmented for independent motion pictures or your particular genre, and how do your film projects fit in this arena?

Beside movie theaters, there is the home video market and cable television, as well as pay-per-view and regular television. There are also other industry outlets that may or may not come later, depending on the success of your project — including merchandising. All of these markets are a part of the industry and should be touched on. How much are they worth? Is their value growing or shrinking?

If you plan on making films that go directly to a particular partition of the industry — such as the home video market or cable television — you should comment on this as well as present facts and figures from this part of the industry. These facts and figures constantly change from year to year. As ticket prices rise, technology changes, and economic situations fluctuate all over the world, the industry reacts accordingly. To accurately report on present industry trends, then, you must do extensive research and get the latest figures.

Finally, convey your reasoning or confidence on how you and your company plan on taking advantage of the industry in order to get your share of the cash pie. What trends will you keep an eye on? What trends will you engage?

The Movie Market

Many independent filmmakers that are not fluent with the business end of their craft confuse the industry of motion pictures with the actual market. The industry encompasses the sum of all motion picture endeavors necessary to conceptualize, finance, produce and distribute a movie. Motion picture studios, independent filmmakers, financial experts, banks, screenwriting software and classes, film school, cameras, acting classes and talent agencies, movie theaters, distributors, advertising, popcorn and soda pop, home video, cable and pay-per-view, etc. — all of these very disparate elements and more lie within the context of the same business or commerce: the motion picture industry. This is regardless of the genre or subject matter of the films, how they get made or distributed, or how much they cost to make.

The market of motion pictures is the distinct choice of genre and elements your films will be based on, where and how they may be promoted and sold, and to whom. Demographics play a paramount role in the market of motion pictures. Science-fiction, fantasy, horror, action, adventure, comedy, drama, romantic, westerns, etc. — these are all particular markets which your movies can cater to. This marketing is based within the industry of motion pictures.

The individual foreign territories you sell your movies to are markets as well. You can break it all down to continents or individual countries. With the larger distributors, it is usually broken down to simply two markets: domestic (United States, Canada and sometimes Mexico), and foreign (all other countries). Yet another partition of the motion picture market is the way the film was produced. Studio, independent, high-budget, low-budget, domestic, foreign, direct-to-video, etc. — these, too, are distinct markets in that they are produced differently and are promoted and distributed to the masses in dissimilar fashions and with different sources of financing, advertising and support. Certain audiences, or demographics, actually take special interest in these specific types of movies. I know several people, for example, that make it a point of collecting all the independent movies they can possibly find on DVD, regardless of their genre, subject matter or budget.

The leading demographic, of course, has always been the mainstream audience — lured to the movie theater by mainstream advertising and propaganda. Most of us find ourselves in this category.

For this header, you should state how well your choice of genre presently performs at the box office. Is the public seeing a lot of films similar to the ones you propose to produce? How do your films compare to what the major and independent studios are currently developing for the immediate future? Are you in line with the present fad? Are you going against the grain or trying something risque?

If your business plan calls for the production of one film project, then mention it here like you did under the Movie Projects header. If you propose more than one motion picture, then mention your proposed *first* project. How does this project fit in specifically with all the data mentioned above?

Lastly, do a blanket statement about your market in general. List specific successful motion pictures that are comparable to your project. This will give your potential investors confidence that the projects you propose will make money since similar projects are already raking in the dough.

Movie Distribution

It is every filmmaker's desire to have a distribution deal in place before attaining financing or shooting their film. More often than not, this desire is wishful thinking. But there are exceptions, and it has indeed happened more than once.

A bona fide distributor will rarely give a distribution deal to a new and unproven independent filmmaker or production company *before* the movie is made. The more accepted route to attaining distribution is to simply shoot the best possible motion picture, then based on the sheer genius of the project, find an indie or studio distributor to pick it up. There are many ways to do this, including showcasing the finished project at film festivals across the world and self-distribution.

The subject of distribution is complex, and I will elaborate more on this topic in its respective chapter.

Whatever you have in place or decide to do with distribution, you should put it here. Do not play games or be evasive if you have not yet secured such a deal. Simply state the truth. "FireGem Entertainment will seek distribution after the completion of its first project," is a legitimate statement and works just fine. If you lie here or anywhere else in the business plan, you could be setting yourself up for a hard fall.

The Investor's Plan

This header is what the entire business plan comes down to:
How much money do you want?
State the exact amount of financing you are seeking from your potential investors and exactly what the money will be used for. It may sound redundant, but mention what film or group of films the money will be applied to.

You should also summarize the kind of deal you have in mind for you and your investors. The options here are boundless and complex. Like in the Overview header, whatever you ultimately decide, you will need to make this choice on your own or get advice from legal or accounting counsel. Again, the purpose of this book is not to influence your legal or financial options.

I personally suggest you leave this section open. If you present an investment scenario, you may be presenting yourself right out of financing. Financiers may be looking for a deal unlike the one you are offering. Your potential investor could turn you down simply because he is not interested in the way you are proposing to do business. However, if you leave the investment prospectus open, both sides can endlessly discuss the possibilities, eventually arriving at a mutually acceptable deal.

Lastly, give a projection of when investors can potentially start to see a return on their investment.

REMEMBER

The Executive Summary should be written last because it summarizes the rest of the business plan. In order to do that, you must write the business plan first. By the same token, you can write a rough draft Executive Summary and utilize it as a guide or outline as you write the rest of your document.

3

The Production Company

"Choose a job you love, and you will never have to work a day in your life."
— Confucius (551?–479? B.C.)

WHO'S IN CHARGE?

Making movies is a dedicated team effort, with a common vision where all players strive toward the same goal. Each member must work in cooperation with all other members—from the inception and development of the project, to its production and subsequent distribution. This means that all persons involved—from the writer and director to the production coordinator, hair stylist and even the camera assistant — must be wiling to cooperate, follow a chain of command, and perform accordingly if the realization of a motion picture production is to be successful. Otherwise, a company may wind up with a complete technical and financial disaster on their hands rather than a viable movie.

Imagine for a moment a group of people on a drifting raft in the middle of an ocean, all of them with paddles. Now imagine all of them bickering and trying to paddle in different directions. Don't think for one second that this has not happened before in Hollywood. It has come to pass more than most studios or independent producers wish to acknowledge. I don't need to tell you there is an abundance of egotism in the motion picture industry. This ego has gotten in the way of the production of more than one movie over the years— sometimes, luckily, with little to no negative effect on the finished product. Other times with disastrous results. But that's another story and another book altogether.

For now, all you need to worry about is the fact that when all is said and done, financiers will be investing their capital in people as opposed to ideas. It does not matter how wonderful your scripts are, or how precisely you have put a grasp on the industry or market, or how well connected you are to a distributor. Unless investors can gain confidence in you and your business associates as reliable and honest producers who will carry out the task of doing what you claim you will do with their money, you will never see a cent from them.

So who is in charge, then? The partners, managers and executive staff, that's who. These are the people at the top of the food chain. They are the ones who will supervise all activities. And they are the ones who will answer to the investors. They, in effect, are the production company.

As you assemble your production team, be sure everyone is aware of the genre of motion pictures you will be producing. *Knights of Justice* by Philip R. Cable, for instance, was a very successful children's production because of the dedication of the assembled staff.

Although you will more than likely initially attract an investor's attention to your project with other factors, such as your track record, your awards and notoriety, or your conceptual artwork and screenplay, investors will ultimately want to know:

- Who will write or polish the wonderful script?
- Who will supervise pre-production?
- Who will produce the movie?
- Who will direct it?
- Who will star in it?
- Who will manage their money?
- Who will manage the company?
- Who will answer to the investors?
- Who will perform the accounting?
- Who will market and distribute the picture?

Investors want to be convinced that everyone will work toward the same goal, and that everyone has the experience and determination to make it so. They want to see leadership, and they want to see loyalty and commitment. More than anything, investors must believe in the human factor of your business plan. They must believe in *you*. This section of your manuscript — *The Production Company* — is where you will strive to convince them to do just that.

THE HUMAN FACTOR

All businesses, regardless of their product, have one common denominator: people. It is people who will perform all the duties listed in your business plan. It is people who will ultimately be responsible for the failure or success of your projects. And it is people who will handle the financing for the production of your movie. For this reason, this section of the business plan is probably more important than all the remaining parts of the manuscript combined. Here you will introduce yourselves, you will proclaim your experience, and you will toot your horns. In the Executive Summary you listed only the names and titles of your managers and staff. In this section, you will go in-depth into everybody's backgrounds. You will also state your company's legal identity in more detail, your common goals and visions, and your reasons for the decisions you have made.

Whether you already have your production team or company in place, or if you're just now bringing them together, there is one thing you should think about before writing this section of your business plan:

- What positions are required for a viable motion picture team of producers?

Compare your team of producers — the team you will be presenting to your investors, as well as entrust to bring to fruition a dramatic motion picture — to a team of professional football players. In order to play football, you require specific players. No more. No less. You can only have one quarter-back to throw the ball. You can only have a select number of players to catch the ball. And you can only have a select number of players to block or rush the opposing team.

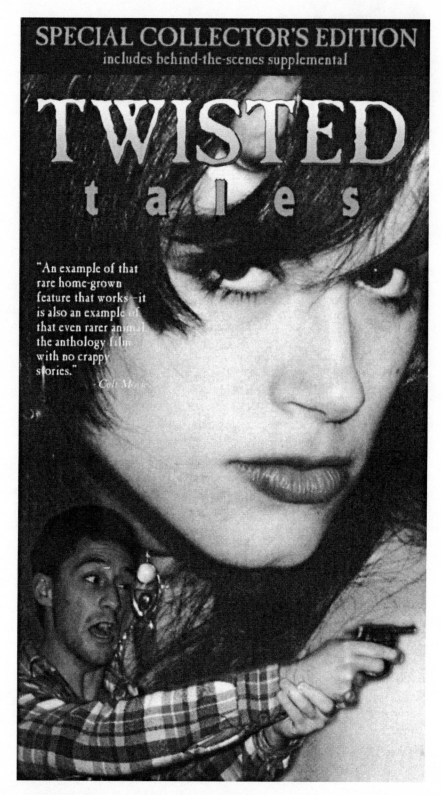

SPECIAL COLLECTOR'S EDITION
includes behind-the-scenes supplemental

TWISTED
tales

"An example of that
rare home-grown
feature that works—it
is also an example of
that even rarer animal
the anthology film
with no crappy
stories."
— Colt M...

Kevin Lindenmuth's *Twisted Tales* summed up the choice of genre his company would be producing throughout the years. Science fiction, fantasy, and horror with twists and turns continue to attract
both fans and collaborators to Brimstone Productions.

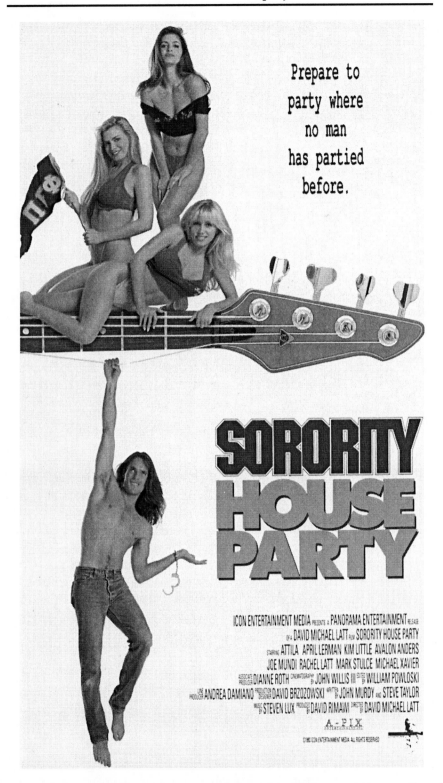

One of the many things a startup company must do is agree on what genre of films it will produce. The Asylum tackled a popular niche with its teenage sex comedy, *Sorority House Party*.

Now imagine the same football team with three quarter-backs to throw the ball. Or with no wide receivers. A team like this will never win, will never prosper.

And so it is with your team of producers or management team. You must have specific people in place to handle specific duties. No more. No less. Before you assemble your team, ask yourself what positions are strictly required and essential, and which are redundant. Do you know people capable of performing all the necessary tasks at hand? Or will you have to search long and hard for able bodies? Do you have too many people in charge of one specific job, and not enough handling another? Figure out who's who, then try to imagine your company as a well-oiled machine, full of muscle and void of fat.

Your management team should loosely consist of at least the following:

• *A creative entity*, often the general partner or CEO of the company (writer or director)

• *An executive producer* (the main force that encourages and oversees the entire project, from creation to financing to production)

• *A financial executive* (handles all matters of finance and accounting and legalities associated within the structure of the company)

• *A development executive* (works directly with the creative entity of the company to handle creative elements for the project)

• *A production executive* (handles the direct hands-on production logistics of the project)

There can be more than one person attributed to each department, and some titles can be shared. Of course you can add more titles not listed here, such as a film editor or cinematographer or production coordinator. You can bring along anybody you want on your management team, but the ones I have listed are the bare minimum titles that investors will want to see before entrusting their hard-earned cash to you.

It is true that a very creative and determined individual can possess all these titles. If you think you are that person, all the more power to you and I wish you the best of luck. However, take my word for it: No investor will consider a one-person management team a viable investment opportunity.

Even if you possess abundant knowledge or experience in all the arenas I have mentioned above, a movie production will nevertheless contain too much responsibility for just one person to handle alone. And if the production is so small that one person could conceivably handle all the logistics, chances are the investment potential would be too small to interest serious investors.

So get your team together now, if you haven't already done so. Remember that investors will ultimately commit their finances to the *people* involved in your project.

Necessary Elements

Let's take a quick look at the positions necessary for your company and compare them to the grand scheme of things:

• A creative entity, usually the general partner or CEO of the company (writer or director)

In order to produce a movie, you need a movie to produce. Simple, right? You can't move on without the blueprint of any motion picture endeavor: the screenplay. For this you require at least one of two creative elements (both if possible) to see it through to fruition. One is the writer. The other is the director. The same person can, of course, be both, and usually is.

Several visions permeate the production of any motion picture. You can have a vision for how you want your company to run. You can have a vision for how you want your team to operate. You can have a vision for how you want financing to be handled. But what it all comes down to in the end is the vision of the finished product: *the movie*. This is the grand end product in the grand scheme of things. All the hard work, all the money, all the effort and sacrifice will come down to a movie for all to see. This is what it's all about. All other visions you or others conceive will work toward this same overall vision.

You absolutely must have a creative entity in your arsenal. He or she is the heart of your project and your company with his or her ideas for the movie. Without a heart, there is no life-blood to pump around to the rest of your company and project.

Of all the factors an investor will weigh when deciding whether or not to take a chance with you, the actual proposed film itself will most definitely be scrutinized. If you don't have a writer you can work with who has already written a screenplay for you, or who plans on doing so—or a movie director—get one now. You don't need both, but you should have at least one. Chances are if you are reading this book it is because you are a writer or director. I have not met too many so-called "filmmakers" who are strictly producers. Most filmmakers are already writers or directors or both.

• An executive producer (the main force that encourages and oversees the entire project, from creation to financing to production)

In the same way that nothing exists without a heart, nothing exists without a *brain*, either. And that is just what the executive producer of a motion picture is. While the creative entity handles the vision, the producer handles all the on-line logistics that will create that vision. A producer has his hand in absolutely everything, supervises everything, and in most instances has the final say. A company without a producer is like an airplane without a pilot.

Certainly you can have someone with no film experience run a company. You can have a Chief Executive Officer or a Chairman or a General Manager. Many large studios have such people running their outfits. Many of these persons have minimal knowledge of the actual hands-on of producing a movie. At the studio level, however, things are handled differently. It's all about figures and politics and foreign relations. Studios deal with corporate strategies on a much different scale. They have shareholders to answer to, and overheads that would stagger any independent production. They have the money to hire all the executive producers they want.

For an independent production company or filmmaker, things are slightly different. It is absolutely essential that among the partners there is someone who knows just what he or she is doing when it comes to the hands-on production of the movie. Preferably, it is someone with experience and a track record. Investors will look to make sure whoever they give their money to will use it wisely and efficiently. If they can not be convinced that the production will be handled accordingly, they will definitely not take a chance with you or your projects.

If you don't have an executive producer on your team, then now is the time to get one as well.

- A financial executive (handles all matters of finance and accounting and legalities associated within the structure of the company).

It is critical that you have a bean-counter on your executive team — someone that knows how to handle finances and knows how to keep track of it all. A financial executive is the person who will effectively take an investor's money and administer it. It is this person's job to know where every penny in the company is at all times. This person must know how to interact with all the banks and financial entities; must know how to allocate any transfers of funds that may be required externally and internally; must know how to effectively report all manners of cash flow; must be knowledgeable in all aspects of film finance and business transactions.

When it is time to produce the movie, this person must also be on top of the budget allocation with the executive producer. Any financial questions an investor might ask during the course of production must readily be answered by the financial executive. The person who fills these shoes will not only handle all aspects of accounting, but will also execute all projections and report the financial performance of the company and the movies it produces. When it comes to financing, this person often has a team of professionals directly under him or her that can be supervised.

The position and responsibility of the financial executive is paramount and crucial when dealing with investors. The person does not necessarily need to be a partner in the company, but had better be a part of the team in some way, committed to assisting the company. Investors will look for someone within your company that they can trust with the actual money they hand you. A good choice for selecting a financial executive might be a certified public accountant or finance officer from a bank or financial institute.

Like all the other positions, if you don't have one, you had better get one now.

- A development executive (works directly with the creative entity of the company to handle creative elements for the project)

A development executive acts as a liaison between the screenwriter and producers of the movie project, and works hand-in-hand with both. A development executive is usually the person who ascertains whether or not a project is viable for production. He or she must look at the project from all aspects and consider all scenarios and elements attached. Can the project be created with the money the company is seeking? Is the project good enough to get A-list actors interested in working on it? Is the project something that the market will accept? Does the project ultimately have potential?

A development executive essentially evaluates literary properties and decides whether or not they are worth pursuing. If a project is close, but requires rewriting, the development executive will work with the writer to get it to where it needs to be. In the case of most independent production companies, the literary properties are already lined up and polished. The scripts are ready to go. So why require a development executive? Because one does more than just evaluate literary material.

A development executive also works directly with the producers and director to attach creative elements to the project, once a project has been selected for production.

Let's say you feel a project would be more viable if Actor X were attached. The development executive would usually be the person to reel that actor in with the assistance of the executive producer. He or she would initially meet or speak with agents or the actors' representatives before scheduling a meeting with the company's other partners. Let's say an investor will only approve a project if the script changed its setting from one city to another, or if a female character were added to the script in which the investor's daughter could play the role — if everyone agreed to the changes, the development executive would work with the writer to make certain the proper alterations were implemented.

Often, the development executive and the creative entity are one and the same. If that is the case, that is perfectly acceptable. However, you might want to ask yourself if you are trying to wear too many hats. You might find yourself burdened with too many production or logistics errands to take care of, with no time to rewrite a screenplay. I would highly recommend you have a development executive that you can work with to handle the appropriate chores for you.

 • A production executive (handles the direct hands-on production logistics of the project)

While an executive producer usually supervises everything from start to finish on a motion picture, a production executive usually oversees only the direct hands-on production of the project. A production executive is usually someone who has experience as a line producer or production coordinator on other projects. This person usually works directly under the watchful eye of the executive producer, who handles the larger and more global tasks at hand. The executive producer usually brings all the toys to the table to play with, then lets the production executive actually manage who gets to play with what.

For example, a producer might handle securing the locations, props, transportation, food and insurance for a day's shoot. The *production executive*, on the other hand, will be on the set to make sure the location and props are utilized when required and not damaged, coordinate where the transportation moves to and when, and tell the cast and crew when it's time to eat.

A production executive is the chief supervisor on any movie set, just under the actual producer. One job the production executive performs hand-in-hand with the producer and director of the movie is the breakdown of the script for daily operations. In order to produce a movie, all the logistical elements of the script must be brought to light and systematically handled. The elements derived from the breakdowns subsequently become the responsibility of the production executive. If there is a prop missing on the day of a shoot, for example, or if an actor was not notified he would be required on that day, it would ultimately be the production executive's responsibility, no matter how many people beneath him should have handled it. It is his or her job to make sure the day-to-day activities go as smoothly as planned.

The various elements a production executive keeps track of in a screenplay breakdown include:

Scenes	Special Effects
Number of pages	Transportation
Locations (Interiors/Exteriors and Day or Night)	Stunts

Cast

Bits and Doubles

Atmosphere

Wardrobe

Props and Set Dressing

Camera and Sound

Wranglers and Livestock

Hair and Makeup

Special Requirements

A producer can technically also do the job of a production executive. However, as I explained in the case with the writer and development executive above, each position has its own responsibilities and time-consuming tasks. You would be wise to find someone who can solely be responsible for handling the hands-on nuts and bolts of daily production when the time arrives.

Now or Later?

You might think you can hire a lot of these people later, when the money comes. You are correct. However, I have found over the years that these bare minimum positions in any company are what investors look for initially, time and time again. This means you would be wise to retain them now, before you go searching for capital.

If we go to one extreme, you don't require any of these people on your team at all. You can simply state in your business plan that you will hire all these executives and more when their services are required. The producers, the writers, the directors and technicians— all will come later. In fact, you as the head of your company don't need to know a single thing about the motion picture industry or making movies except the fact that you enjoy them.

If this is your way of thinking, you might tell your potential financier, "Yes, Mr. Investor, I have been watching movies since I was 3. I know what makes a good movie. When you give me your $1 million, I will go out and buy a script or hire a writer. I will hire a producer to make the movie as well, and I will search for a financial executive to handle the money that you give me. I will also hire the best development executive there is, as well as a production executive to handle all the fine details. You don't have to worry— you're in good hands. Everyone and everything will come later."

Now ask yourself how enticing you think your business plan will be to an investor. Believe me, it won't fly. Now go get your team.

Lack of Experience?

What if you gather a team of dedicated, hard-working individuals who can conceivably handle all the positions mentioned above, but who possess little experience or lack a track record? In this case, it is less likely that you will attain the financing you seek. However, there is one thing you can do to improve your odds and garner success:

• Associate yourself with experienced entities

You can associate yourself with experienced persons or companies in many different and creative ways. Number one, you can try hiring a producer with a track record to be part of your team. Remember, he or she does not have to be a partner if you do not want. Making the producer a partner, however, would be an attractive incentive. The company's general partners and the executive staff are entirely separate entities. Actually, you can be the sole owner of your company, and your entire executive staff can be retained separately under a multitude of agreements.

You can do the same with other high profile entities such as A-list actors, or award-winning cinematographers or writers. Perhaps you know an up-and-coming director who just took first place at the Sundance Film Festival. Have him commit to your projects. List him in your business plan.

Not all credentials and track records need to originate in the motion picture industry. Maybe you have a friend who has worked at the local bank as an account representative for a number of years, and who would love to be involved in the movie business. A person like this would certainly possess financial knowledge, and the credential is a viable one. Have the friend be the financial executive. Perhaps you have a friend who is a bookworm, who has aced all his or her English classes in college, and who has had several short stories published in the local press or other magazines. A person like this would certainly possess certain knowledge to identify viable screenplays and ways to make them better.

The point is, if you can't convince the big boys to be a part of your team, then you must exploit the background and credentials—no matter how small—of the persons you *can* bring to your team. You can even be creative, without being deceitful, and make most anyone stand out from the crowd.

Here is a very bland way to write the credential of your friend who works at the bank:

> *Mrs. Maria Money will handle all the financial affairs of the company. She has worked as an account representative at Bank of New America for over ten years. She began as a teller and worked her way up. Last year she won the nicest employee award.*

Now here is a more creative, more exciting way of describing the same person with the same background:

> *Mrs. Maria Money brings to the company over ten years of corporate financial experience. A self-motivated executive, her talents were recognized recently by Bank of New America, one of the largest banks in the nation. She will manage all the financial affairs of the company.*

By rewriting it this way, you are not lying. Rather, you are utilizing the English language to your benefit by choosing a richer syntax and choice of words. Always try to exploit your credentials in such a way. But be careful—don't cross the line and tell a blatant lie, or exaggerate something to the point of absurdity. You may be called on it, and at such a time your deal will fall through quicker than you can blink an eye.

Another thing you can do to make yourself more enticing to investors if your production team has little experience is to associate yourself directly with an established production company. Sometimes it is easier to forge a relationship and impress such a company than it is to impress investors. With an established production company, you could strike a deal where the two companies would co-produce a project. This would be contingent on your company's ability to raise all or part of the capital. What you've managed to do in the meantime is get an established production entity to support you.

Now when you approach investors, you have the other company's track record to back you.

So why doesn't the investor go straight to the established production company? Because you are going to sell the investor on *your project*. You are going to get the investor excited about what you propose to bring to the big screen. Do you remember the heart of the project, the screenplay?

If you wish to be abundantly cautious, there exist various agreements that you can have investors sign, such as confidentiality agreements and non-circumvent contracts. You can also strike such agreements with the production company you go into business with. Essentially, the agreements would not allow the investor to go around you even if he or she tried. Again, we return to the human factor. That's what this entire section comes down to, and that's what the entire business of making movies is all about.

A Practical Guide

As with the last chapter, you are encouraged to follow along with the fictitious indie business plan at the end of this book. This section is written in direct correlation with the business plan, explaining in detail what is written there and why.

Legal Description

There are various ways to set up a company. Each has its own pros and cons depending on how they are established, and many times where they are formed. The State of Nevada, for instance, is a preferred state for the creation of many corporations because of its favorable local corporate laws.

I will leave the decision of how you establish your company up to you. There is no right or wrong way of doing so. It is all arbitrary and your decision should be a personal one. You would be wise to consult a certified public accountant or business attorney before deciding.

Whatever you decide, document it here. State when your company was legally created and where. You should also indicate the business address of your company.

Background

Tell a little about yourself and your company. What initially brought the company together? What prompted you to seek funding and produce larger productions? What were you doing before this? What are your aspirations now?

Summarize the answers in one or two paragraphs, and put them here.

Theme and Development

This header is tied in directly with the types of movies you wish to make as well as the screenplays you already have in your possession — or will be developing.

Elaborate on your choice of genre and why you chose it to begin with. Is it a popular genre? Has it been successful at the box-office? Do you anticipate that it will continue to be as popular in the future?

Write your answers here in one or more paragraphs.

Conviction

For this header, you will support your answers under the previous header, *Theme and Development*. You don't have to get into hard numbers and data, but you should at least provide an overview of why you believe your choice of genre would be a successful one for your production company as well as the investors. What you want to convince the financiers of is that you can't go wrong with your choice of movie material. Of course you can not guarantee anything, but by presenting comparable successes, investors may feel that the chance they are taking with you is an educated risk.

In the fictitious indie business plan, I present comparable sample motion pictures and television shows that are the same genre the fictitious production company plans to make. You should do the same in your plan.

If you plan to produce a movie about police officers and crime in a major city, for example, list it here. As cliché as the subject matter might appear, it is a very commercial and viable one. Television is full of such shows, and movies are never at a loss for the subject matter, either. It is a proven seller, and that is why producers continue to make programs with such storylines. They make money.

You need to present these facts to the investor. Let him or her know how sellable your proposed projects are.

A simple way to do this is to present a list of all the present or recent productions at theaters and on television with similar subject-matter. But don't stop there. Talk about the demographics and try to explain why audiences want to watch your proposed material. Are the storylines escapism? Do audiences relate to the material? Are audiences curious about the material because they know little about it? You will have to research your choice of material thoroughly and present it here.

The Managers and Executive Staff

Here you present the actual human factor of your company. This is where you let the investor know who is behind the request for financing; who will be handling their money; and who will be producing the movies.

It is important that you present photographs of your immediate team and support staff. It gives potential investors a better feel for who they're dealing with. Instead of looking at cold, hard numbers and facts, they are now looking at photographs of real people. As cold as the business of negotiating for financial backing can be, photographs offer a touch of warmth to the entire procedure.

Remember, potential investors might not get to meet everyone initially. In fact, potential investors often don't meet a single person in early negotiations. Instead, there are a number of people who go-between the investor and the party requesting the money. There can be a number of agents and representatives or brokers who try to get the ball rolling. This is all the more reason to include these photographs. Let the investor know you and your team are real people.

Under the photograph of each person you should include the person's name and title. Then describe their background and the duties they will perform for the company and production. Add anything you feel might add to their worth, no matter how minute.

In the fictitious indie business plan, I elaborated more on the principal of the company, *Mr. Joe Filmmaker*. In most independent companies, you will find a principal creative entity or filmmaker around whom the company is formed. Potential investors will want to know more about this person than anybody else. You should go more in-depth in describing the principal's personal history, education, accomplishments, notoriety and rationale for wanting to produce the motion pictures at hand. Allow this person an extra page or two of information in the business plan if necessary.

Consultants and Outside Support

Any motion picture endeavor requires outside support. To secure funding, for instance, you need attorneys and certified public accountants. For operations, I suggest that you employ the services of a talent or literary agency.

The bare minimum you should list here for potential investors to see is an attorney (preferably an entertainment attorney) as well as a certified public accountant to handle the business transactions if financing is secured. The rest of the list is extra, but it does make a good impression to try to round out the outside support. The entities you include here should all be business related as opposed to production related. These are entities that will assist with the contracts, negotiations, financing and operations of the company.

Invaluable Relationships

Invaluable relationships are also considered outside support as above, but here you should list entities that will assist with the actual production of your projects, as opposed to the business side of things. If you have worked with these people or companies in the past, you might want to mention that fact.

List the companies and persons in no particular order. List where they are located, and what their function is. Are they a production company, a visual effects studio, a hair and make-up artists group? List a contact name, and most importantly, list the company's credentials.

Take a careful look at the sample business plan. Earlier I stated how important it was to associate yourself with established producers with track records, especially if you do not possess a track record of your own. Here is another advantageous place to list your relationship with established entities. You've heard the phrase, "Guilty by association?" Well, this, in a way, makes you *established by association*. Potential investors get to see real-world credits and titles of movies they've watched themselves. Suddenly the entire proposal gets an air of having that much more potential.

If you do not possess any such relationships, you should attempt to establish at least one or two. In fact, the more you retain, the better. Although it is not absolutely vital that your business plan possess this list, it will make it all the more attractive if it does.

Invaluable Assets

This is another list that is not vital to the integrity of your business plan, but will add depth if you choose to include it, or are able to.

Under this header, you should list any unique or unusual assets that would not normally fit under any other category within the business plan. To illustrate what I am talking about, in the fictitious indie business plan I listed the fact that the principal of the company was an award-winning filmmaker prior to the formation of the company. I also cited all the publicity that Joe Filmmaker and his associates had accumulated over the years, as well as all the awards and notoriety.

What the information under this header should tell potential investors is that an entry has already been carved into the public arena. A step has already been taken.

If you've previously produced a movie, you should list that here. Explain how successful your project was. If it played in film festivals, list the awards and recognition it received. If it was distributed, list the box-office receipts and how well it performed in relation to the budget. Did it make money? If your film did not win awards or did not make money, I don't think I need to explain why you should *not* acknowledge that film here.

On-Going Developments

Like any other business, relationships come and go in the movie industry, and companies and filmmakers perpetually strive for more business opportunities and industry kinships. You should mention your on-going developments here. If you have specific business ties you are attempting to secure at the time of writing your business plan, you should mention that here. List contact names and relevant information. This will show potential investors that you are active and will persistently seek bigger and better opportunities.

4

The Movie Projects

"You know ... that a blank wall is an appalling thing to look at. The wall of a museum — a canvas — a piece of film — or a guy sitting in front of a type-writer. Then, you start out to do something — that vague thing called creation. The beginning strikes awe within you."

— Edward Steichen (1879–1973)

WHY YOU DO THE THINGS YOU DO

The truth of the matter is if most indie filmmakers had their way, this is the only section of the business plan they would put together. Just like the creative entity is the heart of your company, this section is the heart of your business plan. This is what all the effort and commotion is about: the movie projects. For most hopeful filmmakers and producers, this is also where all their inspiration was born to seek out a production team and a *plan* to make it happen.

In short, this is the most exciting part of the business plan you will assemble.

SHOW, DON'T TELL

It is a sad commentary, but the majority of film investors that I have met over the years do not have the greatest of imaginations. Most are business and financial entre-preneurs, having earned their wealth in other industries and ventures, away from motion pictures. When it comes to hard facts and data, they are wizards. When you try to pitch them your movie ideas, however, they often draw blanks or miss the point entirely. I'm certain it has something to do with left brain versus right brain influence.

What you must do in this section, therefore, is present more than just text and cold figures. You must visually guide them with artwork. Don't *tell* them what your movies are about, *show* them.

In one regard, this is a good thing. It gives you the excuse to show off your creative genius. You can include conceptual artwork, posters or one-sheets, and storyboards. Decide what works best — what is most striking or engaging — and exploit it here. Perhaps it is an exciting scene from your movie that is difficult to explain, but easy and dramatic to lay out in a storyboard. Or maybe a conceptual poster of the finished movie will work best.

36

Visual Stimulation is important. Conceptual artwork from Gabriel Campisi's proposed *Silent Trespass* has actively garnered the attention of agents, studios — even book publishers. Artwork by Mark S. Pacella.

Do whatever it takes in this section to get a potential investor absorbed in your vision. If you can't do it yourself, then hire a conceptual artist to assist you. I often work with Mark Pacella, a professional comic book artist and Hollywood conceptual designer (see his storyboards and conceptual posters in the fictitious indie business plan). He has been able to instinctively interpret my ideas and thoughts and graphically render them to canvas. You want somebody who can do the same thing.

More Than Just Artwork?

There are many indie filmmakers who go one step further here and actually shoot a trailer or teaser of their movie to present to investors. If the movie is science-fiction or fantasy, some indie producers even make copies of the most crucial props in the movie to exhibit.

Should you do this? That is strictly up to you — there is no right or wrong here. Just how much you should show, or how much you should hold back is strictly an arbitrary decision to be made by you and your production team. There are, however, some pros and cons you should keep in mind when going beyond the typical graphics presentation.

First of all, you never want to overwhelm your prospective investor. I have seen business plans thicker than dictionaries, complete with videos, maps of locations, film stock receipts and the actual screenplays themselves. The purpose of a business plan is to show your investor what you have in mind, and back it up, but it does not mean you should throw everything in your package including your desk and the typewriter. Would you take the time to read a dictionary? No, and neither will a prospective investor. It's just too much information, and that alone could kill your deal.

The saying *less is more* readily applies here. You want to tease your investors, but you also want to back up your representations. At the same time, you don't want to give them data overload, so this becomes a tight-rope balancing act for you.

So how much information is enough, and how much is too much? There is no solid answer. You should use common sense. Also, keep in mind you will never make everybody happy. Some investors will consider your business plan packed with too much information, while others will criticize you for not having enough material.

I mentioned earlier that in Chapter 9 of this book, the varied producers and executives disagree on how long a business plan should be. They all speak from experience, and yet they all have different opinions on the proper length of the manuscript.

The rule of thumb is to have enough material in your business plan to answer all the questions a potential investor might ask. This means even if the investor knew nothing about the motion picture industry before meeting you, by the time he is done reading your material he should at least have a general understanding of the entire process. As stated earlier, a good overall size for a business plan would be between 40 and 60 pages, complete with photos and artwork.

So getting back to the movie trailer question — when considering putting one together for your proposed movie, you have to consider whether or not you are presenting too much material to the investor. Is the trailer really necessary? Again, there is no right or wrong answer. Only you can make the decision, but seriously consider whether or not a trailer or movie props or other material beside graphics are warranted.

Before embarking on going beyond the business plan, consider:

- The ease of presenting the material
- The commercialism of the material
- The creativity of the material
- The professionalism of the material

On the same note, you should ask yourself whether or not you are even qualified to put together a proper trailer or movie prop. The question might appear absurd, since you are no doubt in the business of making movies. But before you have financing in place, you may not have all the necessary resources and people to put together this extra material. Rather, your movie trailer or movie props may turn out less than adequate.

To illustrate my point, I helped an indie filmmaker put together a business plan a few years back. The presentation was very professional and it had just enough material to entice investors. I had showed the initial business plan to an investment entity, someone who represents private investors and venture capitalists. He was impressed enough with it that in a matter of a few weeks, he called to let me know we should send a copy of the business plan to one of the investors he represented. Because it was the filmmaker's responsibility to make copies of the business plan to mail out, I called him and asked him to prepare a package for me. I picked it up and mailed it out the same day. Unbeknownst to me, the filmmaker had shot a movie trailer on video over the course of a few weekends and included it in the package.

The investor never called back.

A few days later I spoke with the investment entity who told me the investor in question never even looked at the business plan. He only looked at the video presentation which the indie filmmaker had produced and it had killed the entire deal.

I contacted the filmmaker to ask what this video thing was all about, since I knew nothing about it. He showed me the video which he had produced, and it was not bad, but it was *not up to par* with what you see in movie theaters. First of all, it looked like cheap analog video, not film. The actors were far from believable, and the camera was static, with little motion. The filmmaker explained he just wanted to present a rough idea of what the project was all about, that he needed the money to make it better, to hire a crew, and of course the stars and money for special effects, etc. I explained all he did was shoot himself in the foot because investors do not want to hear excuses. In effect, the video trailer backfired. The investor saw the video and perceived it to be what the finished project with financing would appear like when completed. The investor gained no faith in the filmmaker, even though, when working on client assignments that are fully funded, the filmmaker has produced award-winning work.

So if you're going to go beyond the presentation in your business plan, it had better be top-shelf material, or forget about it.

On a positive note, if you are able to put together a top-notch preview of your movie, it could work wonders and get prospective financiers hyped about your project even before they read your business plan. In fact, many investors have been hooked on this presentation element alone.

So do your homework, use common sense, get opinions from friends and family, and present the most exciting preview of your film project or projects that you possibly can.

HOW MANY FILM PROJECTS?

You can present as many film projects as you are seeking funds for. Some indie filmmakers only present one project. Others present the total number of projects they plan on producing over the course of the ensuing four or five years. And yet others add more than they need.

What you need to base this decision on is your overall plan for financing and business. If your desire is to produce just one movie, then that is all you are required to present here. In the fictitious indie business plan, the financial plan calls for three movies to be produced over the course of four years. They are part of the broader scheme of things in that they are incorporated into a four-year schedule, and the financing, as well as income, is anticipated and projected accordingly. Investors are asked to invest in all three projects, or the company, as opposed to just one film.

The choice of how many film projects to include here is yours, and it is an arbitrary one. If you do not have a substantial track record, or relatively few credentials, you would be wise to seek funds for one film at a time until you are able to put more credits under your belt. There are pros and cons here, however: many distributors are more interested in multiple-project deals as opposed to a single movie — and this could hamper your distribution efforts down the road. If you have enough experience or are allied with prominent entities already in the industry, you can and should take a chance and seek funding for more than one project. Some financiers also see more potential in being on the ground floor with a company that plans on doing several films as opposed to one. It tells the investors you are in this for the long haul, you have thought out your options well ahead of time, and you are capable of carrying this venture through several years of effort.

If you are pursuing the latter — that is, funding for more than one project — you would be wise to list more projects than you plan on producing, even if they are just ideas or you are still negotiating their rights. In the sample business plan, FireGem Entertainment plans on producing three movies in four years. However, the Movie Projects section lists *eight* properties. That's five more than are anticipated to go into production.

Many investors like to have a hand or say-so in the projects they fund. While their role is usually contractually limited to just putting up the cash, it will not hurt you to allow them to pick and choose from your list of potential projects. It gives investors a broader sense of interaction and more participation than they're really contributing. The trick is for you to make sure all the projects you present are projects you would be equally thrilled to produce.

THE RIGHT TO PRODUCE MATERIAL

If for some reason you have not yet secured that all-exciting screenplay to produce, you should be aware of the many ways to procure such literary properties. Even if you are the writer of your own film, you will have to contractually sign it over to your newly formed company to produce. Although you are the head of both entities, a transaction must be secured whereby you the writer grants your company full permission and rights to theatrically create a motion picture out of it. As simple as this might sound, you would be wise to seek literary rights consultations from an intellectual properties attorney or a

Philip R. Cable decided early on to attract investors to his company's projects by offering comedies with sexual overtones. *Hollywood Fantasies* is one of the filmmaker's most successful projects.

literary agent. If your movie becomes a breakaway hit, you will want to make sure you positioned yourself in a lucrative enough situation to reap your just dues.

Places to look for literary properties to turn into exciting motion pictures include:

- First and foremost, yourself
- Writers Guild of America — signatory literary agencies
- Book publishers and authors
- True stories in newspapers and magazines

The keyword to all of these is *rights*. Who owns or controls the rights to the property you are interested in? The production of any motion picture involves securing these rights before you can proceed. Without them, you are literally stealing intellectual property in most cases, or invading privacy in others.

If you write the screenplay yourself, it becomes a matter of formality to sign the rights of the script over to your production company. If you read a book you find exciting, or know a book publisher who often forwards material to you before it is released to the public, you will have to negotiate the rights to said property. You can outright purchase the rights, or you can negotiate an option-to-purchase, which is effectively a way to pay less money for the rights until such a time that full funding is attained — at which time, you can pay the writer a pre-agreed larger sum of money.

The same rules apply to properties offered by the Writers Guild of America signatory literary agencies, and true stories found in public accounts, such as newspapers and magazines. Be careful with the latter. Just because a story is found in a public newspaper does not mean you can run off with it. A lot of people erroneously believe it is free for the picking because it is in the public domain. This is not the case. There are a lot of specific intellectual property laws that govern true stories, and in most instances, rights must be purchased from the people featured in the news. Sometimes getting to the bottom of who actually possesses such rights in this case is a serious undertaking unto itself, especially when more than one person is involved. By the same token, there are ways to write a screenplay around a true story without having to secure the rights. Some elements of the news do, indeed, fall under public domain. For the most part, this creates a scenario where the writer is extremely limited in what he or she can and can't include in the script.

Either way, if you have a true story you would like to get your hands on, you would be wise to consult an intellectual properties attorney or a literary agent for the proper way to go about things.

For most indie filmmakers and producers, screenplays are generally written by the creative member of the company. Make sure the rights are negotiated properly, then proceed accordingly.

ATTACHMENTS

Another way to make a project more attractive is to attach elements crucial to the success of a motion picture prior to seeking financing. The more common and accepted elements include:

- Star actors
- Established directors
- Movie rights to a bestselling novel
- Added funding

In addition to the strength of your screenplay, these elements will add an air of acceptance by outside entities. It's as if their inclusion in your business plan screams out, "We've already accepted this company and this project, and we are on the bandwagon. What are *you* waiting for?"

Star actors guarantee a certain amount of pre-sales based on their following by loyal fans who will pay to watch almost anything they appear in. Established or award-

Vampires are a staple of Kevin Lindenmuth's preferred choice of genre for film production. The *Addicted to Murder* trilogy, in particular, has met with worldwide success. A multi-million dollar studio spinoff is actively in development at Brimstone Productions.

winning directors have proven they can direct a successful motion picture that audiences will pay to watch. If you have obtained the movie rights to a novel, preferably a bestseller, you now have on your hands a pre-sold audience already hooked on the book. They will more than likely eagerly anticipate the release of the movie version (look at the success of the *Harry Potter* and *Lord of the Rings* movies). If you have added funding (from another investor or financier), potential investors will feel less intimidated in taking a chance with you. They will likely reason that if another investor has already committed his hard-earned cash to you and your project, it must be a worthwhile and sound investment.

Are attachments mandatory when presenting your projects? Absolutely not. But if you are in a position to include one or more, you should make the extra effort to do so.

BUDGETS

Another thing you might want to summarize in this section is the movie's budget. You will go into much more detail in the finance chapter of your business plan, but it is okay to mention the budget here. I do not recommend that you give a detailed budget of your movie or movies here or in any other part of the business plan. Instead, present only a figure or a budget top sheet to give an overview of how much the project will cost or where the money is going.

The reason for this is often a financier will want to put his two cents in, and for the most part a financier is not a person who knows anything about film logistics. If he sees that you'll be spending $2500 a day for a special piece of equipment, he might blurt out that he thinks that piece of equipment is not necessary. You will find yourself on the defensive, perhaps explaining every last cent and why it is being utilized in such a way.

Ultimately, if the investor really wants to see a complete budget breakdown before he will turn over any money to you, you will no doubt have to give it to him or her. But until and unless it is asked for, you should not present it freely, unless you are a person that thrives on headaches and inconvenience.

A PRACTICAL GUIDE

As you've done in the last few chapters, you are encouraged to follow along with the fictitious indie business plan at the end of this book. This section is written in direct correlation with the business plan, explaining in detail what is written there and why.

The Movie Projects

One thing I always do to get this section going for clients is to put up a notice that states the actual screenplays themselves are only available to serious investors who sign a non-disclosure form. Is this necessary? I think it is. As much as I hate to admit it, I think I have met more phonies in this business than bonafide investors. Unless your investor comes highly recommended from your rich uncle in the stock and securities business, sometimes you really just don't know who you're talking to or eating dinner with. Unless you're willing to take a chance on your material being stolen from right under your nose, you might want to consider having interested parties sign some documents to protect yourself.

The mere act of potential investors having to put all their contact information on a form is enough to dissuade most thieves and predators.

Next, you should talk about the project you have in mind for your first production. Who wrote it, and what is it titled? Does it fit in with the company's vision? What about future projects? Do you have them all in place, or will you be looking for material?

Try not to limit yourself in this regard. Open yourself up to limitless possibilities by working with outside writers and material. Have a plan in place and stick to it, but be open to anything unexpected in the future that would benefit you, your company and your investors. In this case, you might want to mention that you'll be working with outside writers in an effort to find the most exciting literary material — material that you might not be in possession of at the current moment.

Outside Material

If you decide to work with outside material in addition to your own, then you should list it here. Otherwise, disregard this header and move on to the next one. There are some filmmakers that have no intention of working with outside writers. That is perfectly acceptable.

If you choose otherwise, however, and are working with a literary agent or have writers sending you material, mention it here. Explain your company's stance on outside literary properties. Perhaps you have professional writers writing screenplays for you that were not completed at the time of putting your business plan together. Mention that fact here. Anything that has to do with projects other than your own, that you plan on producing, make a quick note of it under this header.

Intellectual Protection

For the sake of safeguarding all entities involved, it is a good thing to mention how your properties are protected or will be protected. The two most common organizations involved in literary rights integrity are:

- The Library of Congress in Washington, D.C.
- The Writers Guild of America West (Los Angeles) or East (New York)

The Library of Congress offers actual federal copyright registration of your literary material. The Writers Guild of America does not offer actual copyright registration, but rather establishes a date of when the material was registered with their organization. Most filmmakers and producers register their projects with both entities. They even modify their registration as the project progresses. They often start with the treatment, then the screenplay (various phases of it, until film production is actually completed), and finally a copy of the actual motion picture is sent in.

Some independent filmmakers and producers take their projects a step further, especially with particularly successful properties. They register the titles of their projects with the United States Department of Commerce, Patent and Trademark Office in Washington, D.C.

To illustrate when a project is trademarked or registered with the Patent and Trademark Office, think of a movie with a common name. Let's say, *The Killer*. A title as common as this might be used repeatedly over the course of many years on different productions, especially if the projects are not high profile or largely successful. If you wanted to make a movie with this title, chances are you would encounter no legal ramifications. Now consider titles such as *Star Wars* or *BattleStar Galactica*. How about *Rocky* or *Godzilla*? You can't do it. You can't use them. If you shot a movie using one of these titles, you would very quickly find yourself on the receiving end of a certified letter from someone's attorney.

The Titles

What you should do next is list the titles of your projects. Immediately under, list the writers responsible, following a copyright notice. Mention the bottom line of your projected budget, as well as how long you anticipate the production to last. Next, give a synopsis of your project.

When you mention your first project, you should elaborate on its content more than any of the other movie properties you have in mind. Remember, the creative entity is the heart of the company, and this section is the heart of the business plan. What it all comes down to, then, is the heart of your first proposed project. In essence, this is the heart of hearts. Treat it accordingly.

Take extra space to describe the story behind your first movie. Like all other elements in the business plan, don't overdo it. Be direct and to the point, be dramatic and creative, but whatever you do, *don't be boring.* The easiest way to be boring is to write a dozen pages describing your movie idea. If you're going to have them read that many pages, you might as well hand them the script. So don't do it. One to two pages, maximum, is good enough to describe your project's premise in this section of the business plan.

You might want to quickly tie in the content and genre of your project to the marketing aspect of the industry and demographics. Touch on the specific elements of your movie that will appeal to your choice of audience.

Mention any other cursory facts that might make your project stand out as a production headed toward success. If you have commitments from any actors or special effects people, or prop masters—anything above and beyond the scope of this business plan—mention it here.

Also, take advantage of your artwork that I mentioned earlier and place it here. Any storyboards or one-sheets or conceptual artwork—any visual aides that will facilitate the conveyance of your ideas to the potential investors or other parties—place them here for all to see. In the sample business plan, you will find I placed artwork by Mark Pacella to support the visuals of FireGem Entertainment's proposed first project, *Confused Unicorns and Ogres.* The storyboards visually show some great action, and one of the creatures that would otherwise be so difficult to explain, jumps right off the page.

Some indie filmmakers like to mention potential cast players here as well. Feel free to do this, but be careful not to impart the wrong idea. If you have an actor that has read your script and is interested in discussing the possibility of working with you on your project, by all means mention his or her name. But if you have not actually spoken to your choice of actors, and you mention them here, you should be careful to not make it appear as if you have already touched base with them. If a potential investor calls you on it, you may lose any chance of financing for lying to them.

Never lie in your business plan. Lies last about as long as the flu, and if you come across as a con-man, word will spread quickly and effectively. It's just not worth it.

Very recently I was handed a project to look over and consider whether or not I felt I could attain financing for it. The cover letter stated that two major studios and several A-list actors had read the script already and all agreed it was the best thing they had ever come across. I could not get past page 10 of the script. It was horrendous. It was obvious the cover letter was an outright lie. I returned the package and told the person that major studios are in the business of acquiring wonderful scripts. If they had truly said what they did about his material, I asked him why they hadn't bothered to make him an offer for his screenplay? After turning beet red and stuttering out a half-baked response, the man admitted it was all a lie.

This is a person I will never deal with, nor present to any of my investors—ever. Why? Because if he's lying to me from the start, what else will he lie to me about in the future?

Back to your business plan, state the status of your proposed movie project. Is it now owned by your company? Is it being actively written? Do you own an option-to-purchase on the property? Whatever the legal status of the property is, mention it here. List the director and any stars that may be attached.

Do the same as I described above for the rest of your literary properties, except do not have them be as lengthy. Summarize them more rapidly, but try to include the same information as before: title, copyright and writers, budget, number of shooting days, synopsis, and status. If you only have one project you are representing, that is fine. Move on to the next header.

Market Research

Although no doubt this header belongs mostly in the Marketing Chapter, you should briefly mention your company's stance when it comes to your overall take on demographics and your movies. The reason for doing this here is because the movie projects will still be fresh in your potential investor's mind. Before moving onto any other section of the business plan, you should take advantage of the fact your reader just finished sinking his teeth into the heart of your material.

This might seem a little redundant because you touched on this from a different angle at the beginning of this section, and you will do so in detail in the marketing chapter. Remember that a business plan by its very nature is a redundant document. Everything is tied together. Everything feeds off the other. Nothing exists without the other. So you will often find talk of the "market," for example, in each and every chapter of this book, or even in each and every section of the business plan itself.

Do not be too concerned. This is the way these documents are put together. Investors will not be put off by minor redundancy. They see such things in legal contracts all the time. Most long-form legal agreements repeat the same things over and over and over again, each time from a slightly different perspective. Your business plan luckily does not fall into this category of such severe redundancy.

Selection Criteria

If you have decided you will be working with outside writers and agents, you should mention your selection criteria here. How strict will you be when looking for third-party screenplays? What kind of quality must they possess? What exactly will you be looking for? Who will handle it all, and how? Write it all down here. Be clear and concise.

Remember for every movie that ever gets made by studios or indie filmmakers, there exists over a thousand hopeful writers with scripts that will never see the light of day. The sad truth is the majority of the scripts making the rounds, even by experienced agents, are not up to par with the main-stream. With so much material floating around, then, you must make investors feel confident enough that any such material that makes it to you or your company will be screened in the strictest manner. They want to make sure you will not be allowing "junk" to filter into your company.

Further Protection

This is another slightly redundant header, but you should put it here to wrap up this section of your business plan. Mention one more time the fact that interested parties must sign a confidentiality agreement before viewing your scripts, as well as before entering into any kind of negotiations.

Some people might think this signals paranoia. I believe it signals the fact you take your material very seriously. After all, it is proprietary information and it is what will keep your competition at bay.

Some indie producers like to keep their projects under wraps the entire time they are developing and shooting their project. That is to say, they prefer to keep their production secret, and not allow story or character elements to reach the public before the release of their movie. If done right, and if you can leak some information to the press about your picture, the secrecy surrounding it can become a great ploy in that it creates mystery and breeds curiosity. You might get unexpected press coverage on this fact alone.

Whatever might contribute to the integrity or security of your movie projects, list it here.

5

The Movie Industry

"There's no business like show business."
— Irving Berlin (1888–1989)

More Than Just Movies and Popcorn

The motion picture industry is comprised of various intrinsic elements and sub-industries that are all tightly related to one another in a symbiotic fashion. Like most every other industry in the world, it is always fluctuating with figures, trends and change. The future of the movie industry is always in motion, providing independent filmmakers the opportunity — if they seize it — to seek advantages and niches, and prosper tremendously.

The industry is more than just the physical act of producing a movie — it is everything along the way from concept to realization. It is comprised of art, craft, business, finance, technical and leisure arenas all rolled into one.

Loosely, the motion picture industry incorporates the following elements:

- Talent development (actor, writer, technical — software, classes and books)
- Film school (education)
- Agencies (representation and management)
- Equipment (cameras, lighting, audio, grip, transportation and accessories)
- Film, video and multimedia stock
- Production (studios, sound stages, recording)
- Special effects (digital, pyrotechnics, puppetry and models)
- Stunts and dance (choreography, equipment)
- Make-up and hair (gear)
- Distribution (physical distribution of media)
- Movie theaters and concession stands (exhibition)
- Home video (VHS, DVD — hardware and software)
- Television (cable, satellite and pay-per-view)
- Marketing (strategic promotion, magazines, Internet, talk shows, radio)

One could conceivably break the elements down further, and in different directions. But the ones I have listed here make up the bulk.

To take advantage of the industry's various overlapping segments, filmmaker Philip R. Cable combined comics and film to forge the very successful *The Comic Book Kid.*

For this part of your business plan, you should mention the facts of the motion picture industry, straight-forwardly and to the point. There is little room here for creativity. You should list figures and data, and if you are so inclined, include graphs and charts as well. The latter is a personal choice, and there is no right or wrong way for presenting your material as long it is presented in a cohesive manner. This is the nuts and bolts of the industry, and your information should contain only solid data.

Mix action, adventure, bullets, explosions, and a slew of beautiful women, and you have a fantastic vehicle to attract investors to your project. Ted V. Mikels did just that in 1973 with *The Doll Squad*.

While investors might not be fluent in the business of making motion pictures, they certainly are fluent in business and finance in general. How else did the bulk of them become so wealthy? Because of this, investors will want you, as a filmmaker or independent producer, to be just as fluent in your line of work as they are in their line of work. They will expect you to know your industry like the back of your hand. They will ask you questions, usually indirectly, to test you. You might not even know you are being tested, but the bottom line is you had better be able to answer any questions the investor throws your way, especially when they are of a technical, business or financial nature.

If you are not fluent with the industry, you need to bring someone aboard who is. This is not negotiable. The lack of an industry expert on your team will be perceived by an investor as a sinking ship — even if it hasn't set sail yet. In order for any business to thrive, the managers of the company must be well attuned to the variables and factors of the industry that influence the ocean of currents and trends in order for the company to steer clear of problems and sail toward success.

Even if you make just one movie, and even if you are planning on handing over your finished project to a distributor to handle everything for you, you still need to know how your industry functions overall and how to achieve success in perhaps one of the most aggressive industries in the world. How else will you know that your movie will be produced properly, with enough money, the proper elements, and that it will be suitable for the competitive marketplace? Better still, how else will you convince your potential investors that you will lead them to success?

BUSINESS IS BUSINESS

Describing the industry in the business plan can be a tedious task because it encompasses so much information. Any motion picture project, from concept to realization, is a long and winding road. When describing the different elements of the process, you do not need to go into excruciating detail, but it is a good idea to include enough data so that there can be no mistake about what you are attempting to outline.

When you do your research and compile your data, information you should cite about the industry includes:

- Industry figures (or trends) for the past five years, minimum
- Industry figures (or trends) anticipated for the forthcoming five years, minimum
- Theatrical box-office (gross) figures, both domestic and foreign, for the past five years, minimum
- Theatrical box-office (gross) figures, both domestic and foreign, anticipated for the forthcoming five years, minimum
- Home video sales (sell-through and wholesale) figures, both domestic and foreign, for the past five years, minimum
- Home video sales (sell-through and wholesale) figures, both domestic and foreign, anticipated for the forthcoming five years, minimum
- Cable television and pay-per-view programming revenue, both domestic and foreign, for the past five years, minimum
- Cable television and pay-per-view programming revenue, both domestic and foreign, anticipated for the forthcoming five years, minimum

- Figures broken down as much as possible by studio and independent motion pictures
- Figures isolated with regard to your choice of genre and market

This is a lot of information to gather and compile, but it is out there. All you have to do is look on the Internet, in bookstores, at the library, and check with the government and specialized companies such as Big Horse, Inc. You can also check with the Motion Picture Association of America (MPAA) and the American Film Market Association (AFMA) for the latest figures and trends. I have included a list of resources in Appendix B of this book for your convenience, but what I have listed is only the tip of the iceberg.

Once you have scoured all the necessary databases for your information, you should present it in a cohesive manner for potential investors to readily grasp. If you mention very specific figures, quotes or trends, be sure to give credit where credit is due by citing the source somewhere in your presentation.

Keep in mind many investors are interested in motion picture production only for the potential financial return. Sure it's a risky venture, but the odds are such that if it pays off, it may well pay more than any mega-jackpot in Las Vegas. This is why this section is so important, and you can rest assured it is one part of your business plan that will not be overlooked by interested parties.

YOUR PLACE IN THE SCHEME OF THINGS

As you assemble your data for your business plan, you must keep your specific movies and your company in mind. Compare your personal data with the industry figures you have gathered, or separate them entirely, but present them one way or another. It's up to you how you do it. Ask yourself how your film fits in with all those numbers and data you are giving your potential financier? What budgets will you use on your films? What returns do you anticipate? What are the odds for success, and why? What are "safe" figures? In other words, what are the minimum returns seen by films similar to yours? What budgets would be considered "safe," whereby the potential minimum return would possibly cover the investment?

Be careful with usage of the term, "safe," if you choose to employ it. Nothing in the investment of motion picture production is truly safe by its very definition. The word is used loosely to refer to current trends only, but there are never any guarantees. If you choose to apply the term, do so in such a manner where you clearly disclose how it is being utilized. To use it without regard to its proper definition is reckless and can get you in trouble. If you do not feel confident employing it, then please do not.

As you take your investor by the hand and show him the ins and outs of the industry through your business plan, continually point out your place in the scheme of things. Illustrate how you fit in, and how your choice of genre is a popular one. Show how your decisions parallel those that have reaped financial and critical rewards. Identify market trends and demographics, and clearly point out how your projects easily fit in. Investors will want to see that the projects you propose are in line with the main stream of the industry.

A powerful screenplay and outstanding artwork by Mark S. Pacella helped launch Gabriel Campisi's *Last Chance* into active development.

OFF THE BEATEN PATH

There are many independent producers and filmmakers who seek funding outside the studio system because their projects are *not* in line with the mainstream, and no studio will finance them. If this applies to your projects, you are stacking the odds against you by limiting the number of potential investors that may be willing to take a chance with such a project. If you have a small track record, or none at all, the odds become that much worse.

Don't lie to yourself. Film financiers are in the business of making money. Certainly they take high risks, but believe me they have no intention of losing their capital. On occasion you will find investors just looking to be a part of Hollywood, and willing to lose it all for a taste of glamour and stardom. You will sometimes even find investors looking for a tax write-off—actually seeking a loss of their investment—who will be less picky about the projects they choose to invest in. But these investors are *extremely* rare.

The bottom line is that making movies is a business, and you should treat it as such, especially if you intend to stay in the game for more than one movie. You would be wise, then, to stay on the beaten path and not wander from it. Choose projects and subject matters that are tried and true in the industry, whose track records indicate audiences will pay to watch them.

If you wander from the mainstream and propose a project with questionable material, that is okay, but you will likely have more difficulty convincing your potential investors. Consider why you want to produce such a project in the first place, and then put yourself in the potential investor's shoes. How can you convince him or her to fund your movie? You might elaborate on the project's artistic or human values. Perhaps there have been a small number of similar movies over the years—small, but successful. If that is the case, everything else in this chapter should readily apply to your project.

If you are an unproven independent filmmaker, I would suggest you stick with mainstream fare your first or second time out. Then if you wish to make material that is not considered popular, you at least have a track record to show that you know what you are doing.

ENCOUNTERING LESS-THAN-FAVORABLE DATA

Often, not all the data you locate is favorable. The industry might be on a downslope when you go to write your business plan. The delicate condition of world politics might be affecting markets on a grand scale in specific markets or regions. You might find, for instance, the United States or foreign countries in a state of economic turmoil, thus affecting the bottom line of your box-office figures.

An entire array of variables exists that can affect the motion picture industry as a whole at any given moment. On a smaller scale, these variables include your choice of subject matter and target demographics in the marketplace. The popularity and viability of film genres comes and goes, then randomly recycles over the years. For example, you will often see a dozen or more westerns put out by the major studios in the same one or two-year time-frame. Science-fiction might be the hot ticket for a year or two, then its popularity might dwindle, giving way to romantic comedies or horror films. Ten years later, the westerns return. In no particular order, subsequent genres follow suit.

You might, therefore, find the movies you plan to produce are old news. Figures might show producers losing money hand over fist on a particular genre, until the genre is temporarily suspended. This could influence your potential investor to decline, especially if you are an independent producer with little or no track record.

There are several things for you to consider at this point:

1. If an alternate strategy or exploitation of demographics will constitute a more lucrative scenario, you should contemplate doing so. Consider a different choice of genre, target audience or budget for your film(s).

2. Nobody can truly second-guess the marketplace. Just because your choice of material isn't presently popular does not mean you can't spark interest in it anew.

3. Nobody can truly second-guess the industry. World politics and economics are a randomly and constantly changing force — healthy one day, ill the next.

4. The motion picture industry, for better or for worse, will forge ahead with or without you.

5. If you work hard enough, you can find the opportunity to take advantage of any situation.

Whatever the reason for any negative information you might come across, you need to realize this is how industries function. There is no getting around it. At times, industries can be a roller-coaster of data, at other times, smooth sailing in placid waters. It is okay to press forward if you have little to no control over the circumstances affecting the industry, and if you honestly and truly believe in yourself, your team, your strategies and your projects. After all, life must go on, right?

But if it is convenient, you might consider rethinking your position — *especially if you have control over the circumstances.* If you want to make horror movies, but the industry saw dozens of horror movies over the past year, with depreciating interest and weakening box-office grosses over the course of that same year, you might be wise to select a different genre for your movies. While it is admirable to believe your movies will be superior to anything already put out by other filmmakers, most investors will see it only as a death wish and a hopeless investment opportunity. Even fully established producers and filmmakers with track records have a hard time getting projects off the ground that are not timely with trends in the industry.

So if you've considered all your options and you decide to press forward, what do you do with the information you've gathered? Do you present it to your potential investors with all its negative glory? The answer is yes and no. You must intelligently decide how to present all the data in a manner that is truthful but nonetheless shows potential. Analyze the material, then seek out an opportunity for yourself. Impress your investor with your savvy. Why is there a slump in the movie industry? You might decide it is because audiences are not getting what they want to see — and you are here to fix that problem. Perhaps there is turmoil or war in parts of the world that affects everybody everywhere. You might decide the movies that are being made are too "real." Audiences are seeking escapism, away from all their troubles. They want science-fiction, but they're getting horror. They want comedies and to laugh, but they're getting serious movies about real-life drama.

You are here to change things. You have just the right movies that everyone is looking for. You have the enthusiasm, the production team, the intelligence and knowledge.

Vampires

AND OTHER STEREOTYPES

VAMPIRISM...DON'T BELIEVE THE HYPE!

A BRIMSTONE PRODUCTION Presents
BILL WHITE • WENDY BEDNARZ • VAMPIRES AND OTHER STEREOTYPES
Starring ED HUBBARD • RICK POLI • ANNA DiPACE • SUZANNE SCOTT • MICK McCLEERY
Original Soundtrack THE KRYPT • Special Make-up Effects IMAGEFFECTS STUDIOS
Director of Photography TULLIO TEDESCHI
Written, Produced & Directed by KEVIN LINDENMUTH
Copyright © 1994 Brimstone Productions. All Rights Reserved

Well before the onslaught of television series with vampires, slayers, and things that go bump in the night, Kevin Lindenmuth led the industry with his very own production, *Vampires and Other Stereotypes.*

You have a strategy that you have analyzed from every conceivable angle. You know how the industry works. You know where it's going. You know what to do. And you have your trusty business plan to prove it. Now all you need is the money from your investors to make it happen.

Think positively if you encounter bad data. There is a silver lining to every dark cloud. There are two sides to every coin. Use your positive thinking to your advantage and include it in your business plan. What information you ultimately choose to include or omit is up to you. Do not be deceitful, but be fair and truthful.

Let's look at a different scenario with less-than-favorable data. Let's pretend the world as a whole was in an economic slump the year prior to you writing your business plan. Industry everywhere, including studios and independent producers, lost money. The motion picture industry hit all-time lows. Rather than simply introduce these negative figures, start by citing the years prior to the one in question. Perhaps the years before saw record highs in box-office grosses and total number of movies released. Perhaps attendance at movie theaters was recently at all-time highs. Find something positive — an angle or an edge — and build on it. Now take all your positive information and present it before you introduce anything else in this section of your business plan. Portray a pretty picture — an aura of success— before showing any less-than-positive material. Now when it comes time to post the unfavorable matter, do not talk about it in a negative way. Mention it as if it doesn't surprise you. You expect bad times, and you're prepared to deal with them head-on.

Quickly move on to your place in the scheme of things and how your projects will fit in even in this time of economic turmoil. Refer to the examples I employed above. Then just as quickly move onto future projections. Like I said, nobody can second-guess the future. Certainly there is educated forecasting. And there are trends to help plot a course for any industry. But forecasting is not guaranteed. It is at best an educated estimate that takes into consideration current influential factors—factors that often change without a moment's notice.

In Hindsight

What you have just done is taken your potential investor's attention off current figures and trends, and shown him or her an overall picture of the industry. You've taken their sights off the tree and shown them the forest. You've basically shown them that despite current woes, the industry is a multi-billion dollar industry with plenty of room for success.

Never be deceitful with your information. Be fair. But be positive and search for the silver lining. Identify sources, and if you decide to go against the grain, be sure to provide plenty of supporting documents and information for the decisions you make.

The Money Trail

There is one more very important thing you will be required to include in this section of the business plan for potential investors: the money trail. Every industry has a money trail—that is, where the money wanders throughout its various stages as it makes its way through the system — and the motion picture industry is no exception.

Investors will read this section carefully to get an idea of how you will potentially make lots of money for them. The only thing most of them might know up until they read your business plan is that any transaction would mean they give you their money, you deposit it in your bank account, and you use their funds to produce a movie. That's it.

Of course they want to know more. How will that investment potentially come back to them, and how will it very possibly return a profit? You must explain in detail how the money flows from entity to entity, beginning with the investor's capitalization, working its way through production, picking up again at the box-office, and concluding with the investors. Therefore, your money plan must *begin* with the investor, and *end* with the investor.

I wish I could say laying out the money trail is an easy task. It is not. Although there are several fundamental thoroughfares that are prominent in most cases as capital works its way through the system, every motion picture deal is set up differently enough to warrant distinct financial returns.

Several factors that affect the money trail include:

- Source of funding
- Terms and conditions of funding
- Interest rates on advances, presales and/or loans
- Terms and conditions of distribution
- Terms and conditions established with exhibitors
- Taxes and foreign tariffs
- Gross participations
- Promotions and marketing
- Distribution and/or sales agent fees
- Box-office performance

These factors usually play some role, together, in part, or in various combinations, in most motion picture production and distribution deals. Just how much each element contributes to or hinders the money trail on its way back to you and your investors depends on the arrangements you and your company have made with your financiers and your distributors.

THE TOTEM POLE EFFECT

Generally, once funds have been spent on the production of a motion picture, the only way to retrieve any of that money is to get the product to the public as soon as possible via a distribution outlet. Simply put, if you can't arrange distribution or sales of your finished production, you have just blown all your investor's capital. You *must* get your product to market to recoup the capital.

Money is spent all along the way. From making prints of the finished movie to exhibit in movie theaters, to paying for advertising to get audiences to go see the product, distributors often spend more money on their responsibilities than the budget of the actual motion picture.

Finally the movie plays in theaters. From here, no two money trails are identical. There are several ways to set up financing, distribution and exhibition — and all the hoops and loops the money goes through — as well as several creative ways to pay for services during production, and each imparts its own influence on what has come to be known in the motion picture industry as *The Totem Pole Effect*. Essentially, it is a trickle-down effect, where the money generated at the box-office filters endlessly down the totem pole until it finds its way to the producers and ultimately the investors.

Let's say your movie rakes in $20 million at the box-office over a period of a few weeks or months. The first entities to see that money are the exhibitors, or movie theaters. Those movie theaters are the highest entities on the totem pole. They are the first to get their share of the money pie. The customers that pay to watch your movie give them the money. Depending on what kind of deal they have in place with the distributor, the movie theaters will keep their share of the money right there at the source. What is left of the box-office money is trickled down to the next head on the totem pole. In this case, it is the distributor. Now remember all the promotions and marketing that took place to generate publicity for your project? That was the distributor who probably paid for most of it. In some cases, the producer will provide some of the funds to assist the distributor, but for this example only the distributor takes the risk. Now the distributor takes its fee out of the money it receives. This fee was predetermined when you struck your deal. The distributor will also now take out its expenses and overhead involved in the promotion and distribution of your project. This could be several million dollars alone. If the distributor advanced any money to you, let's say on a negative pick-up deal, it will also get that money back now, plus interest. Once the distributor takes its share of the capital, what is left trickles down to the next head on the totem pole. Will it be the producer? Perhaps. But what if you struck a gross participation deal with an actor, for example? Depending on the contract, the actor may be next in line before the producers. Finally, the money will trickle down to the second-to-last head on the totem pole. This head is the investor. Usually an investor will get all of his or her money back and then some before splitting any of it with the producers. The producer is always the last head on the totem pole, and rarely sees any profits unless the movie is a substantial hit at the box-office.

Sounds pretty depressing, right? Well, like it or not, this is the way it has been done for decades. And if it's been done this way for so long, and movies keep getting made, someone must be busy making money somewhere.

There was a time when the major studios, distributors and theaters were the same entity, or were owned by the same company. This created an unfair market competition for outside producers, and subsequently this arrangement was outlawed by the federal government.

Today, production companies, distributors and movie theaters are all *officially* owned by disparate entities.

As for money trickling down to you as a producer, remember you will get paid for your services during the production of your movie. You need money to take the time off to shoot your project, right? Well, you should take your fees to shoot the movie during the production phase. Remember that the investor is taking the risk, not you. You are being compensated up front even if the movie bombs. You have collected your fees. So what finally trickles down will go to the investor long before you. These deals all vary, and you would be wise to consult with an entertainment attorney regarding these matters.

Typically, your investors should first and foremost get all their money back, plus a profit. If they put up, let's say, $2 million to shoot your movie, they should get the first $2 million to $3 million that trickles down the totem pole to your camp. Once they have their initial investment back, plus a profit, they can now split some of the remaining funds with the producers. These subsequent numbers are often 50/50 or even up to 80/20, usually in favor of the investors.

These figures and variables apply equally to all other sources of income and all other structured deals, including the home-video market, cable television and pay-per-view programming.

FilmProfit Software

Because these figures can be overwhelming, and trying to keep track of all the money can be burdensome, I highly recommend you seek the services of the FilmProfit™ Software designed by Jeffrey Hardy and his associates at Big Horse, Inc. (see Sample Distribution Reports by FilmProfit in the Fictitious Indie Business Plan at the end of this book).

A Practical Guide

You are encouraged to follow along with the sample business plan at the end of this book. This section is written in direct correlation with it, explaining in detail what is written there and why.

The Movie Industry

When you write this section of the business plan, you need to stick with the facts and nothing but the facts. Explain right away how the movie industry functions in general, what it is comprised of, and what makes it tick. What is it all about? As I explained above, the industry is more than just making movies.

Give a breakdown of the different elements indigenous to the motion picture industry. Then elaborate on how they are linked together — how they function by feeding off of one another and why.

An Overview of the Central Process

For this header, go into more detail elaborating on the entire process of the creation of a motion picture. Take your potential investors by the hand and walk them through each step, from concept to writing to producing.

Pretend you are a professor in college and your investors are your students. Now assume your investors know nothing about this business and it is your job to educate them on the workings of how movies are made. Your goal when writing this section should be that by the time your potential investors complete reading this section of your business plan, they will be experts in the entire field of motion picture production, even if only in theory.

As you take them by the hand through the process, give examples, cite anecdotes, and really make them comprehend how everything works by way of example. Write out questions in the course of assembling this section, then answer them yourself. Give investors an overall view of the process so that they can grasp what it is that you are trying to accomplish with their money.

What are the differences between studio films and independent films? Besides the financing, how do both sides think differently? What projects do they prefer and why? How does a project get started? How does your company fit in? How will it perform?

Explain the actual process of writing and producing a movie. Although everyone has seen the behind-the-scenes of how movies are made on television and in documentaries, you must assume your investors never had the chance to watch one of these.

Lastly, wrap it all up by stating approximately how long the entire process you just described will last. Investors want to know how long it will take to get their money back, and getting an idea of how lengthy the creation process will be should help them get an idea of this time frame.

Promotion and Exhibition

For this header, you continue your lecture to potential investors on how the entire business functions. Once you have a completed movie in hand, it must be promoted to the public if you desire to draw audiences to pay to watch your masterpiece.

Start by describing the present state of motion picture promotion and exhibition. Highlight any changes or particular trends. For example, as I write this, there are a small number of movie theaters popping up across the country with special high-definition digital projectors as opposed to the standard 35mm or 70mm film projectors. This could signify a coming change overall to the way we watch movies in the future, or you might decide it will just be an added bonus, and film projectors are here to stay. Whichever you believe, and whatever information you can find to support your thoughts, this is something that investors will no doubt find very interesting. Bring it to their attention, and have fun explaining all the pros and cons.

Describe how you, as a producer, will work with distributors. How will your movie be promoted, exactly? How much will it cost, and who will put up the financing? Have you secured a deal where the distributor will put up all the money for prints and advertising, or will you be asking the investors to put up the funds? How does a movie make its way from you, the producer, to movie theaters across the world? To television sets and video-cassette recorders everywhere? Are there any differences between domestic and foreign exhibitors? For you, this might be a simple bit of trivial knowledge. For investors, it could mean clearing up a nagging question.

Be clear and concise, and never assume your potential investors know too much. This is not to say that you should be condescending in any way. Just think of yourself as the professor, and your potential investors as the students. State all facts clearly and logically.

Video, Cable and Ancillary Outlets

There are, of course, other outlets for making money with your finished movie project than just movie theaters. For this header, you should explain to your potential investors exactly what they are, and how they relate to theatrical exhibition.

Home video and cable programming are the two more prominent outlets that usually follow a project's theatrical release. In fact, many movies never play in theaters and go straight to video release or cable television, such is the revenue potential of these outlets. While certainly a successful run at the theater most often increases revenues for the same project in home video sales and cable programming, these markets stand on their own merit, capable of generating satisfactory revenue for any quality production.

Explain to potential investors how success in one market can lead to success in another, and how producers and distributors strategize to exploit each avenue without depleting the next. List the rest of the ancillary outlets, including merchandising, broadcast television and the Internet. Describe their potential, their likelihood, and your plans with them. Is it your desire to entertain these markets? Perhaps you have a book deal in place to coincide with the release of your movie. It might be your plan to tie both products together. Or perhaps you might decide the Internet is still too insecure and you will pass on it this time around.

Whatever your thoughts and plans are in relation to these various arenas, your investors will want to know everything about them.

Present Trends

It's research time again, and heavy-duty research at that. Grab a stack of *Hollywood Reporter* newspapers or *Daily Variety* magazines and start jotting industry figures and information down. You might want to contact some of the data services I have listed in Appendix B.

Wherever you get your information, for this header you should list what the present trends are for the motion picture industry. How much money is presently being made? What were the revenues last year? Is the trend up or down? How much money are other producers spending on shooting their projects? Tell investors about theatrical revenues as well as home video and cable programming and any other outlets you personally feel worth mentioning. For the sake of clarity, your figures should always be broken down to domestic and foreign revenues.

How will you and your company fare in this industry? What are you plans? What is your strategy? Back up all your claims.

A Long Term Prospect

In the last header you touched on present trends. For this header, you should make an educated assumption of the future in general. Take all the information you've just compiled and make a projection. Industry publications and analysts make projections all the time. Feel free to use a published one, but be sure to give proper credit and cite the source.

It is usually better for you to take the strategies and markets that you have in mind, run them past figures and information you have compiled that points to the future, then present a custom observation based on your personal knowledge. If your observations are mostly in line with professional forecasts, then you should feel confident with your predictions.

It is not wise to go against the grain on this one. If, for example, you decide to make horror movies, and such films have rapidly been declining in revenues at the box office during the past five years, I would not recommend you state that you believe the next few years will see a revivification in the genre. It is not a logical assumption, and it will come across as wishful thinking at best.

I can't emphasize this enough: *don't just state your opinions.* Support your conclusions with facts and figures and solid information. Are the markets growing? Are foreign countries getting more access to cable television? Are VCRs and DVD players reaching more homes in South American or Asian countries? What are the facts in America, Canada

Action is the number one selling genre world-wide. Combine that with a touch of science fiction and a sexy star and you have a recipe for success. *Battle Beast* performed above expectations for filmmaker Philip R. Cable.

and Mexico? What are the revenues in India? Find all of this information and more, and present it in support of your forecasting statements.

International Appraisal

Take all your facts and figures and look at them strictly from an international perspective. Which countries are the biggest buyers of American-made motion pictures? Look back approximately five years, describe the trends in all arenas—theatrical, home video, cable and satellite. Take a look at the present and describe the same. Now do as you did before by creating a projection for the future, but this time break it down by dominating countries. For example, Germany and Japan have been two of the largest foreign consumers of American-made motion pictures in recent years. Describe their exact figures and data to investors—past, present and projected future.

Once again, support your statements. Cite specific articles or reports. Be sure to list your sources.

6

The Movie Market

To market, to market, to buy a fat pig;
Home again, home again, jiggety jig.
To market, to market, to buy a fine hog;
Home again, home again, joggety jog.
— Old Nursery Rhyme

NOTHING HAS CHANGED

If you look back just a few hundred years to when most public trade was done at open-air markets— when farmers showed off their fresh-picked fruit, and craftspeople bargained with their wood-carved pottery and relics— you will find the basic structure that drives and governs the motion picture marketplace. In fact, in many parts of the world the open-air market still reigns supreme for daily activity, trade and bartering— and in Hollywood, believe it or not, the same instinct thrives.

The market, today as it did then, holds fast to the rules of supply and demand. Essentially, nothing has changed.

APPLES AND ORANGES

Open-air markets were the epicenter of commerce in historical civilization, and they prospered because the people who sold their products were also a part of the crowd doing the buying— so they knew what was required, what would sell, what wouldn't, and what people needed to get them through the drought or winter storms. The markets were a symbiotic circle where everybody's needs were met. Everybody always knew who was selling what, what was in demand and what was not. If it was cold, you were sure to find blankets, hides, wools and scarfs offered by the local hunters, tailors or shepherds. If it was hot, you were sure to find plenty of fresh-picked and varied fruits brought out by the local farmers. There was a balance. The size of the crowds were anticipated and enough merchandise was brought along to sell, share, trade or deal.

Often a stranger would show up with a new product— a new fruit, for instance, or a pet, from a far-away land. Curiosity would abound, and some brave folk would venture to buy the oddity. Many, however, would move on without a second glance, not really feeling any need for something so unusual and out of the norm — something so out of the mainstream. Something they could do without.

Usually the seller who made plenty of noise to attract attention to his product or services would make more sales than the one who stood idly by waiting for somebody to purchase his offerings. If the nearby land had plenty of apples growing on trees, and it was widely known that two or three of the locals brought apples every time to the market, not too many people would want to compete with them. They would not want to bring more apples to a saturated market. Instead, they would look for something different yet equally in demand to offer — oranges or nuts, perhaps.

KNOW YOUR PRODUCT LIKE THE BACK OF YOUR HAND

And so it is in a nutshell the same with the market of motion pictures. In order to go to market, you must know your product. You must know where it will fit in with the rest of the offerings, how it will be perceived by the masses, if it will potentially sell, and just how much competition it will face. You must effectively become a part of the crowd in order to participate in a consumer-driven arena.

In order for any motion picture production — no matter how large or how small, studio or independent — to be a success, you must know who potentially will pay to watch your movie and then find a way to get the product to them. The only way to do this is to be very aware of your film's potential. You must know what you have on your hands. Otherwise, how will you possibly know the best way to convince others to pay to watch it or buy it?

Let us consider the open-air market. For the sake of discussion, let us pretend every fruit or vegetable sold is a different genre or movie in the marketplace of motion pictures. Apples are horror films, oranges are love stories, bananas are comedies, grapefruit are action-adventure films, lettuce heads are science-fiction, and tomatoes are movies with fantasy themes. Imagine you're walking through the marketplace. Now take a look around and ask yourself:

- Which fruits or vegetables are the customers buying most of?
- How large is the crowd of buyers overall, and do they appear content with the market or dissatisfied?
- Which merchants are selling more, and why?
- Which merchants are selling less, and why?
- How much competition among the merchants and similar products is there?
- Do you find the identical product at more than one stand?
- Is there a shortage of or demand for a particular product?
- Who is doing the most talking and "advertising" their product? Is it working?
- What's happening to any new, untested products? Are they selling? How is the crowd reacting?
- Could you conceivably offer a fresher fruit or vegetable than those already being offered?

You might find this analogy silly, but I assure you it is anything but. Let's take your

Ted V. Mikels' *Blood Orgy of the She-Devils* is representative of the filmmaker's conscious effort to mix the horror and sex genres — a successful combination of market niches.

movie now and run it past our little model. Let us say your movie is a horror film. In the analogy, that would make it an apple. Now let us take your apple — your movie — to the marketplace and see how well it performs. The two distinct scenarios we will study are as follows:

- The first scenario will provide a successful offering of your apples to the public.
- The second scenario will provide a dismal reception of your apples from the public.

The sun is rising, and the roosters are crowing. The clouds dissipate as the morning dew comes calling. The common folk — the paying public — are waking from a long night's rest. You get up early and race to work. You pick several dozen apples from your favorite tree, wash and shine them, then head out. As you approach the open-air market with your bucketful of delicious red apples, you find that another group of farmers has already set up a display of apples, nearly identical to the ones you plan on selling.

You pay the fact little attention. It doesn't bother you. Apples, you are perfectly aware, are a common product that almost always sell out. Apples, you feel, are mainstream merchandise. People will always pay for nice, juicy apples. As night approaches, you head home with an empty bucket and a pocket full of money.

That is the first scenario. You did well. Your product sold because you brought the people something they knew all too well and demanded.

Now let's look at a different scenario with the same product:

You approach the same marketplace in the morning with your bucket of apples. This time you find that there are a dozen vendors selling the same apples, and the marketplace is about half as full as it usually is. You notice the apples aren't selling as well as the exotic fruits a lone vendor is peddling a few yards down the aisle from you. In fact, the vendor with the strange fruits sells out before you put your bucket down, and by the end of the night you only manage to sell half of the apples in your bucket. You head home with most of your merchandise and barely enough money to buy bread and bacon for your family.

That is the second scenario. You didn't do as well as in the first. Your product failed because the market was saturated and you were offering something people have had enough of. Audiences were looking for something new and refreshing.

ANALYSIS

Let's stick with the open-air model and analyze the pros and cons of both scenarios, then compare them to the motion picture market. Why did you make off like a bandit in the first example and barely survive the second? What went right the first time, and what went wrong the second? Because this is a metaphorical rendering of the basis of a motion picture's market, only the two scenarios which I have presented will be discussed. Keep in mind, however, that these represent but a minuscule combination of the multiple possibilities when it comes to all the factors that affect the marketplace.

In the first scenario, the open-air market was full of customers. They were eager to buy merchandise, and they did. Apples were being sold by relatively few merchants, including yourself. The demand for the apples was strong, and the supply was solid. Despite a little competition, you managed to sell all your stock. When you replace the

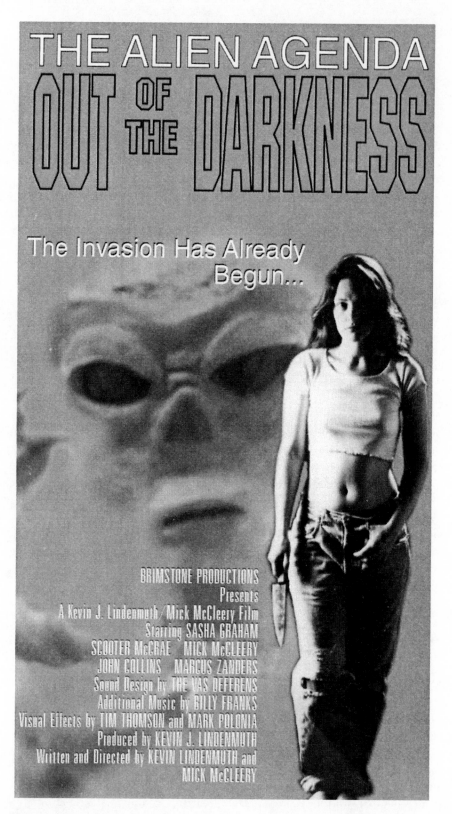

Capitalizing on the market's demand for the genre, Kevin Lidenmuth produced *The Alien Agenda: Out of the Darkness*, a sequel to the very successful first installment subtitled *Endangered Species*.

variables in this model with the motion picture market, it would go something like this:

The domestic economy is strong, and people are driving in droves to movie theaters. Business is booming, and audiences are looking for solid entertainment. Horror films have always been solid sellers, and presently there are only a few good horror films showing—yours included. There is essentially little competition and enough interest for each horror film that box-office sales are strong for everybody. Enough money trickles down the totem pole to you so that you are able to pay a profit to your investors as well as have enough money to personally finance your next picture.

Let's look at the other side of the coin with our second scenario. The open-air market was not as full of customers as it normally is. Customers were extra picky, asked a lot of questions, and weren't quick to buy. There were clearly more apples available than customers would ever care to buy, yourself included. The demand for the apples was dismal, and the supply was beyond saturated. Down the aisle, exotic fruit was selling more than anything else. After a heart-wrenching day, you walk yourself home with over half of the stock you took with you in the morning. When you replace the variables in this model with the motion picture market, it would go something like this:

The domestic economy is staggering, and people are conserving their finances, holding back from frivolous expenses. Business is slow, and audiences are not particularly looking for any kind of solid entertainment unless it's really and truly unique. Horror films have always been solid sellers, but presently there are over two dozen scary movies showing at the local cineplex—yours included. There is essentially too much competition and minimal interest in horror films—box-office sales are lacking for everybody. The only kind of films making any money are the independent films with themes the studios would never touch in a million years. No money trickles down the totem pole to you, and you are forced to sell your children, your cars and get a third mortgage on your Hollywood Hills cottage to stop the Internal Revenue Service from auctioning off your business. Your investors lose all their money, and you have a lot of explaining to do if you ever wish to make another movie again.

I can't explain the market any more clearly than this. When you make a movie, be sure it is commercial and has market potential. I know no one can guarantee the sale of your movie or how well it will perform at the box office, but you can make an educated guess and proceed accordingly. To not do so is reckless and you may as well take your investor's money and throw it on a craps table at a Las Vegas casino.

INDEPENDENT OR STUDIO?

You might stop and consider the open-air market in our model as being governed by the studios, and consequently ask where the independent filmmaker fits in. The answer is simple. With a good product, you will always find someone to take your apples to the open-air market. Or you could yourself set up a small stand with unique products that none of the main-stream vendors want to touch. If you see everyone eating all the mainland fruit (apples, oranges and pears), you might want to try bringing in mangos or kiwi fruit—a departure for the open-air market, and a niche for you.

When put in motion picture terms, a good film will always find a distributor. There will always be an outlet for independent films, even if it is done on a smaller scale. In

Killers did so well financially for The Asylum, a sequel was quickly produced to capitalize on the market's demand for the genre.

our model, mangos and kiwi fruit are the exotic or specialty fruits—or lesser known independent films. They have their place in the market.

As for the comment that all good films always find a distributor, it is my experience that there are too many filmmakers who are biased with their own product, produce something entirely unmarketable, then complain that their *good* film can't find an outlet. The truth, most often, is if a film can not find a distributor, it is for good reason. That is why you have to consider absolutely everything in its entirety—from every conceivable angle—within this book.

Many small films obviously will *not* find their way to movie theaters. Releasing a motion picture to theaters costs almost as much money as producing the film in the first place. Studios and distributors spend tens of millions of dollars for producing the many prints of the finished film and all the advertising that goes along with it. Sometimes the numbers just don't add up or make any sense when considering a theatrical release. Sometimes a direct-to-video, television or cable release is a more guaranteed way of recouping an investment and making a profit on top of that.

So why consider theatrical releases at all if you plan on making a $1 million movie that chances are will never play at a movie theater? Because you must always aim high and you must always show investors the entire arena in all its glory. You must show the possibilities, and you should never write yourself out of a potential theatrical release. Describe to investors all the possibilities, even though chances are great your product will go straight to video, or that is the way you plan it from the beginning. In the world of distribution, anything is possible—look at *The Blair Witch Project*.

SECONDARY FACTORS TO CONSIDER

While the story and presentation of your movie will speak for itself and sink or swim accordingly, there are secondary factors for you to consider when taking your project to the marketplace. These attributes can enhance or restrict the performance potential of your motion picture. In fact, these are things you should seriously consider before selecting your project for production. Loosely, secondary factors that directly influence the performance of your movies are as follows:

- Subject matter
- Demographics
- Movie ratings

To know these elements well and how they function will serve to enhance the success of your financial road to the marketplace. Each attribute works hand in hand with the other, equally influencing the viability of the overall motion picture.

SUBJECT MATTER

It goes without saying that the subject matter alone of any motion picture can make or break a film. Imagine a stunning screenplay, brilliant directing and award-winning acting in a movie about child molesters. It does not matter how well crafted the screenplay is, or how much time the director took envisioning the story, or how well rehearsed the actors are in a movie like this. The moment audiences hear what the subject matter is about, you can rest assured a large percentage of audiences will stop cold in their tracks before proceeding to the local theater to watch this movie. Certainly you will still get people to watch your movie — but you will lose a large number of potential customers based on your choice of subject matter alone. People do not want to watch material as aberrant and disturbing as this. The subject matter is taboo.

DEMOGRAPHICS

Your understanding of demographics is another equally important factor that can influence, enhance or restrict audiences when it comes time to watch your movie. When selecting which project you will produce, think of the demographics— think specifically of which audience groups you will be targeting.

People are a vast and complicated bunch of individuals. Different populations and ethnic groups enjoy different kinds of stories. Religion or economic strife might influence an audience's choice of viewing pleasure. Just because you enjoy a particular kind of movie does not mean everybody else will. Study who enjoys what and *why*. Then act accordingly in your selection of material.

Again let us return to the great movie with top-shelf writing, directing and acting. Let us consider religion and imagine the movie is about Christians taking over all of Asia, and in the story, all other religions— Buddhism, Islam, Hinduism, Taoism, etc.— disappear. You can rest assured your movie will never play in any country where those religions prevail. You've just killed off an entire part of your potential audience with your choice of story line.

On the other side of the coin, you might very well attract a large number of Christians who otherwise would not have taken the time to watch your movie. Based on your advertisements and word of mouth reaching the intended target audience, Christians everywhere might want to see what all the fuss is about and you suddenly have a hit movie on your hands.

MOVIE RATINGS

One of the most influential attributes a motion picture can possess is a movie rating from the Motion Picture Association of America (MPAA). You have no doubt seen them on posters and advertisements everywhere. Movies are Rated G (General Audiences), PG (Parental Guidance Recommended), PG-13 (Some Material May Be Inappropriate For Children Under 13), R (Restricted), and NC-17 (No Children Under 17).

Whichever rating your movie receives will influence, in some capacity, which audiences will pay to watch your movie. In effect, the rating of your movie will restrict who can and can not watch your product in theaters, as well as who *will* and *will not*. If you produce a children's movie, for example, it is obvious the content of your motion picture had better receive a G or PG rating. Otherwise, you've made a movie for a target audience that will not be allowed to watch it and the financial outcome goes without saying.

Interestingly, audience groups such as young teens often will not watch movies unless they have at least a PG-13 rating. They just don't consider it *cool* enough. If you shoot a tough cop movie with a lot of action adventure and romance, some audiences will not consider it worthy if it doesn't possess at least an R rating. They think the movie will be cheesy or less than exciting. Some producers actually re-edit their movies after they receive their rating from the MPAA in order to satisfy their target audience. If the movie is too violent, for example, and the target audience is children, producers will go back and tone down the material to get a PG rating as opposed to a PG-13 or R. And the same holds true the other way around — if a movie that producers wish to promote as terror, for example, receives a PG rating, then it is obvious the material is not scary enough. Disaster is almost certainly guaranteed at the box office, so producers go back and re-edit or re-shoot parts of the movie to attain a preferred rating.

Then there are those producers who opt to not have their films rated at all. Many independent filmmakers do this. First of all, it is not cheap to submit your motion picture to the MPAA for a rating. Smaller films usually can not spare the extra funds required. Some producers will actually put "Not Rated" or "This Film Is Not Rated" on their promotional material. So if a film rating is not really necessary, why obtain one? The answer is simple — *demographics.* Audiences do not always know what they are paying to watch. They are lured into the theater through advertising and word of mouth. But they have not seen the film and do not know what they are ultimately in for. Audiences have learned to trust the MPAA rating as a guide to let them know what they will be watching on the screen when they pay their hard-earned money to watch your movie. Some people, for example, are offended at nudity or foul language. They will not watch such a movie, so an R rating lets them know they should expect offensive depictions and language. Parents want to take their kids to watch wholesome entertainment. They want to see a G or PG rating on the film before they pay to watch your movie. Others are not interested in the mild stuff and only want to watch movies that are Rated R or NC-17.

COMPARISONS

You must keep marketing in mind from the moment you conceive of your project to the moment you produce it and release it. You must also keep marketing in mind at all times when dealing with your potential investors. After you've thought about all your marketing options and considerations, and after you've gone over every marketing angle, you should present your findings in a clear and concise manner to your investors. A page will do, or several pages will do. The point is it must make plenty of sense.

- How viable is the market for your type of motion picture and why?
- What audience will you target and why?
- What MPAA rating will you aim for and why?
- How well has your intended market performed in the past and what are its current trends?

You have your work cut out for you yet again with research. You must convince your potential investors that you know exactly what you are talking about, but you must present him or her with facts to back up your convictions.

Information can be obtained from various sources such as industry magazines and periodicals or data services (see Appendix B). If you study long enough, you will find performance figures for similar films and you can even form your own trends analysis based on such numbers. One of the things I highly recommend you do in this section of your business plan is put together a table comparing films that are similar to the ones you plan to produce. This will provide your potential investors with a clear cut black and white overview of past performance figures on films similar to yours in budget and genre. I recommend you get these figures from Big Horse, Inc., as opposed to hunting them down on your own in the various publications. There are just too many figures to go searching for.

However you get your information, the data you present to your potential investors should include:

- Comparable titles in terms of genre or budget
- The cost to produce the movie
- The cost to distribute and promote the movie
- Domestic theatrical box-office performance
- Foreign theatrical box-office performance
- Number of screens the movie played theatrically

- Gross profit/loss
- Specific genre of the movie
- Domestic distributor
- Date the movie was released
- Domestic video performance
- Foreign video performance
- Video units shipped

By providing this information, you are giving your potential investors a hands-on overview of what to expect with the performance of your films. The investor can look over the information and essentially make up his or her own mind. The data should speak for itself.

A PRACTICAL GUIDE

You are encouraged to follow along with the sample business plan at the end of this book. This section is written in direct correlation with it, explaining in detail what is written there and why.

The Movie Market

When you write this section of your business plan, you should assume your potential investor knows nothing about marketing in general. Introduce this section of your business plan by defining the movie market's role in the entire scheme of the motion picture industry. How does it fit in, and why is it so important? What it comes down to is that the market is the only way a project will be able to get its money back, and then some. Without a market, there is no audience to pay for your product, and without an audience to pay for your product, you will lose your entire investment.

You should then describe how the market is broken down and why. Describe the various genres and types of films— independent versus studio, low-budget versus high-budget, etc. Break down the various themes movies take on, and how they influence an audience to get them to rush to the theater. Describe the various demographics, their viability, and why you are targeting specific audiences. Take the potential investor by the hand, and cite specific examples and movie titles when mentioning the various genres. Provide poster artwork or one-sheets if you have to, to let them see the movies you refer to, and then describe their performance in the various markets. Describe how domestic and foreign performances of the same picture can vary, and why. Talk about how dissimilar audiences will react differently to the same movie, and why.

All of this will serve you when it comes time to present your choice of movie project to produce. If you can show the potential of your product, you will have little explaining to do to your investors in this department. For the most part, investors want to see dollar signs. They want to be convinced they will get their money back, and then some. Often they care less about the choice of genre than they do about the financial viability of the project. By presenting this information to your potential investors here, you are paving the road for your movie straight to the market — and for your investors, straight to the bank.

Continue describing the importance of marketing to your investors, and focus now on where your independent film will fit in. The motion picture world is dominated by studio films with studio distributors. So where do independent films fit in? How can your films compete with the big boys? Take all that we have talked about in this chapter as well as the rest of the book and describe your place in the market, and how and why you believe your products will perform successfully. Support your statements with recent news of similar independent films performing as you expect yours to. Always write with confidence. Unless you are 100 percent certain of what you speak of, do not relay it. Do not exaggerate figures or facts. Do not modify them in any way. Remember, facts and figures can easily be verified by anyone, including accountants and attorneys.

Competitive Advantages

Here you should list the unique strengths and attributes that you and your production staff possess to facilitate the production of your movies, as well as an educated approach to the marketplace.

How will you and your company do things slightly differently — *with an edge* — than most producers in Hollywood? Will you watch the money better, thus be more economical and efficient? What about your respect for the audience? Will you take special care to give them what they want to see — effectively facilitating your place in the marketplace?

Show your potential investors that you are serious. Talk about yourself and your team-mates here. Boast about your accomplishments, and why they should take a chance with you. Make them believe without a doubt that you know the market better than anybody else, and that you've done your homework.

One thing to be cautious about here is the following: If you gather information and present it eloquently in writing, you had better be prepared to know your material in person as well. There is nothing worse than presenting a package of material that is breath-taking, only to be speechless when a potential investor quizzes you on it. This does not mean that you should commit everything that is in your business plan to memory. Certainly specific sections will pertain to specific individuals and their responsibilities. If you are questioned about marketing, for example, but that is not your department, just pass the buck. But whoever the buck is passed to had better come through with flying colors. Otherwise it will appear as if all you did was copy everything out of this book or some other source without any idea of what you typed. Your cover will effectively be blown and you will come across as someone who does not truly know what he is representing. Your potential investor will be no more.

Competition

While we discussed your competition in the marketplace in other sections of this book as well as in the sample business plan, for this header you will very specifically describe your competition to your potential investors.

Rather than discuss the different kinds of movies and studios in general, here you should discuss the behind-the-scenes of your competition to give your potential investor a better idea of how things function. What kinds of deals are struck at the studios? How are they different from the way you will handle your business and marketing? What about other independent producers? Discuss the strengths and weaknesses, pros and cons, of handling things on a studio level versus an independent level.

You should also specifically name your competition. This would of course include all the major studios, mini-majors, as well as independent producers. Now, it might very well seem overwhelming and daunting to describe so much competition. I mean, you might scare your investor away, or send him running to invest in the competition, right? Perhaps. You might ask yourself why even do it, then. The answer is because you want to present a fair and accurate overall picture of what you're asking your investor to take part in. Making movies can be a fun experience in one way. But what it all comes down to is that it is a business, and in order to beat the competition, you must treat it like a business. Some independent film-makers even use the term *war* rather than business. And they are correct in more ways than one. You might in fact be wise to pick up a book on history or war strategies as dictated by *General Douglas MacArthur* or *Attila the Hun*. The first rule in war, you will always find, is know your enemy. And so it is with the marketing of your motion pictures— know your competition.

In order to be successful, then, you should very accurately describe your competition and discuss its weaknesses or rather your superiority and ability to compete effectively. How will your business deals compare to the competition? What about your screenplays? An indie producer can easily possess a much more elaborate and entertaining literary property than a studio. The only difference will be the resources with which to shoot it, but the bottom line is an independent producer with a solid script is a force to reckon with.

What about distribution? Do you have a special deal with a distributor that guarantees your movie will reach the masses? What about genre magazines or Internet outlets? Do you have special connections or relationships that will assist you with marketing? Whatever you have that can convince potential investors you stand a solid chance of success, be sure to list it here.

Risk

As tough as it might have been for you to discuss your competition in detail, you now must describe something even more crucial for your potential investors to be aware of— the inherent risk in taking a chance with you.

There is no getting around it. All the planning, big name stars and careful research in the world will not guarantee the success of any motion picture. When all is said and done, it all comes down to the audience and whether or not they pay to watch your film. The bottom line is if your potential investor takes a chance with you, he could very well lose every single penny he gives you. Although this fact might appear obvious, you nonetheless must present this fact under this header. You must spell it out for your potential investor to read.

There is no way whatsoever to guarantee the performance of any motion picture. You can't put a gun to people's heads and force them to pay to watch your movie. You can, however, do the best research possible and make an educated decision as to what might work.

After describing the risk to your potential investors, describe briefly the various ways a movie can make its money back. Illustrate how as an independent producer it is sometimes easier to get your money back since you are trying to get back less than a studio needs to get back to break even. A studio film, for example, that costs $50 million to shoot, with an additional $25 million for prints and advertising, has to gross over $100 million at the box office just to break even. An indie film that costs $1 million and goes straight to video and cable, both domestic and foreign, might only need to gross a few million dollars before it starts generating a profit.

From a practical standpoint, the indie film in this example is financially more viable.

Rationale

Now that you've presented the good, the bad and the ugly of the business, wrap it all up with an upbeat and very positive and confident analysis of the entire situation. Describe your plan of action in a nutshell. Take everything you've just laid out for the investors and give them your bottom line — your convictions and why you will succeed.

7

Movie Distribution

"Hollywood is the only industry, even taking in soup companies, which does not have laboratories for the purpose of experimentation."
— Orson Welles (1915–1984)

SINK OR SWIM

The time has come. You've completed your masterpiece epic production, you've spent every last dime of your investor's money, gone weeks without sleep, taken out a third mortgage on your home to cover the budget cost over-runs, got a divorce from your spouse in the process, are now seeing a psychiatrist weekly, and are contemplating filing for bankruptcy protection. Your children don't recognize you any more, and the last time you visited a hair salon was before the first time you set foot on your live movie set. Your life is in shambles, but out of the dust and debris you've managed to do something absolutely wonderful; magical — you've completed your movie project.

In hand, you firmly grip your film negative or video master. This is it. There is no going back. It is do-or-die time. You must sink or swim. Your project will be a success, or it will be a total disappointment. It is time to show the world why you've suffered so dearly for the past six to nine months or more, and try to regain some sense of dignity, as well as your sense of sanity. It is time to distribute your movie to the masses.

OUT OF YOUR HANDS

I have talked about distribution in the other chapters and have given you an overview of the basics and how it all works (see Chapter 5). I do not recommend you attempt to distribute your movie project by yourself. There are simply too many variables in an already complicated system, and if you don't know exactly what you're doing you could potentially ruin the chances of an otherwise successful motion picture ever seeing the light of day.

Instead, I highly suggest you seek a distribution deal prior to shooting your movie if possible, or attempt to garner one immediately after the completion of your project. As you gain experience with your projects, you may in the future decide you can take a chance with self-distribution. If that comes to pass someday, I wish you all the luck and patience in the world. Until then, I urge you to seek out a bona fide distributor for your movies.

So what do you put down in this section of the business plan for your potential investors to read and consider? If you're going to take your project outside the company once it is completed, what exactly are you supposed to impart to them?

The answer is just enough for them to grasp the process and their place — as well as yours, the producer — in the scheme of things.

First of all, you should know that no two distribution deals in Hollywood or abroad are the same. Depending on the elements attached to your project, each factor might play a paramount role in the distribution deal you strike. For instance, many high-paid actors and celebrities demand gross participation for the movie projects they perform in. The common belief is that by lending their name to the project, they are bringing in audiences and box-office revenues that otherwise would not exist. For the most part, they are correct. But their participation is always up to debate, and where exactly on the totem pole they will take their share from is also a subject of negotiation.

Secondly, you should never strike a distribution deal without a qualified entertainment attorney to represent you. I can not stress this enough. An improperly handled distribution deal can lead to serious frustration for the uninitiated independent filmmaker who is unaware of all the pitfalls inherent in any such deal. This is not to say that distribution deals are a negative thing or that all distributors will take advantage of you. It's just that unless you know what you're looking at and agreeing to, you may not understand it until it is too late, and then there is nothing you can do about it.

VARIOUS CONTROLLING FACTORS

It is not the intention of this book to instruct you about distribution of your movie project, other than to advise you to secure a deal with a reputable distributor and with the assistance of a qualified entertainment attorney. The distribution process is an entirely separate and complex procedure that comes after you have secured your financing and after you have produced your motion picture project.

Nevertheless, because distribution is so directly tied to the success of your motion picture, I will introduce you to some of the components involved in a distribution deal. As I stated above, you will need to educate your potential investors on the distribution deals you seek or have in place, so this chapter will serve that need as well. When you work on this part of your business plan, do not overly explain the process. Instead, convey just enough information to make your potential investors satisfied that they know how the procedure works and how they may potentially see a financial return. In this part of your business plan, less is more. And less is better. The reason for this is that the deals can tend to get so complicated, your attempt at explaining them might unnecessarily overwhelm your potential investor even before you've secured the deal.

To illustrate just how much information is proper when describing the distribution process in this part of the business plan, consider the following analogy: Imagine you are explaining to potential passengers how the car or bus you're going to transport them in functions. All you need to do at the most is explain what the vehicle does, how it moves forward on tires, and how it goes from point A to point B. You might want to talk about the steering wheel for direction, elaborate on the gas pedal and brakes for speed, and illustrate the air-bag system for safety. But there is no need to explain the inner workings of the combustible engine, fuel absorption, aero-dynamics of the chassis, tire tread or electrical components that govern the rest of the vehicle. It just isn't necessary, and so much description may just confuse your passengers. It is too much information and serves no purpose *unless it is specifically asked for.*

BREAKING IT ALL DOWN

Some of the factors that fluctuate from deal to deal, thus altering the structure and bottom line of distribution, include:

- Studio or independent distributor
- Middlemen, producer's reps and agents
- Domestic and foreign rights and parameters
- Rights negotiated: theatrical, video, cable, etc.
- Scope and magnitude of distribution
- Source of funds (distributor or producer)
- Presales and box-office advances to producer
- Interest rates on advances, if procured
- Distributor overhead with definition and limits
- Cost of prints and advertising (P&A) with definition and limits
- Producer's (percentage) take of box-office
- Gross participants, usually entities above-the-line
- Sliding scale percentages

These factors are the tip of the iceberg when it comes time to negotiate a distribution deal. This is why I highly recommend that an entertainment attorney handle this kind of deal for you — there are usually a lot more constituents, and trying to protect your assets from all of them can be a trying task.

Remember that the movie business is a business. Everyone involved is out to ultimately do one thing—*make money*. That is why it is a multi-billion dollar world-wide enterprise. As an independent filmmaker, you want your movie to make money in order to entice your investors to keep investing with you in future projects. Your investors want to make money for the same reasons— they are in the business of having their money make money. And it is no different with movie distributors. They want to make money, too, and this usually means getting all they can at the negotiating table. As a movie producer with a product to send to market, it is your job (and your attorney's) to make certain the distribution deal is fair and solid. A qualified entertainment attorney will find all the loopholes and patch them up for you before you sign. In many ways it is like a poker game of cards— each side tries to get away with as much power and agreed-upon percentages as they can without breaking the deal.

STUDIO OR INDEPENDENT DISTRIBUTOR

The biggest difference between studio distributors and independents is money. Studios are capable of pumping millions of dollars into the printing of the film negatives and an advertising campaign to get the public to watch one of its pictures. A smaller independent distributor can not compete at that level.

A good way to ensure the distribution of your projects is to build on the success of prior projects. Kevin Lindenmuth's *Addicted to Murder* trilogy did just this with *Bloodlust*, the third, being the most ambitious.

It has been rare for a low-budget independent motion picture to get picked up by a studio distributor. Even the higher budget independent films rarely made it. It just hasn't happened. Lately, however, a lot of the larger studios have noticed the impact of independent films on the market scene. They have seen the financial potential and have consequently created corporate arms to handle these smaller films. So, the studios are in fact distributing independent films—but they are doing so under the banner of sub-corporations.

In essence, it is common for both independent and studio distributors to pick up an independent motion picture through one of their acquisitions departments. So if given the opportunity, which do you go with? The studio distributor will no doubt give your film a much larger exposure. The independent distributor will give it less. With so much money being thrown at the prints and advertising by a studio, however, chances are more than likely you will never see a dime for you or your investors. With an independent distributor, on the other hand, chances are more than likely that you *will* see a return.

The reason for such a difference between the two is the more money a distributor throws at a project, the more money is necessary to recoup their investment. Remember that distributors usually throw millions and millions of dollars at the promotional campaign for their pictures. Since they are on the front line with the theaters, they will contractually get their money back before you as the producer. Just who puts up the money and how much money is allotted to the project for distribution will influence how much is required to break even for the distributor, plus their fee and their gross participation.

MIDDLEMEN, PRODUCER'S REPS AND AGENTS

Some independent films work with producer's reps and agents as opposed to full-fledged distributors. These films are usually smaller and they find their audience one territory at a time. In effect, the producer's rep does just as his title alleges—he represents you, the producer, to domestic and foreign markets, and attempts to license your project accordingly. Bona fide producer's reps will usually have the same connections to the market as distributors, but on a smaller scale. They will present your completed film to potential customers domestically and abroad. They will make direct calls or make the rounds at markets such as the American Film Market (AFM). The bottom line is the producer's rep attempts to license your project to as many territories as possible for a fee, a percentage of the licensing, or a combination of both.

For the most part, this type of distribution is different from the norm because it usually does not work off the percentages of the box-office grosses. Instead, the completed film is usually licensed for a flat fee, for a specific amount of time. For instance, a producer's representative might find a customer in Japan or Germany, two of the most valued customers for the export of American films. Depending on your project and the rights granted, your producer's rep might license your film to either of them for anywhere from $5000 to $500,000. Your producer's rep then moves on to the remaining territories of the world and attempts to strike similar deals with the rest of them.

The disadvantages of this kind of distribution deal are that it may take longer to get your film exposed and subsequently money returned to you. It may actually take several years for your film to be fully distributed to all the markets. Also, if you license your film to a particular territory for x amount of money and the film performs beyond all expec-

Social Intercourse was entered into and won several film festivals before the filmmakers decided the best way to handle distribution.

tation, you will not see any funds over what you licensed it for. This means if your film becomes a sleeper or breakaway hit, you will not see any income over what you received in the original deal.

Some advantages of this kind of distribution deal on the other hand, are that you could actually study the market and make educated estimates of how much you could license your picture for, then set up a budget to fit within that anticipated income. I know several independent producers that do exactly this. One of them estimated he could license his picture worldwide for about $500,000 total. So he shot his independent picture for $100,000 even. He was able to get his investor's money back, give them a substantial profit on top of that, and have enough left over to put money down on a new house and bankroll his next picture.

Whatever fees or percentages you agree to pay your producer's rep or agent will greatly influence the bottom line and overall distribution deal.

DOMESTIC AND FOREIGN RIGHTS AND PARAMETERS

Most studio distributors will negotiate for worldwide theatrical rights to your project. That means they will have the right to exploit your movie domestically in the United States and Canada, as well as in all foreign nations that import American motion pictures. They may assign the rights to various sub-corporations that handle specific titles in particular countries.

In addition to theatrical rights, most studio distributors will also negotiate for video rights, as well as television and cable distribution. They want the whole thing. Independent distributors on the other hand will often offer a deal where they handle either all domestic distribution, or foreign.

As a producer, you can mix and match the various territories and their respective distribution by assigning different deals to different entities. For example, you might strike a deal with an independent distributor to handle all the domestic theatrical rights of your picture, and a separate company to handle all the domestic video rights. Television and cable can come later, so you might opt to leave those out of the equation for now. As far as foreign, you can mix and match the same. You might deal individually with each distinct territory — with several producer's reps handling pre-defined territories for you, or an independent distributor handling a specific continent. You might also break down the rights offered, such as allowing one producer's rep to handle your theatrical rights in Argentina, for example, and a different one to handle the television rights.

The mix and match possibilities of rights offered — domestic, foreign, theatrical, video, television, cable, multi-media, etc.— can make for a very interesting bottom line and contract. These factors greatly affect your financial take, and again, it is all the more reason for an entertainment attorney to assist you.

A final word on this. Although I expressed the many possibilities of breaking down the rights to the various distribution entities, you should be aware that most distributors, studio and independent alike, do not see the potential in obtaining fragmented rights to your project. In other words, they like to have as many rights granted as possible, as opposed to very limited rights. They want to make as much money as possible on any given project, and to limit its release potential is not an attractive option to them.

Therefore, I do not suggest that you work with so many distribution entities if you have expectations of working with a large distributor. I merely illustrated the varying factors that can influence a distribution deal to give you an idea of the options.

Rights Negotiated: Theatrical, Video, Cable, Etc.

As mentioned above, the multiple rights you have access to and are in a position to distribute accordingly, will greatly affect any distribution deal, as well as your bottom line. The more distribution rights you deal away, the more financial gain you expect in return. However, the more rights you give away, the more money a distributor will pump into the prints and advertising campaign to promote your picture. It's a give and take tug-of-war of rights offered and percentages seized between the distributor and producer. Only experienced negotiators will do a distribution deal justice.

Scope and Magnitude of Distribution

Another factor that will greatly affect any distribution deal is the scope and magnitude of the actual distribution itself. More prints going out to theaters means more money is necessary to cover costs. The more advertising there is, the more money spent. This also usually means the distributor will ask for a larger fee and a larger cut of the cash pie. Studio distributors will pump the most money into distribution, hence it is more difficult to see a financial return from them with an independent picture. Independent distributors will provide distribution on a smaller scale, requiring less financial return to break even and make their profit.

Source of Funds (Distributor or Producer)

You will often come across a distribution deal where you, as the producer, request or are asked to put up the money or part of the money required for the distribution of your picture. Essentially you would be *hiring* the distributor to perform the specific services of physically marshaling your picture to all the theaters, video and television outlets, and coordinating an advertising campaign to get movie-goers to watch your film. There is a grand debate over this type of distribution. Basically, you and your investors would be the ones taking the risk with the release of your picture as opposed to the distributor doing so. There are those who argue this grants the producer and investors greater financial returns. This part is true. The more money one puts up, the greater a percentage of the cash pie he is entitled to in return.

However, there are those who argue that a distributor has little to lose in such a scenario. The distributor is paid its money up front for its services. Whether the movie triumphs or flops is irrelevant. The distributor has it's money, do or die. This kind of arrangement greatly affects the kind of deal you strike with a distributor and the kind of money you might potentially see in return for your picture because of vested interest — or the lack thereof.

PRESALES AND BOX-OFFICE ADVANCES TO PRODUCER

A common denominator found in many distribution deals includes the arrangement of monetary advances to the producer upon completion of the picture. This is normally called a Negative Pick-Up Deal. This means that when the distributor *picks up the negative*, it signs over a check for a pre-agreed upon sum of money. The money is considered an *advance* payment to the producer from the anticipated box-office revenues. And as an advance, it is loosely considered a loan. The distributor now must not only make its money back from its prints and advertising campaign, it must now also recoup the advance it paid to you, the producer. Since it is loosely considered a loan, the distributor will not only recoup the advance, but *interest* on that advance as well. The interest rate varies from deal to deal, and is the subject of negotiation.

Presales are another form of advance payment to the producer. A presale is just what the name implies: the sale of your picture prior to its being produced. Although presales are not as common or powerful as they were over a decade ago, some distributors still engage in this kind of deal structuring when given the opportunity. There are independent filmmakers who also attempt this kind of deal as a way to finance their first picture. They sell their picture before it is made based on the strength of the concept or attached elements, promise to deliver the movie by such and such date, then take the money and shoot the movie.

Presales are very difficult to obtain by independent producers, but if you or your distributors can facilitate them, by all means do so. Unlike negative pick-up deals, presales are usually not considered a loan in which the distributor will charge you interest. It usually depends on who secured the money — your distributor, or you directly.

Presales and negative pick-up deals — any kind of advance — must be handled carefully as they can greatly affect your distribution agreement as well as your bottom line. These are two elements to keep a careful eye on in your negotiations.

INTEREST RATES ON ADVANCES, IF PROCURED

In direct correlation to the last header, if you've entered an arrangement where interest rates on advances will be administered, be advised you can negotiate these interest rates. There is a loose formula that distributors utilize to capitalize on this kind of investment for them, but they are negotiable. Unless you are experienced in this kind of deal-making, you must allow your qualified entertainment attorney to handle this for you. An interest rate can actually mean the difference between you and your investors seeing a return on your picture or not.

DISTRIBUTOR OVERHEAD WITH DEFINITION AND LIMITS

It is hard to believe, but there used to be a time when distribution agreements would not define the overhead of the company. A movie could rake in over ten times its budget and cost of prints and advertising at the box office, but the distributor would claim its overhead wasn't met and the producer and investors would get robbed of any financial gain. Distributors would spend the money they received on everything and any-thing—from wild parties, new cars and fine dining, to lavish trips, new offices and private jets—then charge it all to the company overhead and claim they were all necessary evils in the overall function of their company. When the producer asked for his share of the box-office, the distributor would print out a financial statement showing a *loss* for the producer's movie. The producer would not get a cent.

It is sad but true. Although creative accounting still goes on today in one form or another, entertainment attorneys should be sure to look out for a clause that stipulates how much overhead a distributor can claim before it must share the box-office with the producer. Usually this means very specifically breaking down the overhead and defining it so that there is no misunderstanding when the movie goes to market.

This part of any distribution agreement, with its limits defined, can greatly influence your deal and ultimate financial take on your project. You can rest assured distributors will argue for the most money possible. It is true unforeseen circumstances may arise where the distributor will be enticed to invest more money for the good of the film than was previously agreed upon. When genuine reasons present themselves, it is okay to go back to the negotiating table and discuss new terms or exceptions. For the most part, a financial cap is normally stipulated to keep the amounts from becoming exorbitant.

Cost of Prints and Advertising (P&A) with Definition and Limits

Another area where your contract with a distributor may greatly be negotiated is the resources required to physically print your film negative for distribution, as well as the amount of financing that will be used to promote the picture. Depending on your distribution arrangement, this may also apply to the distributor's handling of the home video market and the cost to print VHS and DVD copies of your film.

While running prints of your movie's negative or making video copies for the home video markets is a pretty cut and dry figure to agree upon, advertising can conceivably take on multiple facets. Just how much advertising is enough, how much money is enough, and where the line is drawn on what is considered advertising or not is all up for debate. An advertising budget must be clearly defined so that huge amounts of money are not spent frivolously. This will also ensure that expenditures are accounted for.

An example of financial abuse under the guise of movie advertising is the wining and dining of a potential customer. Certainly money can and should be allotted for this, but what is the limit exactly? If a distributor wants to impress a potential customer, why stop at the wining and dining? Why not buy the potential customer a new car, or send him or her on a trip to Spain, or send them on a wild shopping spree? This doesn't happen only in the movie industry. It happens in all industries across the board. It is called creative accounting, and in your case if you don't set a limit with your distributor, all the money that should be coming to you might wind up blowing away in the wind somewhere on good food, partying and gifts to complete strangers.

Producer's (Percentage) Take of Box-Office

Keeping in mind all the variables we've discussed up to this point, a distribution agreement will stipulate a pre-agreed upon percentage to be allotted to you as producer from the revenue of your movie at the box-office. This percentage will be dispensed to you once specific prerequisites are met, such as the distributor recouping his investment in the advertising of your picture and the recoupment of any advances plus interest. Once these amounts are recovered, the distributor will split the remaining box-office revenues according to the percentage that was negotiated. Although this figure usually falls between 30 and 70 percent, depending on the factors involved, ultimately it is an arbitrary number. This means it us up to you and your entertainment attorney to get the best percentage figure possible, with the least conditions and attached prerequisites.

This figure is perhaps one of the most significant in the distribution agreement. It can probably affect your deal and bottom line more than any other factor. You must negotiate its value accordingly.

Gross Participants, Usually Entities Above-the-Line

I touched on this factor briefly before. You should be very aware of how it works, where it fits in, and whether or not you will want to play with it. A gross participant in any deal means the person will be entitled to a percentage of a revenue stream of money before the receiving party is able to debit any expenses to the funds. If you as producer of your film require $500,000 to pay back your investors just to break even, and you receive a check for $100,000, you would be considered to be well in the red. If you have a gross participant attached to your gross revenue, it does not matter if you are in the red or about to file bankruptcy — you must pay your gross participant whatever percentage you agreed to.

A gross participant is usually an actor or director with name recognition who asks for gross participation. A gross participant might also be a valuable entity that you were not able to pay up front to work on your picture, but you made a deal to pay him or her out of your gross revenues. A gross participant might even climb the totem pole to participate in the distributor's gross revenue. There is more money higher up on the totem pole, and it's all a matter of who can out-negotiate whom in the grand game of Hollywood.

I would advise you as an independent producer to stay away from any gross participation deals at this time. It will be challenging enough to get the money back for your investors as it is. You don't need to have whatever gross revenues you do collect siphoned off like water in a drain before you are able to repay anybody. If, however, you do enter into one of these agreements, proceed with caution. This kind of deal can greatly affect your contract and financial take.

Sliding Scale Percentages

One last common factor inherent in most distribution agreements is the sliding scale percentage. Simply explained, this means that the percentages the exhibitor, distributor, producer and gross participants are entitled to *change* as the box-office revenue changes. These figures, like most others, are arbitrary as well. You might find yourself in a 60/40 percentage deal with the distributor, which means that the distributor — after recouping his investment — will split his share of the revenues with you 60 percent by 40 percent in his favor. As the movie gains momentum in theaters and as more money trickles in, that figure can change in your favor. For example, your movie cost $1 million to shoot. Your contract might stipulate that the distributor/producer split will be 60/40 until the movie grosses $10 million at the box-office. At that time, the split might change to 50/50.

Most distributors, of course, will not offer you a sliding scale percentage. They would rather keep the 60/40 split all the way through the life of your motion picture, even if the movie grosses over a hundred times what it cost to produce and distribute. It is up to you and your entertainment attorney to try to include this kind of deal and keep it in check. This is yet another factor to watch when striking your distribution deal as it will very greatly affect your contract and ultimate bottom line.

THE BOTTOM LINE

All of the contributing factors I listed above are but a fraction of the elements that can influence any given distribution agreement. There is no need to explain it all to your potential investors, but you or one of your associates should be very well aware of how such an agreement may be constructed should you find yourself needing to explain more than you expected to. You should also be aware of these factors as you accompany your entertainment attorney to any negotiating session, or if you find yourself dealing with someone who requests gross participation. The more you know, the better off you'll be, and as the saying goes, it is true that *knowledge is power*.

A PRACTICAL GUIDE

You are encouraged to follow along with the sample business plan at the end of this book. This section is written in direct correlation with it, explaining in detail what is written there and why.

Movie Distribution

For this part of your business plan you should write down the mechanics of the distribution process for your potential investor to get an idea of how the system works. As I explained above, please do not explain more than you have to, or do not complicate the text. Be thorough, be precise, but keep it simple. Explain the difference between the studio and independent distributors, how the process interlinks with marketing and all of its elements, and more importantly — how all of this will ultimately bring a return and profit to your potential investor.

List the various outlets that your movie may go through in an effort to find an audience. Talk about theaters, television and home video. Talk about their time frames, and how each influences the other. After giving an overview of the process, you should indicate what you and your associates personally plan to do with the movies you propose to make. What path of distribution are you hoping to take, or better yet, what distribution deal have you already got in place. If you do not have a deal in place yet, that is fine. State the deal you hope to garner, distributors you may have already spoken to, and back it up with reasons why you made the decisions you did.

If you mention a distributor you have a deal with or are speaking with, be sure to briefly outline their accomplishments, track record, and how they typically work. Do they handle domestic or foreign distribution? Theatrical or home video and television? Because you will be taking your project to this third party, your investor will want to know exactly who will be taking care of your baby. Why have you put so much faith in this distributor? Elaborate and support your reasoning.

Talk briefly about the territories your distributor will handle and its take on your movie's demographics. State historical and economic facts to support your view on how your film will perform. Mention how much money you anticipate the distributor will contribute to the prints and advertising of your movie—and why.

To give your potential investor an idea of just who the movie distributors are, provide the names of some of the studio distributors, such as Warner Brothers or Universal Pictures. Then provide names of smaller distributors such as Miramax or Artisan Entertainment. Outline briefly how each compares to the other—such as how many theaters a studio will distribute prints to on opening day as opposed to the independents. You might want to mention producer's representatives and agents as we discussed above. Let your potential investor know some of the alternatives available to you, and give an overview, without going into too much detail, about how such a deal would work itself out.

Explain why you will be handing the headache of distribution over to a third party (if this is what you choose), and state your reasoning for your decision. Will it be difficult to find a distributor? Why or why not? Do you already have a distribution deal or negative pick-up deal in place? Why or why not? The moment your film is completed, what is your next step? Who will be taking your masterpiece to the masses?

And finally, in order to show your potential investors the money trail—which is something all potential investors will definitely want to see—mention the distribution models you will be creating using the Dark Horse proprietary software FilmProfit (see Appendix B), which I highly recommend you utilize.

Advertising and Promotion

If you have any capabilities in providing your own form of advertising for your pictures—such as relationships with genre magazines or television talk shows—you should write about it here. Anything you will do in addition to the services your distributor will provide should be spelled out here.

You might think about competing in film festivals before locking down a distributor; or performing a media blitz where you send screeners and articles (a press kit) to various entertainment outlets. Put it all down.

Media Advantage

In the fictitious sample business plan, Mr. Joe Filmmaker of FireGem Entertainment is listed as being a prior award-winning editor of a newspaper. This uniqueness is exploited in the business plan in order to allow the company to stand out from the rest of the crowd. I stated earlier in this book that you should always stress your differenti-

One of Kevin Lindenmuth's most successful projects, *The Alien Agenda: Endangered Species,* was distributed worldwide on VHS and DVD.

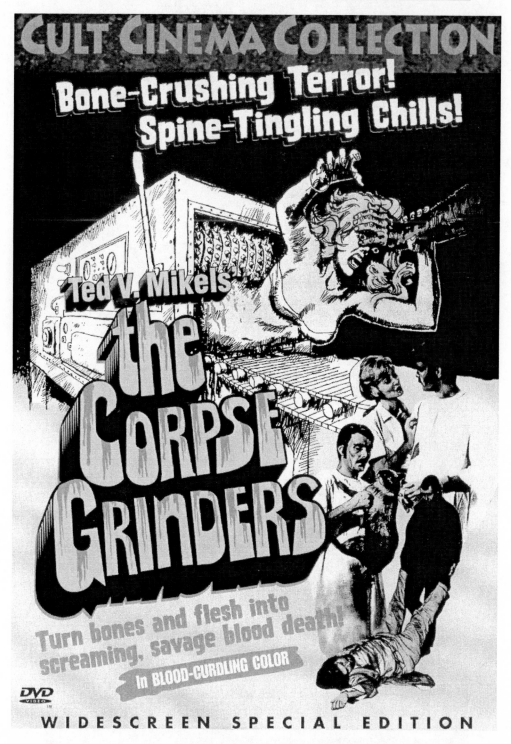

When *The Corpse Grinders* opened in theaters across the country, filmmaker/distributor Ted V. Mikels had beautiful nurses in ambulances check moviegoers' blood pressure before entering the theater to watch the film, citing the fear factor inherent in the movie. The gimmick worked, and the movie became one of Cult Cinema's best known properties to date.

ating qualities while creating your business plan. I must reiterate it here. Always stress any advantage you may have over the competition, and always indicate any unique features or assets you or your associates control or retain. The more the better — investors should see it all.

Publicity Strategy

Any person or company that creates entertainment material sooner or later falls under the watchful and often critical eye of the news media. While this header is not entirely necessary, you might think about including some information on what kind of image you would like to convey to the public with your motion pictures, and how you might go about monitoring a strategy to keep positive in the public's eye. Define your strategy and reasoning for your choice of action, name who will be in charge if applicable, and who or what will be the target of your campaign.

Trade Shows and Conventions

This is another header that is not entirely necessary, but often a good idea nonetheless. In recent years, trade shows and conventions have become extremely popular among genre fans. They give audiences a chance to meet their favorite stars and directors, and they are also a way for you, your associates and your investors to meet the movie-going public. They are a great way to find out first-hand what audiences like and don't like, and for you to see if you are on the right track with your projects.

If you haven't been to a trade show or convention in recent years, the only way to convince you that they are worth your time as a producer is for you to actually attend one.

8

The Investor's Plan

"Business? It's quite simple: it's other people's money."
— Alexandre Dumas (1824–1895)

DON'T BELIEVE EVERYTHING YOU HEAR

If you talk to filmmakers, investment advisors or entrepreneurs, most will agree that investing in motion pictures is high risk and you'd be better off putting your money on a craps table in Las Vegas. They will tell you the chances of finding an investor for your film are worse than finding the proverbial needle in a haystack, and that most banks will not even take a chance on lending capital to such a venture. But before you believe everything you hear, I want you to do yourself a huge favor and pick up the latest movie of one of the naysayers (whether they directed the film or invested in it) and watch it. Watch a movie from a so-called authority on moving-making and film finance who has nothing positive to say about the industry. After you've done so, I want you to seriously scrutinize the movie and ask yourself if you feel your money spent at the theater or video store watching *their* movie was worth your while — and then ask yourself if, given the opportunity, you would have invested in their picture.

Hollywood is full of a lot of *bad material.* Bad movies, bad acting, bad writing, and bad producing. Certainly nobody plans to make a less-than-standard production, but it is the people behind these failed projects who have a hard time finding money and live to tell tales of awful experiences dealing with investors and venture capitalists and distributors. It is these filmmakers and their investors who will tell you to *keep out* — and yet, if you watch closely, these same filmmakers and their investors keep making movies, over and over again. And Hollywood in general keeps the same wheel moving as well, turning out bad movies hand over fist. Want to know why? *Because often even the bad movies make money.*

That's right.

Now I am not telling you that you will make a return on your picture no matter what, and that all movies make money no matter what. I am *not* saying that. What I am saying is that if you know how the game is played and you study your demographics and market potential, and you create even a mediocre motion picture with an arbitrary and controlled budget — one that fits in with your strategy — there is a chance that sooner or later—even if it takes several years—you will likely get your money back and possibly even a profit on top.

So why do so many movies purportedly fail at the box-office? Because a lot of filmmakers are in it for themselves, period. They don't think of the industry as a whole, or their audiences or even their investor's money. A lot of filmmakers want to make the projects that they want to see up on the screen without taking the time to sincerely put it up against the scrutiny of market research or demographics analysis. While I'll be the first to tell you that you should make movies that you feel passionate about, you need to realize passion is a *conditional* prerequisite.

Imagine that you are psychedelically awed by colorful sweaters and are mesmerized by how they are manufactured at the local factory. (First of all, someone like this probably needs psychiatric help, but that's another story.) Does the mere fact that you are passionate about something as obscure as this mean it will make a good movie and send mobs to the theaters to watch it? Probably not—and a simple common sense analysis of the marketplace would demonstrate this.

I can't tell you how many filmmakers and producers proceed with their projects without any regard for the most important element of any production—the audience. But now comes the paradox. Many of the filmmakers responsible for bad movies continue to make films to this day. They may have a more difficult time convincing investors, but sooner or later they get their funds anew and press forward with a fresh project. It makes no logical sense, but it's like I said before—there is more money to be made in Hollywood than one can dream of. Some filmmakers, as bad as they may be, still carry a list of produced credits under their belt, and in the eye of investors, this is good enough to bankroll their next picture. It's all about the *image* the filmmakers have created. With all the posters of the movies they've produced stacked high on their office walls, they suggest the persona of success.

You've probably heard the phrase, *smoke and mirrors*. In Hollywood, this game goes on day in and day out in terms of creating a successful image. Certainly there are those persons who do not need to play games, but most of the hustlers, go-getters and wanna-be producers engage in this to some degree. You can't attract the movie star without the money in the bank, and you can't get the money in the bank without the movie star committed to the project. It's a catch-22, and smoke and mirrors usually work wonders in such a case. What smoke and mirrors means, then, is that you try to convince someone of something that isn't exactly true, but isn't an outright lie either. In the case of a company that's produced movies that haven't made much money at the box office, a producer might choose to leave the financials out of the business plan altogether in hopes the investor will be so impressed by all the posters and produced credits, he'll never ask just how much money such and such project raked in. So the producer is not lying about the success of his movies—he's just leaving out the particulars, hoping they won't be requested.

I know several smaller production companies that shoot films in the $1 million to $5 million range that change their company's name every five or six years. Once their company gets a reputation for putting out bad movies, they reinvent themselves with a new image and continue shooting films—and attracting new investors. There is more money to be made in Hollywood than one can dream of. You have to stop and realize that if movies were such a losing investment, the industry would die out faster than you could blink an eye.

So let me be the first to tell you something that goes against the grain — something that goes beyond the establishment and what you're used to hearing, even something that goes beyond what I've mostly touched on in this book:

> *Investing in motion pictures is not the high-risk venture everyone would like you to believe.*

Yes, there are horror stories and well-publicized financial disasters that have taken place on multi-million dollar levels in Hollywood. That is a given. But that is typical for *any* industry. You win some, you lose some — even when it involves millions. More often than not, successful motion pictures and their ancillary licensing churn out millions and millions, if not *billions*, of dollars for their Hollywood investors and stock-holders annually. That's exactly right — investors are making more money than if they had put their money on that craps table in Las Vegas.

It's all a matter of knowing your capabilities, your product, your industry and market, and your audience. Cater accordingly to each of these, and your chances for success improve greatly.

So now you're thinking that if it's that simple, you will have no trouble finding an investor, right? Wrong. I did not say it was *easy*. Nobody consciously wants to be responsible for a bad movie or a project that takes ten years to recoup its investment, if ever. So nobody is going to blindly invest in your project or anybody else's for that matter. Nobody ever consciously bets on a losing horse. So the industry proceeds, with safeguards and checks and balances to keep everyone out but the most determined individuals. What this means, then, is if you do your homework, prepare a project that will fit in with the mainstream, show potential investors that you know what you're talking about, and are serious and persistent, it is possible you will find an investor for your projects. This will be no easy task for you. The monumental effort involved will be akin to mounting a strategic rescue operation in the Antarctic or planning the military attack of a nuclear-armed country, while simultaneously trying to rescue hostages. You must become an expert in your field — a General in the army of motion picture production — or at the very least, surround yourself by experts. If you approach this business this way, learn, get up every time you're knocked down, and persist, it will only be a matter of time before you get what you're reaching for.

Sound impossible? Nah — it'll be fun. If I can do it, so can you. And the best way to launch your campaign is by putting together your plan of attack — your business plan.

SHOW ME THE MONEY!

Okay, so you've done what I said and researched all your material to the bone and put together the best business plan ever assembled, and now you're ready to approach your investors. The last thing you need to include in your plan is your investment strategy. This part of your business plan is two-fold. It will also be one of your shortest sections of the business plan, as you've already explained everything to your investors that they need to know. In this part of your manuscript, all the intellectual and sophisticated begging and groveling for money that you've been doing to this point will come to an end. You will now ask the investor to *show you the money*.

This section should include the following components:

1. The investment setup of their capitalization of your project (i.e., business setup — rporation, partnership, limited liability company, etc.)
2. The investment forecast which includes capitalization and anticipated time-table on financial returns.
3. The investment allocation or budget (where the money will go).

Let's take a look at the first one. In the second chapter of this book I explained how the legal setup of your company was a personal choice, and that you would be wise to seek the advice of a certified public accountant or business attorney before deciding which route to take. Although this part of your business plan is supposed to lay out your decision on how to set up your investors' money, I strongly urge you to explain to potential investors that you are leaving this option open. There are several ways to set up your company and even more ways of handling a financial investment. There are pros and cons to every possibility, and trying to decide which setup will best suit you and your investors could be a trying experience in itself.

But even if you come to a decision, you must consider how your potential investor may want to conduct business. What if your potential investor has no interest in doing things the way you've lined them up? Will you get the chance to explain to him or her that you're open to changing your setup? Maybe. Maybe not. Your potential investor may not want to waste his time asking. So why take the chance? Instead, leave this option open, and state your decision as such. If your potential investor comes to the point where he likes you, your projects, and the investment request, sitting down to figure out the particulars of your deal should be a pleasure to perform. Be prepared, of course, with several options of your own, but advise your potential investors that the financing plan is negotiable and open to discussion.

As for the second component above, you will once again have to do research that will encompass the investment plan. What this research will mainly be comprised of is a time-table. You will need to explain to your investors where their money will go, and more importantly, *when*. You will also need to elaborate on your anticipated time-table for a return of their investment, as well as a potential profit. Of course there are no guarantees if your movie will make any money back — but the anticipated time-table will give investors an overview of when they might expect to see something.

In order to satisfy your investor's need to know where their money is going, you should also create a budget top-sheet for them to peruse (the third component). This budget top sheet should break down the main elements of your movie and show where all the capital will be disbursed to. Do not include a complete budget breakdown, unless it is specifically asked for — and even then, you should do everything within your negotiating powers to dissuade any inquisitive investor from obtaining such documents. An investor's role in a movie is just that — to invest their capital and for the most part, nothing more. I have been present too often in meetings where overcurious investors think they are producers. If they get an 18-page budget breakdown of your movie project, you can rest assured they will scrutinize every last penny they feel is unnecessary. The problem is that they have no idea what is necessary and what is not.

So unless you have nothing but time on your hands and you'd enjoy explaining at length why you're paying the hair and makeup lady $2000 a week instead of hiring the investor's Aunt Mathilda who would work for free just to get her name in the movies, keep a complete budget breakdown away from your potential investors.

Many indie filmmakers take it one step too far, and this is entirely unacceptable. They balk at presenting any kind of budgetary breakdown to potential investors—even a single-page budget top-sheet. They feel that it is the producer's job to establish how much money a film project will cost, and the investor should freely hand it over, no questions asked. In many ways, the indie filmmaker is correct. After all, an indie filmmaker and his or her company are ultimately responsible for the financing and they are the ones in the business of making movies. They should know what it takes to get the film made. For an investor to throw his thoughts in usually only complicates things—they are usually not, after all, in the business of making movies. Of course there are exceptions.

A budget top-sheet, however, should always be included in the business plan at the very least. Investors want to and must know where the money is going, even if it is only summarized. A budget top sheet, again, will satisfy this inquiry. I highly recommend you use the software *Movie Magic* (see Appendix B) to assist you in this part of your business plan.

A PRACTICAL GUIDE

You are encouraged to follow along with the sample business plan at the end of this book. This section is written in direct correlation with it, explaining in detail what is written there and why.

The Investment Plan

It is time to wrap your business plan up in this section of your manuscript. Imagine you are a trial attorney closing a major lawsuit in court before a jury. Over the past several weeks you have been making your case against the defendant. But now you have to wrap everything up in a few choice words. Imagine the pressure. Well, you must do the same thing here. What you should do is present a single paragraph indicating your overall desire, tenet, strategy and reason you believe the potential investor should take a chance with you.

Your business plan at this point will achieve one of the following:

- Hook your investor to commit to the project.
- Instill curiosity in your investor and a desire to learn more before taking a chance with you.
- Make your investor decide not to take a chance with you at this time.

Whatever the final outcome, always remember that you never fail until you quit trying. So act and respond accordingly. If you don't get it right the first time, learn from your experience. Find out why you were turned down. What can you do to make things different the next time around? What was missing from your business plan?

Also remember you can't satisfy everyone all of the time. So present your business plan to more than one financial entity and see what kind of varied responses you get. Just because one turns you down does not mean the next one will. However, if every investor tells you the same thing—that they feel your screenplay is not viable, or the money you're asking for just seems too steep for your type of project—then maybe they're right and you need to re-evaluate your decision-making altogether.

The Risk

Although I expressed earlier that I believe the motion picture industry as a whole, when well-researched and understood, is a sound investment, that comment was only meant for you, the reader — the indie filmmaker. I do not recommend you repeat my reasoning or opinions in this arena to potential investors. They have all heard from their advisors, and have read in the newspapers, just how high a risk investing in motion pictures is. For you to contraindicate their knowledge and what they think they know will only create the need for a whole lot of explaining. It will become a headache not worth the effort.

Instead, under this header you should stay in line with what the establishment has created and what the Securities and Exchange Commission demands you put on your documents indicating the high degree of risk involved with these types of ventures. Elaborate on the reasons why motion pictures are a risky business and how the establishment (i.e., banks and financiers) view the movie industry as a whole. In a way, this header is your disclaimer. You are fairly warning your potential investors that they are indeed taking a chance with you and your projects— and that the risk is inherent in this industry.

Finally, with the high degree of risk in mind, explain why you still feel the confidence to produce the pictures you have decided on.

Movie Fans

In the fictitious indie business plan, I indicate the principals of FireGem Entertainment are first and foremost *movie fans*, and have been avid aficionados since childhood. Although you do not need to include this header in your business plan, you might be wise to include at least something similar to it. The idea of this header is to distinguish the fictitious company, FireGem Entertainment, from its competitors. I've stated repeatedly how you should always think in terms of uniqueness, and this does just that. After writing out the *Risk* header, a somewhat necessary evil, it is a good idea to immediately follow it with something as positive as this one. Indicate your strengths and competence and what your overall game-plan is when it is time to utilize your investor's money.

Facts and Figures

Immediately following this and the next header, you should include financial projections and data tables for your investors to peruse. The investment plan will ultimately come down to facts and figures, and here is where you will present them. Under this header you should set up what you are about to exhibit. Break down every table you will include and explain why you feel they are necessary. Because data tables can be elaborate, you should describe what they will be interpreting and where you got the information.

In Closing

This is your last header, and the last of your typed sentences to your potential investors. Choose your words wisely and cautiously, for this may be the last chance you have to get your investor's attention. Reiterate here what the proposed budget for your movie or movies is, and how the money will be handled. Make a final statement to cover your business plan and your intentions. Finally, if you will be dealing with an entertainment attorney or have a separate prospectus available, indicate this fact here. It would benefit you to include your attorney's name as well.

The Data Tables

You should include at least five data tables to support your business plan. If you wish to include more, please feel free to do so. In the fictitious indie business plan, I included the following tables:

- Data Table 1. Projected Budget for Production Negative Cost
- Data Table 2. Financial analysis of films with comparable themes or budgets to the ones planned by FireGem Entertainment
- Data Table 3. Element analysis of films with comparable themes or budgets to the ones planned by FireGem Entertainment
- Data Table 4. Projected Income Statement For Years One Through Four
- Data Table 5. Projected Independent Territories' Minimum Prices for *Confused Unicorns and Ogres*

The first one is a budget top sheet. This shows how the investor's money will be utilized. Investors can look through this to get a picture of where their money is actually going. As stated before, I recommend you use the *Movie Magic* software (see Appendix B) for this report.

The second and third tables should include information derived from one of the Hollywood data services. I personally recommend you work with Big Horse (Appendix B) to get this information. These two tables should give a fair comparison of productions similar to the ones you plan on producing yourself. It will give investors an idea of what to expect by taking a peek at the performance of past productions by other filmmakers.

The fourth table is set up to actually show the performance of the company and when it may be expected to begin turning a profit. It will also provide a time-table reference for when subsequent pictures will be produced and how they will fit into the scheme of things with regard to the investor's capitalization.

The fifth table is information you can derive from the trade publications or an independent distributor directly. When smaller films are sold to territories, they are actually *licensed* as opposed to striking a deal to take a percentage of the box-office. Most distributors can formulate tables that cross-index the various territories with their respective expected sales price for your projects. If you can put this information together for your investors, you can conceivably provide an educated expectation of the minimum revenues your picture will see. You can then stack your proposed budget against this model to determine whether or not it may see a respectable return.

FilmProfit

The last section of this part of your business plan should include a series of financial reports. With these reports, you can show the money trail to your potential investors, and show where all the funding works its way through a series of different scenarios.

I have mentioned Big Horse, Inc., and their proprietary software, FilmProfit, several times throughout this book. I can think of no better company and no better financial software to assist you in creating and presenting figures that represent the investor's money trail, taking the reader from square one all the way through production, the release of the picture, and finally a 3-year forecast showing potential revenues broken down by market. The beauty of this software is you can input varying degrees of information and create spontaneous scenarios to see how the financing will play itself out.

For example, you can input the budget of your picture, then input high sales at the box-office and high sales in home video software. The report will show your final take, as well as the distributor's take, and exactly where and when the money goes. By the same token, you can input dismal figures to show exactly how much of a potential loss your project can generate. You can play with this software endlessly, with endless combinations of success and failure variables. The program will show you exactly where your investor's money will go and who will get it — and approximately when.

9

Interviews

Nothing beats good advice like a seasoned professional speaking from true and tried practical experience. This section of the book will present varied perspectives on the independent filmmaking and finance arena from independent filmmakers, producers and executives.

What follows is a collection of candid interviews with industry professionals I have either gotten to know over the years as genuine friends, or I have had the privilege of meeting during the course of writing this book. Their knowledge, experience and advice is invaluable. Take their words of wisdom at face value, and for what they are worth. As you read, you will find the opinions and views of the interviewees are similar in many instances, yet clearly disparate in others. This clearly shows the diversity of variables the film finance arena is comprised of. Like hardened battlefield warriors, the interviewees speak with authority on a subject they have come to know all too well.

Q: Mr. Jeffrey Hardy, you are a successful film finance executive with your own unique companies. In fact, you are an icon in the film funding industry. Can you briefly tell readers a little about yourself and what your companies do?

A: We have a fourteen-year old company called Big Horse, Incorporated, and a trademarked name, FilmProfit, under which we operate and provide various tools and services—from our FilmProfit software to full business planning.

We help filmmakers and finance entities understand each other, through well thought-out business plans and articulate visions and strategies that deal with the real world. Most of Hollywood is aghast and mystified when a film hits, and when it doesn't, because they make films for all the wrong reasons—whether that be because they just want to, they just like to, they want the fees, or many of the other bad reasons available.

We study history, the history of performance, the history of deals and deal structures, and the trends and patterns of today, and what is coming in the way of technology, etc. We have built a big database of film performance, one that has more depth than any I've seen, and we use the knowledge of the industry, the deal structures, and the database of performance to help us understand the future. We ask that database many questions, including how one film performed, and how many films within a budget-range performed, or how a prints and ads spend could be optimized, just to name a few. By the time you read this, elements of that database will be available online, under the name FilmProfit ROI (Return On Investment) Reports.

We do audience analysis. That is, we study the demographics and interests of the audience, to understand how a film might do, and how one might think about communicating to an audience to get them to the theaters (this is not about trickery, but about how to let them know the film you have is out there, and why it will be of interest to them so they can make their decision to go). And we study various elements of the market, say the Latin American television and cable industries—*who, what, when and where*; or the role of the Internet in marketing.

What we do is try to bridge the gaps, helping both sides understand what the creative purposes are, and what the business purposes are.

Jeffrey Hardy

You can make a film for purely financial reasons, but those will be limited, and quite often the audience can smell you from a mile away. Or you can make it for purely creative reasons, and then you're merely in a horse race. We try to identify and maximize the opportunities, identify and minimize the risks, through understanding and planning. A great film about horses with a team that understands why and how people love horses and where they hang out has a better chance at targeting and marketing to its audience than a film about horses made just because it's a cute story, with no plan at all about how to get it seen. Maybe horse people don't want a cute story, and they're all online, and they rely on word of mouth to learn of new movies. This is the type of knowledge that can help a film stand out in a financing crowd, because it has a better chance of standing out when it gets into distribution.

Those are the kind of things we do.

Q: What is your view on the whole independent filmmaking scene from a financial point-of-view? Does it have a future? Is it a force for studios to reckon with?

A: Independent films will always have a place.

Makers and Funding: Independent films are a market force in this way: The economics of film are about constant upward pressure on costs, fees and compensations. Growth is the name of the game at the studios, and in the business overall. In this atmosphere, new and different and unique films have a problem being funded, produced and released. Large sums of money seek safety and security. Different is not secure, it is risky. Therefore, artists of any stripe who seek to break in, or to do something different, or who are just different without really knowing it fully, will generally seek independent funding (the only kind they can usually get) to enable them to pursue their storytelling dreams.

Audience Demand: It is not possible for the studios to find, appraise, and/or fund these kinds of projects, but the growth in outlets, the fact that certain segments of the audience require and demand something new, different, discovery, etc., all support the need for independent film.

Indie Distributor Dreams: When the last independent distributor has been bought up by Disney or Turner or Time/Warner, some new somebody out there will see an opportunity to provide audiences with what they can't get from the big guys. And his economics will be small enough that the opportunity will entice him, and he will one day hope to grow to a size that he can be acquired, or he will fight for his independence. There is always a film-loving student who programs at the local college, who hopes to one day start his own company.

Q: You are aware of the digital video revolution. Will this new technology have any effect — good or bad — on the way financiers see motion picture investments? In other words, will financiers steer clear from digital video productions, gravitate toward them, or will this new arena make no difference at all?

A: Digital video production is a long-held dream in the mind of Francis Coppola and George Lucas both. Pixar was born of a Lucas initiative to have a system that could storyboard digitally, then edit and spit out film in a dreamed-of seamless process. That company was sold to Steve Jobs, and digital years and dollars later, it is now a digital production studio (or nearly so). Freedom, financial and creative, offered by a cheaper, smaller, lighter system, has been a dream in the minds of many other producers and directors as well. Though most editors I know resisted the loss of the tactile work of cutting, and the "plastic-arts" nature of scene-building from celluloid, most producers and directors want to make their movies in the most effective way possible.

The future of film is digital, in production, in post-production, in delivery. Concerns of the like of Boeing (owner of satellites) are offering to digitally deliver movies to theaters (via satellite), to be downloaded to hard drives, and then projected by digital theater systems, as this is written. It will be in some form of theater delivery probably by the time you are reading this book. As well, wired homes (cable and Internet) are markets nearing readiness for digital consumer delivery. Digital is here to stay, to develop, to grow and transmogrify the film art and the film business.

Q: Let us say an independent filmmaker approached you to assist them in securing funds for their latest epic. Please describe briefly a typical scenario that would ensue and specific steps that would be taken (either by you or the filmmaker) in order to potentially find such financing.

A: First, I do not go out looking for financing for films. I work with financial people, but I do not hold myself out, or market myself, or propound to be a financier or finance-finder. I prepare films, packages of films, producers, for financing, whether that be for one-off films, or for packages. We function as a third-party source for information and guidance, and, as such, don't actively seek financing for specific projects, so our third-party arms-length status remains well intact.

Typically, a filmmaker, a producer, calls me, and I get the feel for their project(s). What I am seeking out from them is a list of their assets. Assets are what we are selling to financial people, whether it's a first-time producer, or a seasoned veteran with a slate of films he wants to fund. Examples of assets are:

> The story, whether original, or from another source (the source can be a significant asset). I recently helped a documentary filmmaker who had the rights to a New York Times bestseller, a controversial book, but a seller. That is an asset.
>
> The team. Does anyone on the team have a track record that says they can shoot a film, get it finished, and it will at least be a film?
>
> Relationships to distribution, to actors, to music artists or other celebrities. I recently did a package for a radio show to movie, with significant car-racing and music connections, which I encouraged them to tie down. This gave us a great marketing package that has worked.
>
> A unique understanding of the market –– say a snowboarder and his buddies who know exactly what their friends and extreme sports lovers around the world want. Plus, they know the magazines that talk to these people, and have great relationships there.
>
> Craftspeople who are willing to come on board for reduced pay (these are actually investments by these people).
>
> Commitments from a production facility or grip house that save giant sums of money (these are investments by these people and companies). One filmmaker had his own plane, his own plane mount for a camera, and post-production facilities. Those were assets, and investments in his film.
>
> Relationships to money.
>
> Any sum of money already committed.

Q: Both independent and studio films are made with disparate budgets. How significantly does financing contribute to the success of a motion picture venture? In other words, what are the pros and cons for lower budget films versus larger budget fare?

A: It is seldom that studio films are made for under $10 million. Their economics are such that it doesn't make sense to do that. They can acquire those kinds of films. But there are always companies which are vying to be studios— Studios USA, for example — who can take chances, and need to, on lower budgets. So, for certain lower figures, there is a lot of independent financing, and at the higher figures, very little at all. That is one part of the question.

As far as success and lower budgets, this is a hard question to answer. They are quite different economic equations. We are in the business of analyzing films and their success potential, based on historical factors, other performance, etc. The deeper you get into this, the more detail there is. But it is not my view that a higher budget, per se, has a higher chance of success, even with access to more money with which to buy stars and effects. As a matter of fact, that can also easily be a recipe for disaster. Lower budgets allow more room for profit potential, but it can also be harder for a smaller budget film to get the kind of distribution and marketing expense they sometimes need. In general, studio films break even more often, but how does an investor get to make a *real* investment in a studio film?

Q: How important is it for an independent filmmaker or producer to keep a solid financial track record of their past film performances in the face of potential investors? And what about a filmmaker who has no track record –– is he out of luck when trying to secure third-party funding?

A: It really depends on what a filmmaker wants to do with their career. If they want to make movies with some sort of ease, they will focus more on their financial track record. This will also impact the kinds of budgets that their record can support. But if they are more focused on only the artistic issues in their filmmaking, then they may have to accept lower budgets and longer time frames between films.

It should be remembered that many if not most of the world's great filmmakers have been able to make incredible artistic statements with budgets much smaller than those in Hollywood. I think a filmmaker who ignores their financial track record is not giving proper respect to other people's money that they want to demand for their film idea.

First-time filmmakers are entering the ranks of experienced filmmakers all the time. They get their financing from their family, from friends, from people they ferret out through all manner of means. They are not out of luck, but they have to "make their luck" by preparing, by learning what the decisions are in the business, and making those decisions, and being able to articulate all of it.

Q: When you present a project for funding consideration, how important is it to have a clear and concise plan (business plan) in place for what you propose to accomplish?

A: I often like to call the business plan, "the plan for business." This stops people from thinking they are just assembling paper with writing on it and pictures and things, and focuses them on the fact that they are going through a decision-making process, in which they will have to confront all sorts of elements of the business they may have never thought of — and sometimes didn't *want* to think of. "I'm going to shoot the film and then take it to Sundance," may sound like a plan to some, but it's nothing of the sort. "I'm going to make the film for $1.5 million because I can get exactly what I want on screen for that, and I know that, even if I don't get theatrical distribution after festivals and showing it to distributors, I still have a shot at releasing it on video through a company I found out about. And worst-case scenario, we will get close to if not all of our money back with them." Now, that is a business plan in the forming. And both filmmakers can make the same film, but one has a better chance at success because of having a plan.

Q: How much of a role does the foreign film market play in recouping a film's investment efforts and turning a profit?

A: The best way I can think of to answer this question is by showing you a few charts that illustrate the performance of three films according to our studies. The three films, *Pi, The Bad Lieutenant* and *Crash*, all have very different foreign performances.

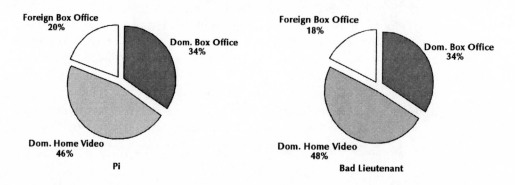

On a macro-economic basis, however, the international market's value to American films now eclipses the domestic value. The performance of each individual film will be according to various factors of appeal. In Argentina, for example, they really seem to like American independent films on cable television. There are things out there you need to know to understand the business end of your business.

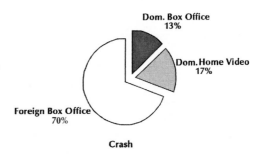

Dom. Box Office 13%

Dom. Home Video 17%

Foreign Box Office 70%

Crash

Q: Writing, developing and shooting a motion picture is the creative end of the medium. Obtaining financing for it, then distributing it to recoup the money and a profit is the other end of the medium: finance and business. Do you find yourself having to move between both worlds on occasion, and if so, how distinct do you find these two arenas? Do you find it difficult bridging the gap between them?

A: Well, I might be a different kind of an animal, since I have a degree in English literature instead of law or some kind of MBA, or marketing focus, which a lot of these folks have. I am exactly here to bridge the gap. That is how I often describe the work I do. I help business people understand the creative side of the equation, and I help the creative side understand the business side. I am totally comfortable here, and feel that it is a good thing to do. I like it. In my mind, the problem with a lot of people in the industry is they understand one side of the question only, and then they want to mess around in the other, resulting in problematic creativity, and problematic business. This is an endeavor which embraces and lives on both.

David Michael Latt and David Rimawi. Independent filmmakers and distributors. The Asylum. *The Source, Killers, Hellion, Sorority House Party, Social Intercourse.*

Q: Mr. David Michael Latt and Mr. David Rimawi, you two are very successful independent filmmakers and producers. Can you briefly tell readers a little about yourselves, your company and your films?

LATT: Rimawi and I first got together in the early 90's putting together a small romantic feature comedy called *Rock 'n' Roll Fantasy*. There were two factors in making this movie that would define our approach to making movies: (a) find out what the market was paying and budget accordingly; and (b) scrape together the budget from friends, family and whatever you can beg, borrow and steal. That's been our approach ever since: finding what the market wants, and making the film with whatever was in the bank.

RIMAWI: When David and I met, we were close to graduating from film school. He wanted to direct and I wanted to produce. So we sort of said, "I've got a barn," and, "My mom can make the curtains." During our first two films, *Rock 'n' Roll* and *Killers*, David and I held down full time jobs. Now we have our own company, The Asylum, with partner Sherri Strain who focuses on international sales. But through all of this, our dynamic stays the same, David makes the film happen while I find the money and secure distribution.

Starting with money from friends and family and now using our own, we focus on marketable genres (action, thriller, horror, sci-fi), but approach them in a stylish way.

Q: What is your view on the present independent filmmaking scene? Does the new wave of cheap digital video and non-linear editors have a future? Is it a force for Hollywood to reckon with, or is it a passing fad?

LATT: As a filmmaker, I say that the indie scene is very exciting. Filmmakers are discovering they can make films for $10,000 (be it film or, dare I say it, video). I love to watch a good film no matter how it was shot (though I am a bit old-school, and like to see a film over video). The problem with the cheap digital revolution is the same problem that plagues the serious writer. Just because you have a computer (or typewriter) doesn't mean you can write. Just because you have your Canon XL1, doesn't mean you can tell a story. As a distributor, filmmakers have to know that DV features are rarely sold. No matter how good it is, the buyer always wants to know that it was shot on 35mm.

Hollywood has never been, and will never be, threatened by real independent filmmakers. These auteurs are making films that cannot compete in budget, marketing, visuals, content, etc. And for the one or two DV features a year that gets wide distribution, it's typically through a studio-owned company anyway.

RIMAWI: With my rather limited perspective on the history of independent filmmaking, I think we're currently on a downturn. The studio's indie divisions are crowding the market place with their own productions; and, a soft world-wide economy has limited distributors' demand for indie films. The bright spots for now are DVD and the ever-expanding digital channels.

The gathering and distribution of information will at some point be entirely digital/electronic. The new 24p HD cameras, along with DLP-equipped theaters, are winning over many in production and distribution. It's years away, but it's here to stay. That being said, while I don't believe "cheap DV" will ever be an acceptable medium for feature films, it will always remain as an option for a filmmaker to at least learn and practice without declaring bankruptcy. Non-linear editors have already "arrived" as a standard in post-production — it's just a question of image resolution.

Killers 2 is one of the most successful titles to be released by Latt and Rimawi's The Asylum.

Q: You have made films with varying budgets, and they range from film project to film project. How important is financing in general and how does it contribute to the success of your motion picture ventures, no matter how small or large the budget?

LATT: As a writer/director you are obligated to tell the best story you can to your audience. Use the best actors, the best sets, the best music, the best ideas. But you also have an obligation to the producer to be on time, to be consistent, to compromise when needed — this isn't about you and your ego; in some respect you are an employee to your investors.

As a producer you have to be smart. Don't make a $500,000 dollar and/or SAG film that does not feature any bankable stars. Find out what the market is paying for a film before you make it (assuming you want to pay back the investors). If the world will only pay $100,000 for a horror film shot on 16mm with Jerry Van Dyke, don't make this film for $200,000 — make it for $75,000. We have survived because we know the value of a film before we make it. We ask other distributors and buyers what they are doing. Our profits may be small, but we've been able to make a profit on every film (which in turn finances our next film).

RIMAWI: There is definitely a correlation between the budget of our films and how much they gross. It's important to be aware of where to spend money. On an action film, put most of the money in stunts and special effects, on a horror film, focus on special effects make-up, etc. Also, as Latt suggests, if you put your money on the cast, be aware of their value in the marketplace.

Q: Both of you have an impressive library of independent films you have written, directed or produced over the years — not to mention an even more striking collection of films your company has distributed. Do you believe these produced credits give you more credibility with financiers and investors as opposed to someone just starting out who has no produced credits?

LATT: To date we've only financed our own films (from $15,000 to $250,000), so there's no need to impress anyone as we've self-financed these films. However, trying to make a film for above $1 million is challenging for us, because people perceive us as "micro-budget" filmmakers.

RIMAWI: To be quite honest, "yes" and "no." With our experience, we would have little trouble raising $100,000 to $200,000 to make a genre film. However, I believe a freshman filmmaker with no track record has a leg up on us in terms of a studio-type film. Studio logic is, "I've seen The Asylum's films and they're real small." With a brand new filmmaker, it's all in their imagination, so it's up to the filmmaker and his/her agent/manager to build the hype.

Q: When presenting your projects to potential investors, how important is it to have a clear and concise plan (business plan) in place for what you propose to do?

LATT: It's important to know what you want. If you want longevity, then plan for it. Make small "genre" films, and keep building up to larger films (by the way, "genre" is not a dirty word. Some of the best films in history — *Alien, Jaws, Star Wars* — are genre). If you don't know the investors, they will want a plan. An investor will also put money in a project because of you, the story, and/or the thrill of making a movie.

RIMAWI: In addition to the plan, if you're going to friends or family, they'll be investing in you. If you go to businessmen (doctors/lawyers), they'll be motivated by whatever money you've already been able to raise. If you are looking to raise money from a studio or distribution company, they'll be interested in the script and your cast. And finally, if you're going to a bank you'll need some distribution deals (pre-sales) in place, as well as a completion bond (insurance).

Q: Your films reach international audiences and are distributed world-wide. How much of a role does this foreign market play in recouping your investment efforts and turning a profit?
LATT: I'll leave this for Rimawi.
RIMAWI: For us at least, our primary market is North America; however, not by much. On the average, 40 to 45 percent of the income comes from foreign markets.

Q: You no doubt handle the production and distribution of your own motion pictures. Writing, developing and shooting a movie is the creative end of the medium. Obtaining financing for it, then distributing it to recoup the money and a profit is the other end of the medium — finance and business. How distinct do you find these two worlds, and do you find it difficult bridging the gap between them?
LATT: Rimawi and I are filmmakers. As such, there is no pre-defined job description. We'll do it all because we love it all. Finding money, selling a film, or developing a character is all part of the same package.
RIMAWI: For me there's little conflict between the "two worlds." I just take the restrictions of making a film and add elements that will make the film as marketable as possible. For instance, most filmmakers already have to work with the restraints of a 90-minute running time, shooting on film, in color with sync sound, etc. I just add to that and say, "It has to be a marketable genre; I can only spend as much money as I think I can get back, etc."
So once I'm aware of all these restrictions and requirements, I then look for a project that interests us. The one area that trips us up is that we are passionate about having very stylish films. Often, independent film buyers are quite conservative and are turned off by films that don't have the standard flat look — bright and in focus.

Q: You are familiar with the business plan found in Appendix A of this book. How valuable do you feel this reference material can be to independent filmmakers seeking funding for their film projects?
RIMAWI: I believe the business plan included in the book, along with the reference materials, are invaluable. In addition to these materials, filmmakers should get a hold of all kinds of documents used in producing and distributing films: talent releases, errors and omissions insurance policies, distribution agreements. These will be instrumental in understanding the details that are critical down the line when you finally want to distribute your film.
My new favorite learning tool is film commentaries. Definitely buy a DVD player and soak up all the extras.

Q: Do you feel the Internet has made an impact on the marketing and distribution of motion pictures — and more importantly, has it contributed in any way to the acquisition of funds for independent films?
RIMAWI: I feel the Internet has had absolutely no significant effect on the commercial exploitation of feature films as the market/demand is minuscule considering the technical limitations. On the other hand, the Internet has perhaps been the single most

important development in short film distribution. However, with the crash of the dot coms, that surge has shrunken considerably.

Where the Internet has made a serious impact on feature film distribution is marketing. In addition to web sites dedicated to particular films, there are endless sites offering reviews, for bad or good, on most every film available and some that aren't.

But "no" in terms of distribution, the Internet is not yet a viable market.

Q: What personal advice can you give to beginning or established independent filmmakers who are seeking financing for their film projects?

LATT: In college my professors always answered the question, "How do you direct?" with, "You direct." So how do you make a film? You make a film. Don't wait for Universal to green light your picture. Don't try to be clever and get Tom Cruise drunk and commit to a picture. Have a garage sale and max out the credit cards. Get deals around town, and make your great marketable film for $100. I have friends that graduated college 15 years ago that are still waiting for their phone to ring with the magic words, "I found the money to make your movie."

RIMAWI: I agree with Latt. As we've always said, "If you want to make a movie, set the date and stick to it." That's really the best advice. Other good advice, not that we've ever followed this, is to make a list of your resources (2 shiny boards, 6 shot guns, Aunt Jane's clothing store, a loaf of bread, etc.) and write a script around those elements.

On a more practical basis, independent financing from the private sector will come from your self, friends and family. How this works is, once you've chosen your project and picked your "date," you go out of your way to mention to everyone you meet that you're making a film in December (or whenever) and you're looking for money. Be sure to mention your Uncle Pete has already put in $6000 and if the person you're talking to has money and is interested, they should make an offer to invest.

In terms of financing from entertainment related companies, you'll need a bankable cast attached or a great script along with an impressive short film/commercial/music video under your belt, so long as these smaller projects are similar in nature to the feature.

Q: Mr. Ted V. Mikels, you are a very successful independent filmmaker. You are also an icon in the independent filmmaking arena, recognized the world over with such cult classics as The Corpse Grinders *and* Astro Zombies. *Can you briefly tell readers a little about yourself and your films?*

A: Well, first of all, *Corpse Grinders* and *The Astro Zombies* represent only a tiny fraction of my life's work. It just seems that the folks who like this sort of film are much more vociferous or outspoken than those who like other films.

I first started making films in the early 1950's, putting anything together that I could with out-dated and inexpensive drug-store film. The footage then had to be shipped to Los Angeles or New York, as I was in Bend, Oregon at that time. During the fifties, I committed myself to making the next ten years dedicated to making films of every sort, to include work in classrooms teaching films, etc. I also had the opportunity and pleasure of working on several major studio productions out of Hollywood that had come to film in Central Oregon. These included Kirk Douglas's *Indian Fighter, Oregon Passage*, Disney's *Tonka, Day of the Outlaw*, and several others. After scouting locations and planning for nine years, I filmed my own and first 35mm feature called *Strike Me Deadly*.

Ted V. Mikels, independent filmmaker with TVM Global Entertainment: *The Corpse Grinders, Dimension in Fear, The Astro Zombies, Strike Me Deadly, The Doll Squad.*

Now, forty-one years later, many people still think it's my best film or at least one of the best. It's an action-adventure with a major forest fire raging throughout. It starred and started Jeanine Riley in her very first exposure to film, and because of it she soon after won the role of Betty-Jo in *Petticoat Junction* and has enjoyed a brilliant career since.

Right after that, after spending a year in Hollywood editing the film, I moved my family to Hollywood. In the years that followed, I held offices at Columbia Pictures Studios, then Samuel Goldwyn Studios, Allied Artists Studios, and Universal Studios. My first offices were in what is now Raleigh Studios, across from Paramount Pictures, where we very often had lunch and the pleasure of seeing and/or meeting such stars as John Wayne himself, Lucille Ball, Henry Fonda, Vincent Price, and countless others.

In all, I think I have made more feature films than any man alive who has never been studio-financed. My credentials list nearly 100 films, which is why I say that *Corpse Grinders* and *Astro-Zombies, Blood Orgy of the She-Devils*, etc., represent only a tiny fragment of my work. *And*, my dream is yet to do my epic, *Beowulf*, which I have been pining to do for 40 years.

Q: *What is your view on the present independent filmmaking scene? Does the new wave of cheap digital video cameras and non-linear editors have a future? Is it a force for Hollywood to reckon with, or is it a passing fad?*

A: Probably those who are intent on making movies will never give up. They will use any means and method available to them to create their movies. The little digital cameras will allow them to develop abilities never before possible with expensive film. The force that Hollywood reckons with is the huge overflow of creations submitted to distributors, who often have time only to look at the box-jacket. A few will get lucky, and there will be some who go on to big time with this advantage as a start in making movies. Non-linear editing seems to have taken over. However, I don't know when I would ever give up my moviolas and video bay to do digital post-production at my own studios.

Things will change as always, and the next year or two might bring on totally new concepts in film-making, new procedures, and new technical advantages/disadvantages. Non-linear makes it much more possible for new-comers, or those without access to film bays, etc., to compete.

Q: You have made films with varying budgets throughout the years, and they range from film project to film project. You have shot some high budget 35mm films and low-budget video films. You have done it all. How important is financing and how does it contribute to the success of your motion picture ventures, no matter how small or large the budget?

A: There is no playable movie made entirely without money. Money is required for film or tape, food, transportation, insurances, offices (work-place), and replacing burn-outs (bulbs). In fact, pre-production phone calls and thousands of pages of Xeroxing of forms, scripts and the like can run into many thousands of dollars even on very low budget pictures. I used to say the main difference between low budget and high budget films is what the performers and technicians are paid. That, along with special costs related to locations, lodging, travel, etc., remains basically true. I have always said the bigger the budget, the more things can be accomplished over the telephone. The more money, the more you can compete with the major studios, with special effects, stars, exotic locations, and picture "mounting" (i.e., great music scores, etc.).

Q: You have an enormous established library of films you have produced over the years. Do you believe these produced credits give you more credibility with financiers and investors as opposed to someone just starting out who has no produced credits?

A: I used to think years ago that after my first film, financiers would flock to give me money. *It does not happen.* Investors want a solid plan to re-coup and make a profit on their investment. A so-called track record does carry some weight, but it is the current project, that one that you are about to do, that must make financial sense. *The Corpse Grinders*, which I released through my own distribution company, out grossed every picture it played against, including many multi-million-dollar epics by the major studios. The difference was that I had to work with a tiny number of prints by today's standards, and move them around the country a few at a time. Shipping and inspection were a huge cost — and umbrella-type national advertising and promotions were unheard of then. So money has always been difficult to raise, especially if you are honest with investors and tell them up front that there are *no guarantees* whatsoever. That's why investors want to see a good solid business plan — to enhance their chances of making money.

Someone just starting out has to look harder and longer for financing or find a rich uncle with a string of pizza parlors who believes in him or her.

Q: When presenting your projects to potential investors, how important is it to have a clear and concise plan (business plan) in place for what you propose to do?

A: When you present a plan to potential investors, you must remember that they often are not particularly enamored with film-making like you are. The way that they can become enthused is if you can show them that making the movie can turn into a profitable investment. You cannot ask them to believe in you and your talents—that is not quite enough. You must point out the logical way that a successful movie could return its costs, then enter into a profit stage.

A step-by-step outline of procedures will help them better understand the complete process. However, what they really want to know is exactly how the money will come back with a great potential for profit. Knowing what you will do with the finished movie will give them confidence that there is more to the project that just creating the film. Knowing that other companies, such as distributors, require a certain number of movies to offer to world-wide markets to stay in business can give the investor confidence that there actually is a market for your product. In your presentations for potential investors, you must explore those steps following the creation of the movie, and explain them in detail.

Q: Your films reach international audiences and are distributed world-wide. How much of a role does this foreign market play in recouping your investment efforts and turning a profit?

A: Actually, if your movie cannot reach outside the United States, you are not reaping the rewards of true international marketing. With some films, the greatest potential is actually from foreign sales and distribution. Remember there are over two hundred countries in the world that utilize movies. Often, the more business your film can generate in the United States, the more interest is shown by countries looking for successful film product. There is no easy way to reach out to all of these markets and receive income from them, so it is obvious you must rely on dependable and honest distributors with the long arms of international sales and distribution.

If your film is successful in this country, these sales will be generated for you. If you are not able to secure theatrical releases for your films in this country, turning to magnetic (all video and DVD) sales and the foreign market may be your key to profit, as some countries are not able to acquire the expensive major studio product—leaving a possible opening for you if they like your film. In past years, foreign sales and distribution have brought incomes to me for my films, and in a couple of cases, foreign sales, which are usually in the form of an outright cash sale for certain rights for a certain period of time, have allowed me to purchase prints of the movie for U.S. theatrical distribution.

Q: Many times you handle the production and distribution of your own motion pictures. Writing, developing and shooting a movie is the creative end of the medium. Obtaining financing for it, then distributing it to recoup the money and a profit is the other end of the medium—finance and business. How distinct do you find these two worlds, and do you find it difficult bridging the gap between them?

A: I have often been asked if I had it to do all over again, what would I have done differently? When I was a distributor, other distributors could not, and of course would not, send any financing my way. Friends of mine who made distribution deals up front with a distributor were often financed by the distributor who then had the ability to start the marketing of the film when it went into production. What I did was make the films and then take on the chores of distribution in addition. This is an entirely different world from production, and the problems are not at all similar. A distributor that has international connections and sales personnel to sell your movie can usually do a much better job of marketing than you can do. They have a vastly greater reach to world-wide and

Ted V. Mikels considers *Girl in Gold Boots* one of his personal favorite productions. Shot on a minuscule budget, it was released in both domestic and foreign theaters.

domestic buyers, and often have departments that create good marketing materials, handle theatrical, television, home video sales, cable sales, etc. It takes years to develop these connections, and it is probably more intelligent to let those people who are in the business of international marketing handle your sales while you move on to your next project. I often think I would have been much further ahead if I had taken that course. When MGM had wanted to give me a large cash advance and a world-wide distribution deal on my film, *The Doll Squad*, I lost out because I had already put in motion the distribution process by offering theatrical rights to sub-distributors around the country. I would not go back on my word, so I lost out on what could have been a sky-rocket ride to success for me.

Looking back, it might have been much wiser for me not to have taken on the distribution processes, and possibly receive financing from those active distribution companies.

Q: You are familiar with the business plan found in Appendix A of this book. How valuable do you feel this reference material can be to independent filmmakers seeking funding for their film projects?

A: If you are searching for investors but can offer them nothing but hope that you will be successful, you probably will never secure investors at all. Reference material is extremely important.

Giving potential investors an overview of our industry opens a new look into a possible financially successful venture. Exposing them to the procedures takes the mystery out of the investment, and can give them the confidence that at least you have a clearly laid-out plan you will follow to bring money back to them with a profit on the movie. Also, you must not make promises that you may not be able to keep. So allowing the potential investor to see the entire plan for doing business is absolutely essential. Without a properly prepared business plan, you probably will never even get to communicate with sophisticated investors who have been offered every sort of investment possible. If your plan makes sense to them, you may get your financing. The plan will answer many questions that they will ask to protect themselves. A good business plan answers these questions.

Q: What personal advice can you give to beginning or established independent filmmakers who are seeking financing for their film projects?

A: The first advice I can offer to those seeking financing is that you must research your market before zeroing in on your script. If your research proves that there is an existing potential market and great interest in your particular classification of material, then with great gusto, pursue it. Your enthusiasm is your first prerequisite. Your personal enthusiasm and confidence is catching, and it can give you an entrée to investors. Again, do your market research first, then bounce your intended project off of everybody who will listen. And you should listen to what they say. If nine people out of ten tell you you're drunk, lie down. These first reactions to your intentions are invaluable — *listen to them*.

Do all of the above before you approach your investors with your business plan.

Of all of the nearly 100 movies I have made, I often didn't follow my own advice, and went ahead. I have suffered many times for not going about the creation of my movies more intelligently. Suffered financially, that is. Until you are a multi-millionaire, you must make your films for the outside world, and give the world what it wants. When you have money to burn, then make films to please yourself. However, be sure you have a good appetite, as you may have to put salt and pepper on them and eat them yourself.

Q: Mr. Philip R. Cable, you are a successful independent filmmaker and distributor. Can you tell readers a little about yourself and your company?

Philip R. Cable, independent filmmaker and distributor with AAA American Entertainment: *24 Hours to Midnight, Shadow Love, The Comic Book Kid, Knights of Justice, Hollywood Fantasies, Battle Beast.*

A: Originally I wrote a lot of plays in the 1960's and 70's, but the problem is you can't support yourself as a playwright. I became a screenwriter because movies were really my first love, but I became very frustrated by the fact that producers would buy my scripts and screw up my movies. So I became a filmmaker in effect to protect my screenplays as a producer, as a director, which I had done in theater anyway. I learned to distribute my own pictures. I had to learn a little of everything, actually. Because I do low-budget movies, I had to learn first-hand about special effects, stunt-work, makeup, photography, still photography and all these other things— the filmmaking process, the economics of film, the economics of distribution. All these things connect together. I think probably because I had to learn all of this stuff, I find that a lot of people, including some from the big companies, heads of major departments, often call me and say, "Hey, uh, Philip, don't tell anybody else I asked you this, but how do you do this thing here?" And I respond with, "Well, you do this." And they say, "That's all you gotta do?" "Yup." "Oh, well, thanks a lot."

The name of our distribution-production company is AAA American Entertainment. Of course, whenever we do different films, we usually do productions in cooperation or co-production with individual production companies. As you know, most films have to have their own individual limited partnership.

Probably one of the most successful films I've made is called *24 Hours to Midnight.* That was made back in '89, I think. That did very well domestically and overseas. I also did a children's film, *The Comic Book Kid,* that did very well, and *Knights of Justice.* On this one we did marketing never done before with a direct line and tie-in to the comic book. Other films include *Shadow Love, Hollywood Fantasies* and *Battle Beast,* which I am particularly proud of. It stars Lorin Taylor, Lisa Todd and Charles Dierkop from *Police Woman,* Dan Layne, who is in the Martial Arts Hall of Fame, and Jim Willis who is in the Masters Martial Arts Hall of Fame. Plus another dozen or so films we've done over the years.

Q: Your films no doubt reach worldwide audiences. How important is the foreign marketplace for recouping your investments and turning a profit?

A joint production effort, *Shadow Love* has become one of Philip R. Cable's most successful projects to date.

A: The foreign market is the marketplace. You have to understand that in the case of independent films anywhere from 90 to 98 percent of your money is going to come from the foreign markets. Even for a major film, anywhere from 42 to 52 percent of their money comes from the foreign markets. The foreign market is the predominant marketplace now. You're just not going to get a theatrical release here in the United States unless you're with a major studio. And even if you are with a major studio, the odds are it won't make any money. It's absolutely vital to remember that: if you can't make your film with the foreign market in mind — and it has to be with a foreign market in mind, not domestic — you're just not going to make any money from it. So what you want to keep in mind is, pair down the dialogue as much as possible because the foreign buyer is going to have to dub that in or subtitle your picture. The more dialogue you have, the more they need to dub, the more costly it is for them, and the more they will take that into account when deciding whether to buy your film or not. Also the more urbanized or Americanized your film is as opposed to a universal type of storyline, the more likely they're going to go, "Wait, this isn't going to make sense to someone who works in a rice patty in Taiwan." That's why if you look at certain Woody Allen films, they don't sell well overseas unless it's France. Whereas, for example, a Chuck Norris action movie does well internationally, simply because the storylines are so simple, anybody can understand them. Lots of action, and a very simple concept behind it. I mean, even if you turn off the sound, you can still understand what is going on.

Q: The indie filmmaker has been around for a while now. How much of an impact will the current digital video trend have on the business? Will we be seeing more shot-on-digital-video movies? Will investors flock to these projects or turn away from them? Is the new digital video a force for Hollywood to reckon with?

A: Yes and no. They will be jumping on the bandwagon simply because the independent filmmaker can now afford to make their films independent of a lot of investors. They can do it cheaper than they could do it before, because it doesn't involve film. The bad thing is you can get a lot of people who don't know how to make films making a lot of very bad DV movies. When foreign buyers hear the word "digital," they automatically assume it's better quality, in the same way that they wouldn't buy BetaSP or any other tape format. They wouldn't be interested. But if they hear the word "digital," they'll tend to buy it. Because, thanks to Lucas, they associate the word "digital" with big superior quality. It's one of those buzz words in Hollywood, like CGI as opposed to optical effects. They're also more inclined to buy it with CGI effects than if it's optical effects. I know filmmakers that deliberately screw up some of their special effects so that it looks more digital, so it doesn't look as good, so it makes it look more expensive.

Now on the other hand, domestically, you can't give away a digital movie to television. They will not buy it. They don't like digital movies because they don't look like film. But now here's the thing — a movie that is shot on film, even a mediocre or lousy film on 16mm or 35mm, overseas and domestically will always be worth more money and be more likely to sell than a really good film on digital. They figure it's film, it's got to cost more money, therefore it has more value.

It's a major issue because too many people came out with bad movies. When these small video cameras made it possible to tape outside, we got to see a plethora of really bad horror movies shot on tape. And when the digital video cameras came out, then suddenly a lot of people got to make digital movies. And most weren't very well made.

The important thing is to find out what the distributors and buyers want and need, and then you make a movie in accordance with that need. I'm not saying to sacrifice your integrity, I'm saying don't make a movie that there's no market for. Otherwise what you're doing is like masturbation—you're just doing it for yourself.

Q: What about Film-look or other processes whereby the video is altered to make it appear like film? What if buyers can't tell the difference?

A: The Film-look is important, but it's a double-edged sword here. If you're going to use a Film-look process or computer process or something like it, you're much more inclined to make sales. The problem with Film-look is that it degrades the image quality of your tape, and by doing this it's harder to make copies of your tape, and when you make copies for your overseas buyers, it degrades the image even more. You're more likely to make a sale, but it's harder for the guy who winds up with it to have an adequate copy. So you're stuck between a rock and a hard place in that respect. I would say, however, if you have a choice in the matter that you always make sure to shoot your video like you were doing a film. Light it like a film. Shoot it like a film. Don't use techniques or even transitions as if you were doing a video. I see people do all these weird video transitions, but then it becomes blatantly obvious that it's shot on video-even if it's been Film-looked. Try to make it look as much like a real movie as possible. That increases your chances of making a sale.

Q: When approaching financiers, how important is it for you to have a clear and concise business plan in place?

A: I'm going to tell you what I prefer to do—what I recommend filmmakers do. Not for established filmmakers—they already know what to do. For the new filmmaker, here's an approach that is simple. One, if you're going to have a business plan, make it as simple and as easy as possible. I don't think a business plan should ever be more than 20 pages long because if it's more than that, the person you give it to, no matter how smart the person is, no matter how well read, is not going to read it. They'll turn it over to their business manager or whoever, or their lawyer, who in turn will read it and say no because it's easier to say no and not get in trouble down the line if it loses money.

If it's too short, on the other hand, it looks like you don't have all the information. So basically try to get the information and boil it down to its essence, whatever you legally have to have in there and what is necessary to understand. And have a good cover. Then, at the same time, try to keep your budget down low so that it's easier to get the investors. And the investors you approach are friends, your family, acquaintances and people you work with, and so on. Now most people say, "I don't want to do that, because what if the movie loses money," and that's absolutely true—those people will hate you. But if you hold off and you make the movie with somebody else's money, and it makes money, and you never approached your friends and your family and acquaintances, they'll hate you because you never approached them. So if you're going to lose anyway, lose for something you did rather than something you didn't do. Friends and family might not always believe in you, but they know you're less likely to cheat them than somebody else who's doing a business deal, so they at least know you're going to give it your best shot.

Q: How important is it to have a financial track record? If one is not present, is it more difficult for indie filmmakers to get financing?

A: I would say having a proven track record is at least between 50 to 80 percent of your success. Now I'm not saying necessarily that your movies have got to make tons of money, because yes, that alone will make people want to invest. But if you have some kind of proven track record, or you're doing business with somebody who has a proven track record, that will help you greatly. If you don't have a proven track record, then do business with people who do. Even if it's someone who hasn't made movies that were huge successes, if you're affiliated with somebody who has a proven track record of having produced or directed other successful pictures, or acted in successful pictures, the people you're trying to get to invest will think you know a little about what you're doing — we're not dealing with people who have high hopes.

Now can you do without this? Yes. But then you're going to be dealing with people who are going to be putting up $500 a piece as opposed to $5000 a piece. If you don't have the means of getting a lot of money, then you try to get people who have very little money to believe in your project enough to do it. On the other hand, if you think you can get a little more money, then you can get someone who has a bigger and better track record than you do if you don't have the experience.

Try to maximize what you have done. Do you have a background as a playwright or a screenwriter? Do you have a background as a film critic? Whatever. Have you gone to USC? UCLA? Whatever. Something that shows yes, you know what you're talking about. You're not just standing there showing off. And that helps convince people simply because you have more credibility now.

And another thing you can do, which a lot of people do, is shoot a trailer. You show highlights of your movie, not unlike people watching a regular trailer in a movie theater. That gives investors an idea of what you're trying to do, because the average person has limited or no imagination and they can't see what you're talking about. But if they see what you're talking about, then you've come out on top.

Q: *How important is money to making a movie, and what are the pros and cons of low budget movies versus high budget movies?*

A: There's no good and bad either way. If you're doing a large budget movie, you lose a tremendous amount of control, which is frankly a fair thing because if somebody else is putting up $30, $40 or $100 million, damn it, they have a right to say what you're going to do with it.

You lose a lot of creative control, you lose control over distribution, and frankly, you almost never see any money back. I mean, unless things have changed in the last couple of years, Paramount was saying that the original Star Trek never made a dime. So, good luck. Certainly you get to work with great people, it's more likely that you can actually reshoot things, or at the very least, have wonderful special effects, and ways of correcting things, because you have the time to do things. That is the main advantage of big budget films — you have *time*.

But when it comes to low budget films, you have a certain amount of autonomy. You can dictate what you want to do, how you're going to do it. You don't have a lot of time, but if you take care and plan, think your shots out, and think your production out, more than likely you'll turn out something great. You have a lot more control. And also if things don't turn out the way you want, at least you haven't lost $100 million and ended up in disgrace so that nobody in town wants to touch you. The risk is less.

I mean there are a lot of filmmakers that did a lot of low-budget movies and maybe they didn't make that much money, but they showed what they could do and then down the line they made bigger budget films. For example, John Carpenter made several low-budget films before making bigger films later on. And even now he likes smaller budget films because he has more control.

I think it depends on what your intent is. Most people want to put a project together and say, "Hey, MGM is going to love this project and they'll want to put me in charge." Well, why? Why the hell should they? If you don't have a proven track record, they don't want to deal with you. They only want to deal with a handful of guys. In Hollywood, most of the major studios are package deals. They get so-and-so director with so-and-so producer with so-and-so actor that are all usually represented by the same people. The odds of someone with no track record and no experience putting together a package deal are slim.

When you're starting out, you're going to be doing low-budget movies, it's just that simple. And you might discover that you ultimately enjoy that more. I prefer frankly, to have a lot of control over my projects because then I can shoot the vision that I have — at least in projects that I've written and directed.

When I did *24 Hours to Midnight*, the distributor took the movie, went back, reshot and added some scenes that were not in the original picture and recut it in a way that some of the scenes really didn't make any sense. That taught me that I never wanted to go through that again. It was a hugely successful film, but to this day it's always somewhat of an embarrassment to me because a lot of people walk over and say, "Hey, you know that scene where that guy *died*? That scene where he's killed by that ninja — how come he's alive in the next scene?" It's because he didn't die in that scene, but the way the distributor edited it, he left out the fact that the guy is alive.

Q: What do you see as the future of independent filmmaking and filmmakers?

A: The fact of the matter, as far as I can tell, is that independent filmmaking is always going to be around. As technology changes, filmmaking has the potential to become cheaper and cheaper. As technology makes it possible to produce a picture for little money, more independent filmmakers will jump on the bandwagon.

The ironic thing is that major films are getting more and more expensive every year. The foreign buyers are simply not willing to buy that expensive material. Frankly, I don't understand. I'm in the business. I know the foreign sales market. I know the foreign buyers. I know the distributors. There is no logic to this, but the studios keep charging more and more money, and the foreign buyers simply don't want to pay, or they *can't* pay it.

The world economy is not that good, and the Asian market — usually a particularly strong market — is not that great right now. The South American and Latin American markets — always important markets — aren't very good right now either. There's just not that much of a market for these films. They're trying to buy some of these big films, but the fact is they just can't afford to buy them.

Basically there's always going to be a need for the independent filmmaker because the independent filmmaker is the only one who can make movies at a price at which there's a guarantee of some kind of profit for the buyers — or as close as you're going to get to a guarantee.

As a general rule of thumb — and this fluctuates from year to year, of course — but as a general rule of thumb you figure about 9 out of every 10 major films lose money; about 7 out of every 10 low budget films make money. Which one would you be more inclined and willing to invest in? And if you deal with films that are genre-related (action, horror, erotic, martial arts, etc.), the ratio of success is even higher. It's like 9 out of every 10 make money — so long as you keep within a small budget.

Q: How valuable do you think the business plan included with this book will be to readers and hopeful indie filmmakers?

A: I think it's great for readers to see what a filmmaker's business plan looks like. Although every business plan will be slightly different — every one will be changed slightly in proportion to what the need of that particular film project is going to be like. If you're doing something for a comic book superhero film, your business plan is going to be different than if you're doing something for, let's say, an erotic thriller, or an action film or whatever. Because different people want to invest in different things. Ironically, film investors are not like regular investors. You appeal to their ego, you appeal to their personal fancy, rather than strictly the financial comeback. The financial comeback is simply the extra added effect. That's the gravy. One guy put it this way — you're not selling the steak, you're selling the sizzle. Whatever it is they personally like about that particular genre or that particular movie, that's what ultimately sells them on it. So that's what each business plan has to cater to. For an erotic thriller, you have to point out the sexy and beautiful women and men, the successful history of other erotic thrillers, and how well those pictures have done. For a martial arts film, you talk about the martial arts stars that are in the movie, the action that's going to be in it, how it will differ from other action films. For science-fiction, you talk about the special effects. Every genre is sold by different things. Science-fiction is sold predominantly by the special effects, horror by the makeup, erotic thrillers and T&A films are sold by the beauty of the women and the men and the locations. Action films by the quality of the stunt work and the explosions and pyrotechnics. Martial arts films by the type of martial arts they use and the stunt work and the frequency of the fights.

All this affects the business plan to a degree.

Q: What advice do you have for aspiring or established filmmakers looking to take "the next step"?

A: First of all, you have to have a project that is worthy of having more money. In other words, you don't just take a movie that can be shot for $20,000 and make it for $50,000. You take a project that you can't do for $20,000. You have to have that $50,000 or $500,000 or the $5 million or whatever it is. You can't cheat your audience by saying, "Well, I'm making the same kind of movie except I'm getting more stars in it." A lot of people like to say, "Well, all they're doing at the major studios is the same kind of movies we make on low budgets," which is kind of true, but they do it in a different way. Everything is bigger, grander, more elaborate. If you're doing a *Charlie's Angels*, sure you're going to get bigger stars, but you're also going to do more elaborate sets, more elaborate location work, a lot more martial arts stuff, which will look totally different from the TV show.

They did two *Blair Witch* movies. The second one was not a very good film — and it cost $10 million — as opposed to the $27,000 of the first film. They couldn't do that second film on the budget of the first. So they had to have the $10 million to do it, because they had to build a lot of sets. If you're doing something that involves a lot of location work, spread out over a lot of places, as opposed to a consolidated one or two places, like a forest, city streets or whatever, that complicates things and you have to have more money and more time. Time equals money in this business.

If you have a choice between spending more money on this or spending more money on that, give yourself the extra time. Give yourself those extra few days. That can be the difference between having a really good film — a really good commercial film — and having a film that is not as good.

Q: Do you see the Internet having any impact on indie filmmaking, and more specifically on their sales and marketing?

A: So far it really hasn't changed things that much. The main effect of the Internet right now is that it can be used to let the public, and more importantly foreign buyers, know more about your films by virtue of your website, by virtue of a downloadable trailer. By accessing your trailer, they might be more inclined to buy the film or take a look at it later on.

The Internet is not a great place to sell movies yet. They keep saying it's going to be, but it hasn't happened yet because the image isn't good enough yet. I am told by one source that one company has claimed that they can do that, but so far it's not available yet. Heaven knows when it will be. It may be five years for all we can tell. Also, the average person simply doesn't have a fast enough modem or fast enough computer to watch movies on the Internet. Until that's done, the Internet is not going to be a viable alternative to television.

One thing to consider is the potential creation of programming for the Internet. This is where the low-budget filmmaker has an advantage. The big studios can't do low-budget filmmaking for the Internet. The low-budget filmmaker can. Once the various Internet services, whether they be Juno, AOL, Yahoo or whichever, get to the point where they have a chance to do something like the television networks with original programming, independent filmmakers can theoretically and potentially be creating a lot of original programming, whether it be variety shows, comedies, dramas, action shows— and they can do it similarly to what they did 50 years ago. Like *The Adventures of Superman* or *I Love Lucy*. One of the reasons those shows were so successful is because they were very low budget, and they didn't take a whole lot of money to be able to make a profit.

The Adventures of Superman back in 1951 cost $15,000 an episode. *Highway Patrol* back in the mid-50's cost $20,000 an episode. And if you can produce that kind of programming for the Internet, it probably would make a profit. Therefore, independent filmmakers and the Internet might be able to make some money. This hasn't happened yet, but I think it's certainly within five years you're going to see this happen.

For now the Internet is a great tool for promotion. Also, it's a great place to get investors. You put your business plan on a website. Several people do that. You can put posters from other films, allow investors to download clips from other movies you've made, or trailers. It allows investors to have a better sense, without even having to meet you, that you're real. You put all your promotional material and business plan on the website and let them "meet you" before actually meeting you.

Q: Mr. Ron Ford, you are a very successful award-winning independent filmmaker. Can you briefly tell readers a little about yourself?

A: Born in Bremerton, Washington in 1958, I have always been interested in film and performing, as far back as I can remember. I received a Drama degree from Olympic

Ron Ford, independent filmmaker with Fat-Free Features: *The Fear, The Song of the Vampire, Witchcraft XI, The Alien Conspiracy, Hollywood Mortuary, Mayday.*

College (Bremerton, WA) in 1980. While in college, I was nominated for the Irene Ryan acting award for my performance as Dodge in Shepard's *Buried Child.* The first play I wrote, *Outlaws*, which was produced for the American College Theater Festival, was nominated for the David Library Literary Award. That same year (1983), I married the woman who played my wife in *Buried Child* in the same theater in which the play was produced.

In 1985 we moved to Tucson, Arizona, where I worked on the production crew of many motion pictures (including *Can't Buy Me Love* and *World Gone Wild*) in many capacities—from driver to make-up artist. There I got my first professional acting roles in the TV series, *Hey, Dude* and *The Young Riders.* I made a public access video of Forrest J. Ackerman's Lon Chaney story, *Letter to an Angel.* Ackerman appeared as the narrator in the short, which won an award in the American Film Institute's 1985 Visions of U.S. video competition.

In 1990 we moved to Los Angeles. I have since appeared in over a dozen motion pictures, including *Killer Tomatoes Eat France, Addicted to Murder* and *The Cool Air.* I played Bottom in *Ill Met By Moonlight*, a screen adaptation of Shakespeare's *A Midsummer Night's Dream*, in 1993. After winning the 1992 Christopher Columbus Screenplay Discovery Award, I wrote the 1994 horror hit, *The Fear*, with Vince Edwards, Ann Turkel and Wes Craven. As a director, I helmed my first feature, *Alien Force*, in 1995 for Wildcat Entertainment, in association with my own company (our first venture), Fat Free Features. The action/karate/comedy genre blender (guest starring TV's "Robin," Burt Ward) was successful enough to warrant two more pictures for Wildcat. A succession of feature directing and writing jobs quickly followed for other production entities, including Sterling Entertainment, Vista Street Entertainment and SNJ Productions. In 1999 I wrote and directed an installment of a long-running Horror series, *Witchcraft XI: Sisters in Blood.* The same year also saw me directing my fist 3-D feature, the sci-fi action thriller, *V-World Matrix.* In 2000, I wrote and directed *Deadly Scavengers* for Vista Street Entertainment, and a segment of the anthology film *The Alien Conspiracy: Time Enough.* Also produced in 2000, I wrote *The Song of the Vampire* for actress/director Denice Duff. Today I can be found busily writing, directing or doing post production work on some production at any given time.

Q: Your films range in budget from film project to film project. How important is financing to you and how does it contribute to the success of your motion picture ventures?

A: Well, money isn't everything. It is possible to make a masterpiece for little or nothing—but it sure is a lot harder! Financing, unfortunately, is the gateway to being creative. Without the bucks, there is no movie. So as dull and uncreative as it may seem

STARS AREN'T BORN...
THEY'RE EMBALMED.

HOLLYWOOD
MORTUARY

FAT FREE FEATURES PRESENTS A RON FORD MOVIE FILM STAR RANDAL MALONE STARRING IN "HOLLYWOOD MORTUARY"
ALSO STARRING TIM SULLIVAN WITH CONRAD BROOKS AND DAVID DECOTEAU
SPECIAL GUEST STARS MISS MARGARET O'BRIEN AND MISS ANITA PAGE
EDITED BY JEFF LEROY MUSIC BY TIM THOMPSON MAKEUP KEVIN PARCHER AND ROBERT VAN
DIRECTORS OF PHOTOGRAPHY JEFF LEROY AND CLARK JORDAN ASSOCIATE PRODUCER MICHAEL W. SCHWIBS
LINE PRODUCER PAULA POINTER-FORD PRODUCED WRITTEN AND DIRECTED BY RON FORD

One of Ron Ford's most successful projects, *Hollywood Mortuary* has been released worldwide on VHS and DVD.

at times, it is a basic, fundamental and all-important aspect of film making. With less money you have to work harder at everything — you have to be as clever as you can and call in as many favors as you can think of. With a larger budget you simply buy exactly what you need, and you can take valuable time to get just the right shot instead of "making do" with what you can get easily and quickly. A larger budget allows you to concentrate more on the creativity and not the nuts and bolts. The irony, however, is that often when the budget is larger the producers who control that money dictate more and more of the creative decisions, effectively limiting your expression more than if you had worked on your own for little money. So no situation is ideal, and you must make the best of each one to get the best picture you can. The best way to do that is to go in with a business plan so that you can get the full value of every cent on the screen.

Q: When presenting your projects to potential investors, how important is it to have a clear and concise plan in place for what you propose to do?

A: It depends on my relationship with the producer. Some trust me and leave me alone more than others. With new producers who I've never worked for before it is absolutely important to have a clear, precise plan. Let them know how you intend to spend their money and assure them that it will be put to good use. There are a hundred guys in line behind you with their plans wanting that money, too, so you better be able to give them a clear reason why they should pick you.

Q: Your films reach international audiences and are distributed world-wide. How much of a role does this foreign market play in recouping your investment efforts and turning a profit?

A: Foreign is the bulk of your money. When I make a movie on video for under $20,000 it has a very limited market in the U.S. But if you think ahead and make a commercial picture with exploitable elements (nudity, gore, action), there is a place for it in the foreign market. Larger movies shot on film can have a wider market domestically, but then foreign is still always a huge part of your returns. Always consider the foreign market when planning your feature.

Q: You many times handle the production and distribution of your own motion pictures. Writing, developing and shooting a movie is the creative end of the medium. Obtaining financing for it, then distributing it to recoup the money and a profit is the other end of the medium — finance and business. How distinct do you find these two worlds, and do you find it difficult bridging the gap between them?

A: They are distinctly different in every way, completely different sorts of disciplines. But money does affect the creative also, because when you are shooting, the clock is always ticking. And that clock is a financial one. The longer you take shooting, the more it costs. On a film set it is absolutely true that "time is money." To answer your question, I don't find it difficult bridging the gap between the creative and the financial. I don't think of it that way. They are the twin blades of the film making sword, and they always work together. If you think of them as a marriage, two parts of a whole, it seems less of a battle.

Q: You are familiar with the business plan found in Appendix A of this book. How valuable do you feel this reference material can be to independent filmmakers seeking funding for their film projects?

A: Invaluable. It will give a clear, practical guide as to where to begin and what steps to take in getting your movie financed. Also, it is an excellent template to judge the professionalism of your presentation. If you go in looking like an amateur, the battle is lost before it has begun. This is a practical tool that I wish I had possessed starting out.

Q: What personal advice can you give to beginning or established independent filmmakers who are seeking financing for their film projects?

A: Follow the plan in this book, always consider your market before beginning, be as detailed and precise as you can be in your preparations and presentation, and keep plugging away—*never give up*!

Q: Mr. Kevin Lindenmuth, you are a very successful award-winning independent filmmaker. Can you briefly tell readers a little about yourself?

A: I've been making movies, in one form or another, since I was eight years old. This started with the family's Super 8mm film camera, when I made short stop-motion animation films and then ten years later, at the University of Michigan, I made some interesting video shorts as a Film/ Video Studies Major. During this time I was working staff at

Kevin Lindenmuth, independent filmmaker of Brimstone Productions: *Addicted to Murder, The Alien Agenda, The Alien Conspiracy, Walking Between the Raindrops, Rage of the Werewolf.*

Ann Arbor Public Access Television, the local television station, and I was able to get most everything I created aired on local television. Oftentimes the scheduling department put a religious show right before my video—and those TV church goers who sat and watched my rather offbeat films afterwards often called into the station to protest the content! After college I moved to New York City, working actively in the film/video business for various companies—at the same time pursuing my own interests in independent filmmaking. From 1990-2000 I either directed or produced over a dozen genre features, five of which were nationally distributed by Blockbuster Video in the United States. Most recently I worked on two projects with my wife, Audrey Geyer. The first was a drama entitled *Walking Between the Raindrops*, which had some festival exposure in 1999, and the second was an hour long documentary entitled *Caring for the Caregivers: Living with Cancer.*

At the end of the 90's I also wrote an interview book entitled *Making Movies on Your Own: Practical Talk with Independent Filmmakers*, which delved into the arena of do-it-yourself independent filmmaking. Over two dozen independent filmmakers, including Mr. Campisi, were interviewed. A follow-up book, tentatively entitled *Interviews with Independent Filmmakers*, will be published by the time you read this interview.

I've also written for such genre magazines as *Epitaph, Pirate Writings, TV Scene,*

World of Fandom, Screem, Draculina, Vamperotica, GC Magazine, Cult Movies, and a slew of Internet film sites such as www.buried.com.

I'm currently in postproduction on three alien invasion movies entitled *The Alien Conspiracy,* and two werewolf anthologies featuring the talents of Tim Ritter, John Bowker, Alexandre Michaud, Ron Ford, Les Sekely, Bruce G. Hallenbeck, and Joe Bagnardi.

Q: Your films range in budget from film project to film project. How important is financing to you and how does it contribute to the success of your motion picture ventures?

A: Well, financing determines exactly what you'll be able to do in your film. For example, my movie *Vampires & Other Stereotypes* (released in 1992) had a budget of $30,000. I was able to build sets, have a special effects crew, and feed and house over twenty production people, etc. It was still very low budget but I was able to get some decent footage. *Addicted to Murder,* on the other hand, cost only $5000 but it was written for this specific budget in mind. The majority of locations were interiors, namely my apartment and the apartments of friends in New York City. Special effects were minimal and the production crew was much smaller. The three *Alien Agenda* movies, done a few years later, had comparable budgets although the effects were more on par with *Vampires & Other Stereotypes.* In part this was due to the advancement in computer effects, and as a more experienced filmmaker I knew what could be "pulled off."

It was these lower budgeted movies that were eventually nationally distributed by Blockbuster Video and sold to such countries as England, France, Germany and Thailand.

Q: Your films get more elaborate and more expensive from film project to film project. They seem to be a natural progression. Do you find financiers more receptive and prone to investing in your movies with each passing film project?

A: Up to this point all of my films, except *Vampires & Other Stereotypes,* were made entirely with my own money. And since they were self-financed, I had more personally at stake — if I didn't make my money back quickly on them I'd directly feel the repercussions! As I obtained more experience as a filmmaker, I was able to get more bang for my buck, as it were. If I made *Vampires & Other Stereotypes* today I could probably make it for one-third the original budget and come out with a superior movie.

With these movies I think I was too impatient to actively pursue getting financing from outside investors. I didn't want to wait around, potentially years, to get my budget to make a movie. I needed to make movies *now.* I had too many films in my mind that I wanted to do. So I simply worked with what I had and did the best I could for the budgets. In reviews and media, these films inevitably get compared to million dollar movies and the phrase, "If only there was a budget," oftentimes pops up. But I always have to remind myself that there are thousands of films out there that never do get distributed. And these low budget movies of mine do get distributed to video stores and sold to foreign countries.

As I embark on increasing the budgets and approaching financiers to make the bigger budgeted movies, I'm sure my track record of making and getting movies "out there" will greatly help.

Q: In the future, when you present your projects to potential investors, how important do you feel it will be to have a clear and concise plan in place for what you propose to do?

"A very serious, disturbing horror feature. The film is filled with horrific and gruesome happenings."
— *SHOCKING IMAGES MAGAZINE*

Addicted to Murder

MICK McCLEERY • LAURA McLAUCHLIN • SASHA GRAHAM
ADDICTED TO MURDER
Starring GORDON LINZNER • CANDICE MEADE • SEWELL WHITNEY
JOLEE BECKER and BERNADETTE PAULEY
Original Soundtrack by STEVE MARUZZELLI and HECTOR MILIA
Special Make-up Effects by RON CHAMBERLAIN and DEREK BECKER
Written by KEVIN LINDENMUTH and TOM PICCIRILLI
Produced and Directed by KEVIN LINDENMUTH

Kevin J. Lindenmuth is perhaps best known for the success of his *Addicted to Murder* trilogy, which was released to both domestic and foreign markets.

A: With making a movie you must always have a clear and concise plan of how you are going to approach it, whether you have a $5000 or $500,000 budget. Once the production is underway, there is no room for mistakes and second guessing. This planning, planning, and more planning was the only way I was able to pull off all the Brimstone movies. All the films were specifically tailored for the budgets.

Q: Your films reach international audiences and are distributed world-wide. How much of a role does this foreign market play in recouping your investment efforts and turning a profit?

A: The foreign distribution market, at this point in time, is far more lucrative than the domestic market. A large part of it is the fact that American distributors always want to have "stars" or "names" in the movies they acquire, believing that this aspect is what always sells the movie to an audience. This is the primary reason why I self-distribute the movies here in the U.S. Yet, I am still able to sell them to video stores. With foreign sales, the distributor simply licenses the movie for "X" number of years and pays a flat fee up front for that leasing of the film. This way you are assured of the money. And you may be able to recoup the entire film's budget with one foreign sale.

Q: You many times handle the production and distribution of your own motion pictures. Writing, developing and shooting a movie is the creative end of the medium. Obtaining financing for it, either personal or from third parties, then distributing it to recoup the money and a profit is the other end of the medium — finance and business. How distinct do you find these two worlds, and do you find it difficult bridging the gap between them?

A: Because I often have a small budget to work with, this budget somewhat determines how the script is written — and also forces me to be more creative in terms of how scenes will be shot, what effects are used, etc. I don't think of the budget as limiting my creativity, just the opposite. I've written a number of scripts, more much higher budgeted films, where I ignored the cost factor, and I can't say that these scripts were necessarily any more "creative." Just different. But there is a *huge* difference between the creativity of writing, shooting, directing and producing a movie and the business end of selling that finished movie. Making a movie, it's a total creative endeavor — I'm not thinking if it's sellable or marketable, that I need this or that specific scene or actor to sell the movie. I'm simply trying to make the movie in my mind's eye, making the movie that I want to make (the purist form of independent filmmaking). When I sell the movie, this creative endeavor is now viewed as "product" by the stores or companies that buy the movie from me. They are the ones who are thinking, "Is this marketable?", "Will people buy or rent this movie?" Often these distributors don't even watch the entire movie — they simply need "product" and base their decision on the box art or genre. The truth of the matter is that fans of science-fiction and horror movies will rent out the movie if they think it's original and a lot of the originality today is being done in independent films. I don't think distributors understand this.

Given a choice between creative and business, I'd stay with the creative.

Q: You are familiar with the business plan found in Appendix A of this book. How valuable do you feel this reference material can be to independent filmmakers seeking funding for their film projects?

A: I think the reference material in this book will be an invaluable asset to independent filmmakers. Since the majority of independent filmmakers plow ahead on their own, oftentimes producing their own films without outside help, their knowledge either has to come from other filmmakers or from material that they read. The reference material will give them a clear basis on how to approach potential financiers.

Q: What personal advice can you give to beginning or established independent filmmakers who are seeking financing for their film projects?

A: Stick with making movies. If you can't get the budget you want to make a specific film, don't wait and do nothing. Make a smaller film with your own money while you try to get the financiers to make the bigger budgeted one. It all comes down to this: If you want to make movies bad enough, *you will.*

Q: Mr. Ed Hansen, you are a successful independent filmmaker. You are probably best recognized for your very successful The Bikini CarWash Company, *and your more recent* Wooly Boys *with Peter Fonda, Kris Kristofferson, Keith Carradine and Joey Mazelli. Can you briefly tell readers a little about yourself and your films?*

A: I started my career as a writer: poems, short stories, sports articles. I moved on to copywriting for ad agencies working on such award-winning accounts as Goodyear Tires, QANTAS Airlines, Volkswagen USA, and American Airlines. I graduated to becoming a Creative Director supervising a creative staff of over 40 people who worked on Chevrolet Dealer Associations, Pennzoil, Cooper Tires, and Great Western Savings with annual billings of over $30 million. After four years, I realized I was losing touch with the creative and becoming more of a supervisor. I started writing creative projects "freelance" to keep my touch: *Sesame Street, Carol Bur-*

Ed Hansen, independent filmmaker with Atomic Hollywood: *The Bikini CarWash Company, Wooly Boys, Robo-C.H.I.C., Rocky & Bullwinkle.*

nett, Smothers Brothers, Pat Paulsen, etc. Suddenly, I was having fun again and set up my own creative boutique to create and produce corporate films, documentaries and low budget features. Vestron Video was the first company to finance my film projects which numbered seven extremely profitable erotic comedies, including: *Eroticise, Takin' It Off, Takin' It All Off, Party Favors,* and *Party Plane.* Because of various experiences, Vestron also hired me to edit and supplement many of their other feature films, which eventually led me to editing promos for *Dirty Dancing, Ghostbusters, Rambo, Karate Kid, The Natural,* as well as a video edit of *9½ Weeks* and all of Disney's *Rocky & Bullwinkle* videos. Everything still starts with a script but, as in the case of *Wooly Boys,* we no longer have to produce everything. But the script must "move" us, make us laugh or cry, arouse sensual feelings or disgust, make us love or hate — or forget it. It's not worth the effort.

Q: What is your view on the present independent filmmaking scene? Does the new wave of cheap digital video cameras and non-linear editors have a future? Is it a force for Hollywood to reckon with, or is it a passing fad?

A: First of all, the best of the new wave of digital video cameras are *not* cheap, and really provide state-of-the-art quality at affordable prices. Of course they have a future. With George Lucas shooting *Star Wars: Attack of the Clones* and the upcoming third *Star Wars* entirely on *digital,* I think we can safely say it has a future — at least, until the next big advancement is made.

Q: You have made films with varying budgets throughout the years, and they range from film project to film project. How important is financing in general and how does it contribute to the success of your motion picture ventures, no matter how small or large the budget?

A: *Nothing* gets made without money! From a creative standpoint we can argue that without a script, without actors, without a director, etc., you can't do a movie. And that's true, but without the money, there are tons of unproduced producers walking around with scripts, actors and directors attached, that still have little or no chance of getting anything produced.

Q: You have an established library of films you have produced over the years. Do you believe these produced credits give you more credibility with financiers and investors as opposed to someone just starting out who has no produced credits?

A: Absolutely! Without credits, you're just talking. With credits, it means you've been there, done that and it's relatively easy for possible investors to find out that the production came in on schedule and made a profit.

Q: What about financial track records? Are they scrutinized by potential investors, or do you find that they are irrelevant?

A: Whether they actually read it or not, which is probably arguable, most of my potential investors want as much material as possible on financial track records, current projections based on similar films, etc.

Q: When presenting your projects to potential investors, how important is it to have a clear and concise plan (business plan) in place for what you propose to do?

A: Each project and potential investor is different and I find you must try to tailor your "plan" to the needs and personalities involved.

However, normally I try, within reason, to give them *everything* I have to which I have access. Despite trying to make the plan very complete, I also try not to verbalize too much and instead try to make the plan well organized and simple and fast to read. It's been my experience that full pages of type tend to "lose" potential investors. Filmmaking is exciting and I believe that excitement must be reflected to some degree in your presentation.

Q: Your films reach international audiences and are distributed world-wide. How much of a role does this foreign market play in recouping your investment efforts and turning a profit?

A: Again, each project is different. As a general rule, action plays best internationally, while "talky" dramas or comedies tend to do very poorly. However, "physical or action" comedies play extremely well if the humor is "seen" and not buried in clever words (which may not translate well into many countries). One only has to look at the success of Jerry Lewis in his early films overseas which usually generated better critical reviews as well as better box office. My film, *Robo-C.H.I.C.*, an action comedy, did huge business overseas and also won a top award at the Moscow Film Festival. I normally project the U.S./Canadian marketplace first, and then add 45 percent for international.

However, my film, *The Bikini CarWash Company*, reportedly did over 200 percent more overseas.

Q: Writing, developing and shooting a movie is the creative end of the medium. Obtaining financing for it, then distributing it to recoup the money and a profit is the other end of the medium — finance and business. How distinct do you find these two worlds, and do you find it difficult bridging the gap between them?

A: For most creative people, I think the creative end of the medium is the easiest. Obtaining financing then distribution is tremendously difficult and filled with slinky characters. Many financing people do *not* have the money, but love to take meetings, even pay for lunches, and call on their cell phone that they are "meeting with their writers and director to discuss their movie." Despite the meetings (which defies any logic), weeks later they suddenly reveal they don't have the money, don't want to invest in a movie because of the stock market, their partner was arrested in Bangkok with all the money, they'll only do it if you can attach Tom Cruise for $100,000 or they've heard you can do a 35mm movie for under $35,000 so why do we need $350,000? The real problem with forcing creative people to try to handle financing and distribution is that it tends to grow calluses over the creativity.

Q: You are familiar with the business plan found in Appendix A of this book. How valuable do you feel this reference material can be to independent filmmakers seeking funding for their film projects?

A: I think it's excellent as long as the reader remembers every project and potential investor is different. Adjustments have to be made. Emphasis should, as in advertising, project the benefit to the investor (be it greed, ego, charity). Unless he or she sees the benefit, why bother? Most of these people have enough money, they just have to be assured that they're going to get a fair shake and that you are aware and hope to accomplish the investor's goals.

Q: What personal advice can you give to beginning or established independent filmmakers who are seeking financing for their film projects? More precisely, when indie filmmakers gather their forces and prepare to meet investors, what personal knowledge and experience can you pass on to them for doing so?

A: Never bullshit anyone, especially an investor. Like a wild animal, I think potential investors can smell fear (lies), so you're always better off just laying it on the line. I've gotten a ton of respect from investors when they asked me a question and I answered truthfully, "I don't know the answer, but I'll find out for you and get back to you." If you try to bluff your way through it, more than likely you're going to stumble and hurt yourself. If a beginning filmmaker doesn't have the experience, admit it and point out the advantages ("lower price, enthusiasm, etc.") If it's an experienced filmmaker, they should point out the advantages ("I've been through it all, my films always get released, ego has been submerged, etc.")

Appendix A

A Sample Indie Business Plan

FireGem Entertainment, Inc.
Quality Motion Pictures

The production of *any* motion picture is a highly speculative endeavor and involves a serious degree of risk for investors. This document is not a solicitation for funds or financiers. It is presented *for information only*. Please use due diligence.

EXECUTIVE SUMMARY

Business Philosophy

The mission of FireGem Entertainment's producers is to utilize their acquired skills and knowledge for the purpose of creating dramatic motion pictures that tell stories of fantasy, ancient mythology and folklore — and to reap financial rewards that will satisfy investors' interests so as to keep them investing in future projects. The partners of the company possess over 50 years combined experience in the motion picture industry, and boast over two-dozen independent writer, filmmaker and cinematography awards.

The partners of FireGem Entertainment intend to take advantage of today's technological advances in digital cinematography and special effects to produce films with high production values at less than conventional production costs — potentially allowing the company and its investors greater financial rewards.

Overview of the Company

FireGem Entertainment was formed earlier this year as a privately held Nevada Corporation with the intent of specializing in the development, packaging and distribution of motion pictures for global theatrical, television and video markets. The partners of FireGem Entertainment will utilize their combined industry experience to promote and sell their films to the popular fantasy and supernatural markets. Strong dramatic storylines will be utilized first and foremost for all movies, allowing for the attraction of A-list actors to the projects, as well as attracting a more diverse and global audience in the marketplace.

The company is seeking $15 million for the production of three motion pictures at $5 million each.

The Managers and Executive Staff

FireGem Entertainment is comprised of four principals, all of whom possess successful prior experience in the motion picture and television industries, as well as a talented pool of experienced support staff. The partners also possess established relationships with a team of outside associates to assist with their productions on an as-needed basis.

141

The principals and staff of FireGem Entertainment are as follows:

- *Joe Filmmaker — (Partner) Executive Producer, Writer and Director*
- *Jane Filmmaker — (Partner) Financial Affairs, Producer and Writer*
- *Billy Camera — (Partner) Operations*
- *Johnny Money — (Partner) Investor Relations*
- *Mark Movie — Production Executive*
- *Jack Billboard — Marketing*
- *Jiffy Typewriter — Development*
- *Mary Microphone — Public Relations and Promotion*
- *Mathilda Helper — Executive Assistant*

Our consultants and outside support include the following:

- *Sonya Bernstein — Entertainment Attorney*
- *Andrew Nelson Mikels — Corporate Attorney*
- *Mark Brown — International Business Attorney*
- *Barnaby Withers — Certified Public Accountant*
- *Shelly Barr — Talent and Literary Agent*
- *Leanne Dalstein — Talent Manager*
- *Fritz Beauford — Independent Producer*
- *Telly Karell — Foreign Distribution Executive*

In addition to these people, there are several dozen industry and production entities with which FireGem Entertainment retains active relationships. You will find a select list of these additional entities with their credentials in this plan (see Company).

The Movie Projects

Confused Unicorns and Ogres is the first film slated for production by FireGem Entertainment. Joe and Jane Filmmaker wrote the screenplay to this film based on Joe's successful published book by the same name. Pre-production, budgeting and preliminary casting on this project has already been performed by the partners.

FireGem Entertainment has additionally optioned the rights to *The Thirteen Elves* and *Medusa's Mirror*, and is actively developing the properties, *Banshees of the Night* and *The Queen's Pegasus*.

Each proposed motion picture project will be tailored specifically to parallel and embrace elements which today's highest-grossing blockbuster films contain.

FireGem Entertainment's slate includes the production of three films over the ensuing four years, with budgets in the $5 million range each.

The Movie Industry

The motion picture industry has gone through various trends and fads over the years, but one thing remains steadfast: the industry's overall monetary worth has grown steadily for the past decade. Worldwide theatrical box-office receipts presently add up to over $20 billion annually. According to reports in *Variety Reporter* and *Hollywood Daily*, world totals are expected to exceed $30 billion by the end of the next decade. It is expected that the production companies in the United States will receive well over 50 percent — or $15 billion — of that amount.

In addition to theatrical revenues, 2002 saw nearly $40 billion in revenue from cable television programming and $22 billion in home video (VHS and DVD) sales and rentals.

A loose summary of these present-day figures is impressive:

Theatrical Revenues:	$20 billion
Cable Television Revenues:	$40 billion
Home Video Revenues:	$22 billion
Total:	$82 billion

The partners of FireGem Entertainment feel confident they can take advantage of this solid stream of revenue, securing the company's position in this highly competitive arena.

The Movie Market

Tales of fantasy, ancient mythology and folklore have survived the test of time. They are the oldest stories known to man. Mass audiences have embraced these genres on all levels—from books and video games to amusement parks and motion pictures, themes of fantasy and the like are embraced by the public, and the market is presently demanding more.

Confused Unicorns and Ogres, the company's first film slated for production, comes with an established literary fan base anticipating the production and release of the motion picture. The book by the same name, written by Joe Filmmaker, sold over 1 million copies the first year in wide release, and spent nearly four weeks on the *New Park Times'* *Bestseller List*. FireGem Entertainment plans on taking full advantage of this massive pre-sold audience.

A careful survey of a string of recent blockbuster Hollywood motion pictures clearly indicates movies like the ones FireGem Entertainment plans to make are not only an accepted public genre, but are also some of the most successful movies ever made. The financial rewards of these type of films are staggering when compared to other genres.

The message is clear: These marketable subject-matters sell.

Movie Distribution

The distribution of motion pictures comes in many guises, each with its own pros and cons. The partners of FireGem Entertainment have explored several of these disparate avenues. They will seek distribution by both major and independent companies, subsequently working with the one which offers the more lucrative financial deal.

Both domestic and foreign markets are already attuned with the types of films FireGem Entertainment plans to produce. The partners of the company anticipate distributors will be quick to acquire the films offered by the company based on the strength and demand of the genre itself, and historical performance of the same.

As FireGem Entertainment builds its track record and a financial base is fortified, the partners plan to eventually promote and distribute their projects worldwide from in-house. That is to say, FireGem Entertainment has an eye on becoming a worldwide distributor of quality motion pictures in the near future.

The Investor's Plan

FireGem Entertainment is seeking an initial investment amount of $5 million for the production of the first film. The staff plans on making a total of three films over the four years ensuing from the day startup capital is received. Each film will cost $5 million to produce. The total investment required is $15 million, to be utilized accordingly over the course of the four years. The plan combines the success of the three motion pictures into one "virtual" investment — effectively tipping the scale of potential in our favor for a more likely capital gain. The plan is based on the adage, "Don't put all your eggs in one basket."

Rather than creating an investment prospectus, the principals have kept this option open—citing the fact that no two investment deals are the same. While certain parameters will be adhered to, the particulars will be negotiated and established in good faith by the legal counsels and representatives of FireGem Entertainment and the investors. It is the principals' belief that this will make the legal process of negotiations more feasible and comfortable for investors.

The first year after the initial investment will be spent on the production of *Confused Unicorns and Ogres*. The beginning of the second year will simultaneously see the production of FireGem Entertainment's second film and the release of its first. Subsequently, box-office cash flow is not anticipated until the end of the second year, and profits not foreseen until the end of the same.

THE PRODUCTION COMPANY

Legal Description

FireGem Entertainment is the legal entity created by the principals of the company to engage in the production of theatrical motion pictures. The entity is a privately held C-class Corporation formed in October of 2002, and registered with the Secretary of State in Nevada. The business address is 5555 Main Street, Any City, Nevada 55555.

Background

Joe Filmmaker, the company founder, used the name of the company several years prior as a banner entity to produce nationally-acclaimed award-winning short-films for the international film festival circuit. Embracing the story-telling passion and filmmaking vision of Joe Filmmaker, the partners and executive staff of FireGem Entertainment have come together for the distinct purpose of creating feature motion pictures for worldwide theatrical exhibition.

Theme and Development

FireGem Entertainment will initially develop and produce action-adventure and thriller films with fantasy, science-fiction or supernatural themes as backgrounds. Special emphasis will be paid to the foreground element, *drama*— the necessary motivating-factor and realism inherent in any successful motion picture. We strongly feel the combination of these elements is the quintessence of escapism today's audiences seek — and actors and craftspeople wish to be associated with.

Conviction

From time immemorial, the public has shown overwhelming passion for these types of stories. More recently, analysis of box-office receipts over the past twenty years in industry and trade publications shows most of the all-time highest-grossing movies share identical themes to the films we plan to produce. We feel the present commercial success of the following comparable motion pictures strongly supports our convictions:

- *Space Blast*
- *Jurassic Fever*
- *Termination-Man*
- *Pixies and Fairies*

- *Unicorn Ghosts*
- *Nightmare on Ogre Avenue*
- *Independence Night*

Television Series:

- *X-Folders*
- *Space Trek: The Last Generation*
- *Babylonian-8*

- *Eon*
- *Xenco: Warrior Prince*
- *Herculean*

After dedicated research, FireGem Entertainment has realized there is a public demand and desire for action-adventure and thriller movies that explore fantasy, science-fiction and supernatural stories with dramatic and emotional intensity. The predominant success of television's award-winning *The X-Folders* series (which investigates unexplainable, mysterious and paranormal phenomenon) as well as *Eon* (similar subject-matter dedicated to unicorns, ogres, fairies and dragons) and the record-breaking success of the motion picture *Independence Night* (which presents a hypothetical Greek God invasion of Earth) readily assures the validity and accuracy of our choice of genre for motion picture production and subsequent distribution.

The company further believes there is a universal awakening taking place in which the public demands to know more about the world we live in, the meaning of life, and the answers to a plethora of recent unexplainable phenomenon such as UFOs, alien encounters and abductions, ghosts and spirits, as well as geographic and other natural anomalies. Ancient mythology plays right into this arena with its historical mysteries.

The screenplay of FireGem's proposed first film, *Confused Unicorns and Ogres*, has been described by industry readers as "*Close Encounters of Medusa's Kind* meets *Lethal Cyclops*"—two blockbuster hits at the box-office in recent years. *Confused Unicorns and Ogres* will feature fantasy and ancient mythology as a background. The dramatic foreground will feature the protagonist's desperate search for his kidnapped daughter. This dramatic element will consequently fuel the action and adventure of the tale as the protagonist stumbles onto forbidden knowledge held clandestine by dark and illegal factions of the population of the time.

Advance marketing tests conducted on behalf of *Confused Unicorns and Ogres* show audience reactions to be outstanding. *Unicorn Universe*, the leading international magazine on ancient mythology, published a preliminary poster and article in one of its latest issues, and claimed readers responded with eager anticipation to the film's arrival.

Other magazines, including *Hollywood Variety, Textbook Filmmaker* and *Cyclops Universe,* have run similar teasers with coinciding reader results.

The Managers and Executive Staff

FireGem Entertainment has hand-picked a select group of professionals to run the company and production of its films by placing them in positions that would take the most advantage of their strengths within the company. With this team of *players*, the company will move steadfast toward the creation of successful and profitable projects.

Mr. Joe Filmmaker — Executive Producer, Writer and Director

Mr. Filmmaker's diverse and detailed production background began early in his life. At age eight, he grabbed his father's Super-8mm film camera and shot a series of random narratives that, although amateur, were notably a sign of things to come. His novice productions became increasingly more elaborate over the years, and what once began as a hobby suddenly signaled the beginning of a prominent career in television and motion picture production.

At age fifteen, he was beating out the competition in film festivals and contests across the country with his intricate low-budget Super-8mm film productions. Films like *The Lost Horizon* and *Creature Killers*—fifteen-minute shorts— took top honors at national tournaments. Newspapers and magazines published several feature articles on him, his sophisticated little films and his unpretentious production crew.

Just two years later, he received several breaks in the industry and took his first steps toward professional filmmaking. He began working in movies and television shows as a camera and lighting technician, script supervisor/rewriter and assistant director. Burt Stallone's *Rockola X* and *Over the Big Top* were two of his first professional productions. Working as an uncredited crowd-control production-assistant, he was able to accomplish what he set out to do— penetrate the impervious walls of Hollywood's stone castle.

At such an early age, Mr. Filmmaker was officially "in" the business of moviemaking from that point forward, working every job available so long as it was motion picture or television oriented.

Over the years, his instinctive drive and enthusiasm for filmmaking led him through the thick and thin nuts-and-bolts of the business. From producing *Mrs. Hello Teen America Pageants* to rewriting shooting scripts at age eighteen for David Mann's television series, *Psycho Story*, he quickly learned the ins and outs and "best kept secrets" of story-telling, drama and production from his hands-on experience.

Mr. Filmmakers's conspicuous creativity provided for an abundance of popularity in high school as well as in college. For his 1986 Teramisu High School senior assembly— where graduating students put on a show for the rest of the pupils— he showed his amateur Super-8mm *Creature*

Joe Filmmaker

Killers film to a standing ovation of over one thousand students and teachers. In college, his obsession with writing and dramatic narrative lead him to the position of Opinion Page Editor for the campus newspaper of the time, *The Screaming Rebel*. He was also given the position of Editor-in-Chief of the campus's Hispanic Association newspaper, *The Hispanic Wind Breeze*. Both publications immediately recognized his writing talent and abilities, and presented him with numerous awards.

His professional screenwriting skills were fully realized by studying with UCMA's critically-acclaimed Professor Richard Watson (author of the book *Screenwriting: How The Heck Do You Write One of These Things?)* in 1989. His first two feature-length screenplays, *When Angels Blink* and *Silent Silent,* garnered him literary representation by a prominent Los Angeles literary agency—a striking accomplishment in itself, as *thousands* of writers year after year are rejected.

The culmination of Mr. Filmmaker's technical experience and passion for dramatic story-telling led to the formation of FireGem Entertainment. A portfolio and selected list of his credits is available upon request.

Mr. Filmmaker's distinguished experience in motion picture and television production will be used to evaluate and select which film projects go into production, negotiate with all pertinent outside entities (investors, distributors, actors and agents, writers, directors, etc.), and oversee every aspect of the entire executive management team. He will ultimately approve all trade, legal and fiscal obligations. He will also push for and approve strategic alliances with other companies and organizations. He will work with one goal in mind—to produce the most exciting motion pictures, thus maximizing returns on investments.

Mrs. Jane Filmmaker—Financial Affairs, Producer and Writer

A graduate of the Cinema School of Bruises and Hard Knocks in Los Angeles, Mrs. Filmmaker is actively completing a Masters Degree in Film Finance and Business Management. A self-motivated executive, she currently brings a vast amount of knowledge and hands-on experience in financial and management affairs from prominent Nevada and California corporations, including Bank of Anywhere, USA.

Mrs. Filmmaker is the second creative and motivating force behind FireGem Entertainment. In addition to her financial obligations as an executive, she will supervise and assist in the development of literary properties and production of the company's films. She is an avid student of literature and co-authored early drafts of the company's proposed first film, *Confused Unicorns and Ogres*. She is currently co-writing the final drafts and polish.

Mrs. Filmmaker's background in literature and creativity began at an early age. By the age of ten, she had amassed over 500 children's and young adult books in her "private little library." Like Mr. Filmmaker, she has established a sixth-sense awareness of what works and what doesn't when it comes to story-telling, screenwriting and filmmaking.

Jane Filmmaker

Mrs. Filmmaker will be responsible for overseeing the company's present financial conditions and forecasting the company's long-term financial strategies for guidance of management. Her tasks will include accounting and managing the budgets of the motion pictures in production as well as the company's budget for administrative operations. She will in essence be the heartbeat of the company by keeping track of every penny the company spends and attains.

Mr. Billy Camera — Operations

Mr. Camera will supervise the company's operations, coordinate all development and production affairs, and will manage the company's subordinate staff. He will be responsible for managing and enforcing the internal mechanics and hierarchy of the company, making sure it performs smoothly and efficiently. He will assist Mr. Filmmaker and Mrs. Filmmaker in all high-level negotiations and contract establishments with outside key executives, associates and prominent entities in the motion picture industry.

Billy Camera

Mr. Camera's extensive background as an investigator for the State of California government will translate vast management skills and experience to FireGem Entertainment. His responsibilities as a government agent included management and supervision of his state division, where he coordinated searches and handling of confidential data between a multitude of state offices and state personnel.

His skills and proficiency in management were recognized in early 2002 by the State of California when he was given the task of revising current insurance and fraud against the land laws and regulations. By analyzing and comparing current laws and regulations passed by legislation in neighboring states, he was able to present specific recommendations in order to expedite the entire fraud prosecution process. His suggestions for new procedures and provisions were implemented after lecturing key government personnel and administrators on the intricacies of hierarchy within such an immense body of state employees.

Mr. Johnny Money — Investor Relations

Mr. Money will serve as executive liaison between the company and private financial investors, both foreign and domestic. He will seek out and secure the budgetary requirements of the company on a project-by-project basis. Where it is deemed beneficial, he will pursue co-production agreements with outside companies to lessen the financial obligation of producing our movies. He will play a decisive role in negotiating and protecting the company's interests where all financial affairs are concerned and deals procured. He will work closely with the company's accounting and legal representatives, and assist Mr. Filmmaker and Mrs. Filmmaker in all high-level negotiations and contract establishments with private investors.

Mr. Money brings over thirty years of combined corporate experience from the hotel and casino gaming industry in Las Vegas, Reno, Atlantic City and Miami. His credentials traverse the most stringent of financial posts in some of the country's most prestigious resorts and distinct establishments.

As Vice President of Foreign Relations at these various companies, it was Mr. Money's responsibility to accommodate "high rollers" from a variety of countries across the globe.

Mr. Money's dedication, skill and distinct enthusiasm for the production of motion pictures makes him an invaluable asset to our company.

Mr. Mark Movie — Production Executive

Johnny Money

Mr. Movie will coordinate with Mr. Filmmaker and Mrs. Filmmaker the actual production of the company's motion pictures once a project goes from the preproduction to production stage. He will supervise the logistics of on-set responsibilities, including budget, schedule, permit and location adherence, cast and crew necessities, as well as camera, equipment and props essentials. He will be assisted by a unit production manager or line producer, as well as a staff of production assistants. He will assist Mr. Filmmaker and Mrs. Filmmaker with all particulars regarding the realization of transferring a screenplay into a vividly staged motion picture adventure.

Mr. Movie will utilize skills and expertise derived mostly from his extensive and distinguished background in multi-media and music video production in the Seattle, Washington "music scene." Talent from early music videos he produced and edited went on to celebrity-status, including *Nervousness, Pearl Oyster, Alice in Drag, Mud Sugar, Sad Mad, The Pleasure Twosome* and *Jagged Drill.*

Of particular interest, Mr. Movie has worked as an audio/video technician and producer of special projects for the World Health & Peace Organization (WHPO) as well as the National Aeronautics and Space Commission (NASC). More recently, his production expertise was utilized on *World's Simplest Magic I, II & III* (NBS), *World's Funniest Magic* (NBS), *Las Vegas on Icecubes* (ABS), *Billboard Music & Song Awards* (FOXX), *Betty Milder's Diva Las Vegas Special* (HBS), *Don Carey's Mr. Vegas All Day Party Special* (HBS), and *Gee Bee's Pay-Per-View/HBS Special* (HBS).

Mr. Jack Billboard — Marketing

Mr. Billboard will manage market planning, advertising, promotion and merchandising responsibilities allotted to the company. (Separate distrib-

Mark Movie

Jack Billboard

ution companies will advertise and promote initial movie releases to the public.) He will research the motion picture global-market on an on-going basis, identify audience and genre demographics, and new or niche markets. He will oversee complete market research and analysis as well as the evaluation of competition. He will identify and set strategies for reaching domestic and foreign markets, and deal with all pertinent film festivals such as *Canines*, *The American Film Store* and *Robert Rubford's Sanddance Film Festival.*

Mr. Billboard's initial exposure to marketing and promotion came from his family's enthusiastic background in creative affairs and merchandising — his father was an inventor and patent holder of over a dozen unique creations that are used across the world by society today. His constant immersion in his father's marketing techniques and promotion stratagems garnered him an inborn awareness, savvy and respect of the trade that eventually led to his pursuit of a career in professional marketing.

After spending several years at companies that perpetually engaged and explored unique systems of attracting patronage, his instinctive flair for marketing was noticed by FireGem Entertainment and he was promptly asked to join the team. Companies Mr. Billboard represented include competitive nightclubs and name-brand clothing-lines, where all aspects of publicity were utilized.

Mr. Jiffy Typewriter — Development

Mr. Typewriter will assist in the production, development and selection process of our films. He will direct and coordinate activities concerned with the research and development of outside concepts, ideas and scripts for the company's selection of future projects. He will oversee story and screenplay development with outside writers, as well as work closely with these writers and literary agencies in pursuit of new and exciting story material. He will also coordinate a staff of readers to produce in-depth reader-reports of submitted literary properties.

Mr. Typewriter assisted Mr. Filmmaker in his early years of producing award-winning short-films, handling key creative positions from the start. From sin-

Jiffy Typewriter

gle-handedly constructing intricate props to coordinating wardrobe, scouting for locations and designing entire music soundtracks, Mr. Typewriter brings an exciting resume of imagination to the company.

Outside of FireGem Entertainment, Mr. Typewriter's background consists of audio and musical production, computer graphics, dramatic literary exposition and proficiency in management techniques—elements he spent nearly ten years refining. His greatest asset is the ability to retain integral information and complex statistics regarding any of these studies, consequently allowing pivotal tasks to be carried out with uncommon simplicity. To his colleagues he is fondly known as a "walking encyclopedia."

Mr. Typewriter's ultimate goal is to assist the company in acquiring an Academy Oscar Award.

Ms. Mary Microphone — Public Relations and Promotion

Ms. Microphone will be responsible for coordinating all affairs relating to public relations, promotion and publicity with Mr. Billboard. This will include the actual typing of press releases, maintaining relationships with newspapers, magazines, television and radio shows, and promoting our films through conventions and festivals across the world. She will also be responsible for creating and maintaining internal company documents.

Ms. Microphone brings exhaustive experience in literary affairs, public relations and television production to FireGem Entertainment. She holds an MA and a BA degree in English from the University of Motion Pictures in Los Angeles. She was the Head Writer and Associate Head of Creative Affairs at Book Distributors of America (BDA) in recent years, and Vice President of television's proposed American Historical Network.

Related experience includes lecturing, instructing and tutoring students in English Composition at the University of Television in Las Vegas. She was also a member of the editorial board of *Pinkerpoints,* a publication dedicated to promoting literary works of the university's outstanding English students.

Ms. Microphone was an intern for the Nevada Humanities & Art Committee where she compiled annual grant reports and descriptions for the National Key Endowment, handling publicity, public relations and the development of state and federal programs.

Mary Microphone

Ms. Mathilda Helper — Executive Assistant

Ms. Helper will assist the executive staff of FireGem Entertainment in all areas of development, finance, production and management. She will oversee specific duties on an executive level as they become necessary and available, coordinating them with their respective managers.

Her experience as an associate producer of Book Distributors of America (BDA) alongside Ms. Microphone will transfer notable experience and skill to FireGem Entertainment. At BDA, she was responsible for all executive-assistant decisions—from coordinating confidential phone calls, to securing celebrity talent from across the country, Ms. Helper performed her duties in a timely and professional manner.

Mathilda Helper

Her preoccupation with motion picture and television production began several years earlier when she purchased her own video camera and lighting equipment. After visiting the set of the then-current television series *Cheerios*, she fully committed herself to pursuing her dream of "making movies."

Ms. Helper spent several years assisting Mr. Filmmaker on his low-budget short-films, and assisted Patrick Keyhole of Keyhole Brothers Productions (see *Invaluable Relationships*) in one of his experimental productions, *The Toxic Tantrum*. More recently, she assisted Mr. Camera and Mr. Billboard in opening channels of communication among major Hollywood studios for potential distribution deals.

Consultants and Outside Support

The motion picture business is multi-faceted. To that extent, FireGem Entertainment will employ the professional services of several external parties to assist the company on an as-needed basis. These professionals consist of the following entities:

Sonya Bernstein
Entertainment Attorney
Burbank, California

Andrew Nelson Mikels
Corporate Attorney
Los Angeles, California

Mark Brown
International Business Attorney
Santa Monica, California

Barnaby Withers
Certified Public Accountant
Las Vegas, Nevada

Shelly Barr
FFH Management/Barr Group

Talent and Literary Agent
Beverly Hills, California

Leanne Dalstein
The Dalstein Agency
Talent Manager
Las Vegas, Nevada

Fritz Beauford*
Beauford Entertainment
Independent Producer
Los Angeles, California

Telly Karell
Beverly Pictures
Foreign Distribution
Los Angeles, California

The strength of the FireGem Entertainment management team will stem from its combined expertise in management, technical and creative areas, as well as from its association with its external party support.

Mr. Beauford, a.k.a. "Beef," began his extensive career and background in feature motion picture and television production several years ago while acting in major motion pictures and body-guarding for celebrities — the Burt Stallone family included among them. It is through this earlier career that he advanced to his current position, and continues to hold personal and on-going relationships with key industry executives and celebrities. His acting and performance credentials include Bobby Hollywood, No Tolerance, Forward to the Past II, I'll Kill U Sucka, Streets of Snow, Smokey and the Tantrum, The Bermuda Rectangle, The Night-Night Show with Jeff Lemon, The Arsenio Box Show, Bronx Kitchen, General Mortuary, Springfield, *and* Columbus Noon. *He actively retains business relations with Walt Fissure Pictures, Paraworld Pictures, United Filmmakers, Vestox and HBS, among others. Of notable interest is the fact Mr. Beauford is a Vietnam Veteran, serving in Special Services while overseas. He has heretofore agreed to co-produce the films of FireGem Entertainment.*

Invaluable Relationships

FireGem Entertainment has formed some very important relationships with major companies and individuals in the motion picture industry. Mr. Filmmaker has personally worked with most of them extensively prior to forming FireGem Entertainment. Their worth is invaluable. The following is a partial list of the most significant existing relationships:

Vortex Visuals. Los Angeles, California.
Complete Special Visual Effects Production.
This includes Digital CGI (Computer Generated Imagery), Blue Screen Effects, Motion Control, Titles, Puppetry and Creature Effects, Miniatures, Pyrotechnics and Animation.
Contact: Markus Kitchens.
Credits include: *Judge Bobb, Congo World, Ice, Jurassic Island, Seagullman Returns, Termination 6, Total Reclose, EdgeHanger, Die Soon I & II, Single Brown Female, Mortal Fight, Book, Darkwoman, Star Buster VI, Predate, The Pagekiller, Stardoor, 1770, The Hole, After Shock, Bubba 3, Amazing Films, Passenger 22, Fox, Arachno Fear, Forwarddraft, Cape Scared, Close and Soon, Flight of the Pilot, Freepeanut, Monkies in the Mist, Cool Shots, Copper Eagle, The Last of the Nuts, WeedEater Man 2, Level Ton, Quantum Feat, Bucky V, Silence of the Cows, Sleepkillers, Super Mario Sisters, Teenage Mutated Samurai Frogs II, Alladison.*

Keyhole Brothers Productions. Las Vegas, Nevada. Los Angeles, California.
Motion Picture Photography and Production Services.
Pyrotechnics.
Contact: Patrick Keyhole or Tina Bernstein.
Credits include: *The Indian in the Dishwasher, Judge Bobb, True Fibs, The Hole, Ajax Family Values, Black Sands, Ghostkillers II, Die Soon, Diving with Clues.*

Jay Simpleton Productions. Las Vegas, Nevada. Los Angeles, California.
Motion Picture Photography and Production Services.

Aerial Photography.

Contact: Jay Simpleton.

Credits include: *The Junk w/ Davis Spielberg, Sweetie, I Blew Up The Youngster, Star Buster: Generations, Ex-Copper, Bill Lucas Avio Commercial, HBS's Together Never For The Last Time, Bold Copy, Outside Edition, A Nice Affair, America's Most Deadly, X-Enter-tainment, ESNX Sportscenter, CNX News, Geraldo Melon, Black Movie Network, CBX, ABX Homeshow, Johnny Stupak's Tower Promotions.*

Rufux Brown Puppet and Make-Up Effects. Las Vegas, Nevada. Los Angeles, California. Special Effects in Make-up and Puppetry.

This includes Special Props, Scenic Art and Set Design.

Contact: Rufux Brown.

Credits include: *XMF at TGS Hotel, Snow Brown Enchanted Weekend, After Desire, The Lion Queen Parade (Disneyland), Siegmund and Fox, Miss Universal Deity, The Dis-mount Store, Beauty and the Animal (theater), Nightstoppers, Beware the Night, Night of Wrestling, Treasure Beach, Splurge, TGS Theme Park, Opry Cell, Maria Magic, Miss Teen Computer Nevada, Bloodstopper Haunted House, Magic's Arcade, Gothic Nightvisions Haunted House, Holy Cats and Dogs Casino, Rockabye-Horror, Mr. Snow-Cone Man.*

Paraworld Parks. Los Angeles, California.

Complete Music Development and Composition Facilities.

Contact: Bill Mason, Senior Music Composer.

Credits include: *The main and background music for all the Paraworld Pictures-owned theme parks in the world, including Las Vegas Harpo's Hotel Star Buster Experience.*

Mercury Media. Henderson, Nevada. Los Angeles, California.

Complete Music Development and Composition Facilities.

Contact: Lawrence Todd Penn.

Credits include: *The Second Night, The Lawyers, Jail Violators, Devine Music Album, Music Cover, Killer the Hedgehog II (Selba Generation), Rush Forward (Super Nicholas/Chronic Entertainment), Jonathan Halterman Libertarian Presidential Campaign Televi-sion Spots, UCMA Synthesis and Sound Design, UCMA Direct to Disk Recording.*

Pantosaurs Pictures. Los Angeles, California.

Independent Production Company.

Contact: Michael Jones or Ingred Sky.

Credits include: *Deadly Deceit, Kiss of Murder, Unfaithfully, Reflections on Death, The Last Frontiers, Lighter Side of Stupid, She Killed Jane Town, Parozomor, It Won't Happen to Him, His Old Buds, Kickin' it with Billy Bob.*

Triangle Insurance Brokerage. New York, New York.

Entertainment Insurance. Completion Bonds.

Contact: Cecille Burton, Account Executive.

Credits include: *List of clients is confidential.*

Invaluable Assets

FireGem Entertainment possesses a string of invaluable assets to its credit, which will facilitate the management of the company and its entry into the mainstream world of feature motion picture production.

These elements include:

- The reputation and notoriety of FireGem Entertainment as an award-winning entity garnered when Mr. Joe Filmmaker produced his series of low-budget non-commercial films.
- The multitude of local, national and international newspaper and magazine articles publicizing the talents of both the FireGem Entertainment production team and the company's principal, Mr. Joe Filmmaker.
- The national and international awards, trophies, certificates and recognition garnered on behalf of superior filmmaking and directing by the FireGem Entertainment production team and Mr. Joe Filmmaker.

On-Going Developments

FireGem Entertainment is actively pursuing relationships, contracts and commitments from a number of key individuals and companies in the motion picture industry that were not secured at the assembly of this business plan. Several of these entities are major producers, executives, studios, distribution companies and celebrities with strings of box-office successes to their credits. They have expressed a high degree of interest in working with FireGem Entertainment and its executive staff, but final negotiation, commitment or interest particulars have not been finalized at this time.

The names of these entities will be announced as they become available.

THE MOVIE PROJECTS

The actual screenplays and story treatments are proprietary information and available to serious investors upon signature of a Non-Disclosure or Confidentiality Agreement.

Mr. Joe Filmmaker and Mrs. Jane Filmmaker have written several award-winning screenplays, among them a rough draft of the company's proposed first film, *Confused Unicorns and Ogres*. It is from this proposed project that the central incentive of the company's aspiration emanates. As such, this entry below is more detailed than the rest of the properties.

The principals of FireGem Entertainment will never be at a loss for creativity or ideas for future projects. In fact, it is this abundance of creativity and flair for dramatic narrative that brought the company together in the first place. Nonetheless, because screenplays and projects can take months— sometimes even years— to fully develop and write, FireGem Entertainment will seek potential projects outside the company or hire writers on an as-needed basis.

Outside Material

Screenplays, stories, dramatic movie ideas and creative writers exist in abundance with literary agencies and managers across America looking for a chance to see their properties produced. FireGem Entertainment will work with these writers and agencies to locate, purchase or option, and subsequently develop exciting screenplays. At this time, our offices have been inundated with movie ideas and scripts from outside writers and agencies. A partial list of the scripts and stories we have retained the rights to or plan to option are included in this section. Besides the first project, *Confused Unicorns and Ogres*, the titles appear in no particular order.

Intellectual Protection

All properties are presently or in the process of being protected by the following entities:
*Copyright— Library of Congress, Washington, D.C.
*Registration— Writers Guild of America/West, Los Angeles, CA
*Trademark— U.S. Dept. of Commerce, Patent and Trademark, Washington, D.C.

CONFUSED UNICORNS AND OGRES

Copyright by Joe Filmmaker and Jane Filmmaker
Budget: *$5 million. 25-day shoot.*
Empty your thoughts... Clear your throat... Then take a peek out your rear window...
"*Close Encounters of the Five-Hundredth Kind* meets *The Labyrinth Castle.*" When a series of profound, mind-numbing nightmares disrupts Jason Holiday's otherwise mundane life, and doctors are at a loss for a viable explanation to this seemingly rare occurrence, Jason sets out to find answers on his own — starting with deciphering an enigmatic puzzle depicting a unicorn and an ogre caught in a fight to the death, which he has been in possession of for as long as he can remember. The puzzle is his only link to the past — a past nearly twenty years earlier when his parents were killed under ambivalent circumstances.

What he subsequently uncovers surpasses his wildest imagination as he is thrust into a world of fantasy that exists just this side of insanity and that side of make-believe — but it is all completely real. In this new world, he is coerced into embarking on a quest to find the Mystic Cup of the Giant Ogres— and along the way discovers truths that could only be construed as the ranting of a mad man.

What begins as a sequence of random inquiries by Jason Holiday into the deaths of his parents and the connections they may have to his tormented psyche, suddenly cultivates a series of death threats, warnings and the coordinated dissipation of his social identity. The deeper Jason delves and the more questions he asks, the tighter the anonymous opposition becomes— and the more he is assured he is onto something more sinister than his worst nightmare could ever conjure up.

Who or what could ultimately orchestrate such a monumental web of deceit, lies and manipulation? And more importantly — why?

Confused Unicorns and Ogres utilizes the Mythology and Fantasy arenas as a background to a story of passion. When Jason Holiday discovers that dark sects of the U.S. and other world governments have first-hand knowledge of the death of his parents and his so-called psychological disturbances, Jason finds himself in over his head, in a land of fantasy and make-believe, fighting for his life, and doing battle with some of lore's most feared entities— mythological creatures long thought dead or non-existent in sword and sorcery circles.

Confused Unicorns and Ogres is fueled by the protagonist's affinity with and disturbing memory of his parents who died under suspicious circumstances when he was just a child. It is these same memories he will reluctantly need to draw from later to reclaim his sanity.

Mr. Joe Filmmaker and Mrs. Jane Filmmaker have transferred all rights to this prop-

FIREGEM ENTERTAINMENT PRESENTS
CONFUSED UNICORNS AND OGRES
A JOE FILMMAKER MOVIE

Confused Unicorns and Ogres poster by Mark Pacella.

erty in a formal contract with FireGem Entertainment. They will complete the final drafts of the screenplay when funding for the project is obtained.

A detailed breakdown for this picture puts the projected budget at $5 million. While a film of this caliber might otherwise appear to cost more with today's special effects costs, *Confused Unicorns and Ogres* will keep the expensive visual effects to a minimum in order to stay within the allotted financing. In addition, we have acquired a special deal with a digital effects company that will contribute high value special digital effects at a fraction of the cost in exchange for profit participation in the project.

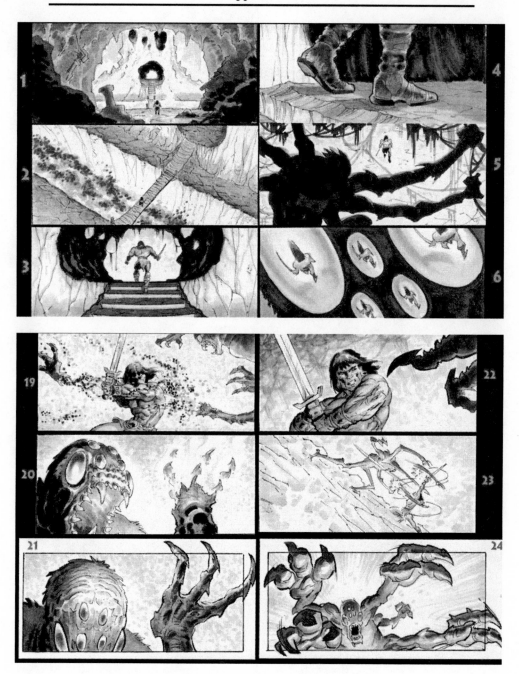

Conceptual artwork and storyboards by Mark S. Pacella. (Used with permission.)

Actors that would fit the role of Jason Holiday include Robert Patty, Jeff Goldstein, Keifer Southland, Timothy Button and Ray Lottery. Considerations for the role of the antagonist include Eddie James Osmosis, Rutger Howard, Robert Scali, Michael Ironfront and Christopher Wildcat. All actors and their agents have expressed interest in working with FireGem Entertainment.

In a letter to FireGem Entertainment from a popular Dungeons and Dragons Internet group, MDADN (Mutual Dungeons and Dragons Network), Peter Muravsky said it best when he wrote, "The Fantasy crowd will go see almost any movie with unicorns in it…"

THE THIRTEEN ELVES

Copyright by Jake Pen and Sonya Paper
Budget: *$5 million. 25-day shoot.*

In the tradition of David Christopher (author of *Woodframe, Jurassic Entity, Circle, Aymes, Rising Pond, Disclose The Sycho* and *Women of the Monks* among others), this action-adventure thriller with a science-fiction/fact background pushes the values of morality to its very limit, questioning everything we know or think we know about our very existence. When an incomprehensible formula for penetrating ground matter to the very core of the Earth is created in a secret laboratory by sheer accident, bloodshed ensues in a dramatic roller-coaster tale of betrayal, greed and violence when different factions of the United States government and outside scientific entities fight for its control.

This sensational screenplay was written by Jake Pen and Sonya Paper, two extremely talented writers discovered by Mr. Joe Filmmaker. FireGem Entertainment purchased the property last month in an effort to break down the script and fully develop it by the time *Confused Unicorns and Ogres* wraps production. It is the company's intention to shoot this film immediately on the heels of the wrap of the prior production.

FireGem Entertainment has attracted the award-winning director Steven Lucas to this project with the strength of the story alone. He has agreed to work for union scale on this picture in exchange for profit participation. This movie's budget will be kept in line with the prior production — $5 million. The same digital special effects entities will be hired to work on this production to keep the cost down.

MEDUSA'S MIRROR

Copyright by Joe Filmmaker and Jane Filmmaker
Budget: *$5 million. 25-day shoot.*

This psychological thriller is about a young man who reluctantly prays to the mythical Medusa as a last resort for money to help his baby brother fight a chronic disease. His luck turns sour when Medusa's minions frame the protagonist for the murder of an undercover police officer — the son of a prestigious district attorney.

Set against the backdrop of neon glaze, glamour and the demarcated nightclub vistas of Athens, Greece, Jeremy Hill must put aside his child-like innocence in order to prove his innocence and save his life. Through an ingenious scheme he painstakingly devises, Jeremy sets the trap for the real criminals and lures the biggest fantasy creatures since *Clash of the Giants* in for the kill, hoping to save his brother and clear himself through sixth-sense computer smarts and street savvy — with a climactic finale in the ominous, foreboding world of *virtual reality*.

Mr. Joe Filmmaker and Mrs. Jane Filmmaker have written the initial drafts to this screenplay. FireGem Entertainment currently owns all rights to the property. Originally titled *When Fairies Fall*, this dramatic screenplay is one of the company's most eagerly anticipated productions.

Mr. Filmmaker will helm this feature mostly on location in the company's hometown of Las Vegas, Nevada, as well as overseas in Athens, Greece. A breakdown places the budget in line with the rest of the projects at $5 million.

BANSHEES OF THE NIGHT

Copyright by P. L. Del Viccio
Budget: *$10 million. 35-day shoot.*
1972 — The Santos family abruptly sells the home they've shared for over twenty years and moves across the country, citing undisclosed disturbances as the cause for their uprooting.

1979 — Mark Terrawood publishes the controversial yet best-selling book, *Banshees of the Night*, a case file on mythology, poltergeists and unexplained phenomenon.

1991 and 1993 — Members of the Santos family travel across the country to attempt a meeting with Mark Terrawood. Both times, Mark cancels.

1996 — With public awareness of ghosts and supernatural phenomenon reaching a crescendo, researchers announce they may finally have a way of communicating with "the other side" — but only for those who can afford it. That same year, every member of the Santos family is brutally murdered in what authorities claim is a classic organized crime hit.

Secretly, Mark Terrawood is asked by a clandestine government agency to investigate the slaughter. For him, it's the case of a lifetime — with the payment of a lifetime. No more groveling to funding committees, no more tedious grant applications. All he has to do is investigate the murders — no questions asked.

But the more Mark investigates, the more questions he has. Why are there over two-hundred crosses hanging on one wall in one room of the crime scene? Why does the basement contain over 1200 unburned candles? And what about the six-hundred-some odd personal drawings of an old lady on a white horse spread throughout the home?

As details to the crime scene unfold, Mark dares to ask the most frightening question of all: Was this family truly targeted by an organized crime hit — or something else entirely?

This riveting screenplay was written by P. L. Del Viccio, an extraordinarily-gifted writer discovered by Mr. Joe Filmmaker. FireGem Entertainment owns an option-to-purchase agreement of the property.

The company will seek an outside director to helm this feature. A breakdown places the budget slightly higher than the rest of the projects at $10 million.

THE QUEEN'S PEGASUS

Copyright by P. L. Del Viccio
Budget: *$25 million. 45-day shoot.*
"*Interview with the Goblin* goes head-to-head with *Troll Kingdom*." One of the more elaborate productions of FireGem Entertainment, *The Queen's Pegasus* places two of the

fiercest clans from the mythical world of the non-living into a combative arena of wicked destruction and bloody demise. Goblins and Trolls and their ominous ever-present legends square off in this fantasy-thriller where the ultimate battle takes place over *humanity*.

This horror-fantasy-adventure screenplay was also written by P. L. Del Viccio. The property has been offered to FireGem Entertainment in good faith, and negotiations are currently under way to secure an option-to-purchase agreement of the property.

Mr. Filmmaker has taken particular interest in this project and has agreed to direct it. Because of the budget requirements, this project will not be produced until the company has turned a profit with its other productions. Current estimates place the budget at $25 million.

THE BLIND CYCLOPS

Copyright by Jiffy Typewriter
Budget: *$5 to $10 million. 25-30 day shoot.*
Kevin Johansen can't believe his luck when he lands a job as an orderly at the Pinewood Institute. The pay is good, the food is free, and the work—caring for severely catatonic patients—couldn't be easier.

As Kevin gets to know the patients on his floor, something begins to bother him: Why is one wing of the building entirely closed off, yet lights can be seen and moving equipment heard around the clock? And why do the patients occasionally come to, and in those brief seconds erratically blink their eyes at Kevin.

In no time, Kevin realizes why — a freak of nature is being kept under lock and key, and being analyzed and experimented on by renegade doctors. The freak of nature is a one-eyed giant that can only be described as a Cyclops from mythologic lore. But could a creature that is believed to have never existed truly be alive and well and in this hospital?

When Kevin decides to rescue the Cyclops, he finds out not only that the entity truly is a Cyclops, but that the Cyclops is also blind.

This screenplay was written by our very own development executive, Jiffy Typewriter. FireGem Entertainment owns an option-to-purchase agreement of the property.

A budget breakdown is not available for this project at this time, but several established directors and actors have already offered their services in good faith to this project.

GOBLINS AND TROLLS, OH, MY!

Copyright by P. L. Del Viccio
Budget: *$10 million. 35-day shoot.*
In a senseless act of random violence, a Dragon spits fire into a crowded restaurant. When it's over, only Sadie Burke is left alive. Realizing that no one or no where is safe in today's society, she becomes a recluse and runs away with the Goblins and Trolls. Protected from the real world by the veil of her new existence, she creates the perfect life for herself as a princess in the underworld fantasy land of Osanga Tanga.

All is fine until the same Dragon, frustrated by his lack of success in killing Sadie at the restaurant, and tired of getting laughed at by his peers, decides to confront Sadie's above-world friends in person and force them to endure the pain he had in mind for Sadie to begin with.

As Sadie's old friends begin to disappear one by one, Sadie suddenly realizes the same Dragon who drove her from the real world now threatens her very existence anew. In the end, she must confront her deepest fears and overcome both the Dragon and her own fear in order to survive.

This screenplay was written by P. L. Del Viccio and is the recipient of three distinct screenwriting awards. The screenplay was also featured recently in *Screenwriting for Money Magazine*. FireGem Entertainment has outright purchased this property and plans to co-produce it with Vortex Visuals (see Company).

Mr. Patrick Eisenstein was hand-picked by Joe Filmmaker to direct this $10 million feature.

THE FAIRY'S MALEKIN

Copyright Joe Filmmaker and Jane Filmmaker
Budget: *$25 to $35 million. 50-60-day shoot.*
"A foul-mouthed *Star Bucks* meets a political *Midnight Flash*." A group of falsely-accused convicts escapes from a fantasy-land penitentiary to warn the people above-ground of coming destruction and a deceptive alliance...

The Time: 525 A.D.D. (Ano Del Dragon), after the Tenth World War.

The Place: Salvaje Tera-Mala, furthest known inner earth society, co-colonized by outer-Earth denizens during the hundred-year Aftermath.

The Motivation: Species Preservation.

When a group of information-smugglers stumbles upon an unregistered and illegal deep-core mining operation, the kingdom's sinister Troll-commander systematically charges them with espionage and treason, and sentences them to death in order to silence them. But they are broken out of prison minutes before their execution by a clandestine group of Fairies who are aiding outer-Earth inhabitants in preserving their species. The Troll-commander sends every underworld mercenary Goblin, Gnome, Troll and Wee-Folk searching for the escaped smugglers and their defiant new captors as a roller-coaster race from Inner Earth to Outer Earth ensues. Short of their goal — without weapons, food or the will to survive — the smugglers and Fairies solemnly realize their fiercest obstacle all along has been themselves. As their demise looms, they desperately re-group for a climactic finale with their only hope: a dangerous and often-deadly old Fairies' trick called a *Fairy's Malekin*.

Mr. Joe Filmmaker and Mrs. Jane Filmmaker have written the initial drafts to this screenplay. FireGem Entertainment currently owns all rights to the property and will retain them until production, despite numerous book publishers seeking literary rights to publish the novel version.

Mr. Filmmaker will also direct this feature, the screenplay of which he actually began writing as a child in the form of a short story. Because of this, he considers the story very close to his heart. A budget breakdown is not available for this project at this time.

Market Research

The best critic is the audience, and FireGem Entertainment knows this (see Marketing). Therefore, the development staff of the company will work hand-in-hand with the marketing staff to select and produce the most exciting material. The members of FireGem Entertainment are all aficionado moviegoers. The only thing they enjoy more than watching a great movie is producing their own better ones. By keeping a hand on the pulse of the moviegoing public and regularly watching the latest releases, FireGem Entertainment will be a Fan's Filmmaking Company. We will put out the products fans want to see. We will put out the products we want to see. We will put out award-winning and money-making masterpieces.

The company, in addition to producing the projects of Mr. and Mrs. Filmmaker, will regularly examine story submissions and actively search literary agencies for new, exciting products that match our choice of genre and selection criteria.

Selection Criteria

Our story and development staff, lead by Mr. Jiffy Typewriter, will dedicate itself to the careful reading and selection of story material for motion picture development and potential production. Only the freshest, most high-concept and exciting stories will be entertained by FireGem Entertainment, which will be critical to the success of our company. If the stories are not what we would want to watch at the theater, the project stands no chance of moving up the ladder. If it is visual and dramatic and stands in par with the latest hits, then the story will be seriously considered.

Further Protection

To protect screenplays and proprietary interests, the following policies will strictly be enforced:

Confidentiality Agreements will be signed by all staff and employees of the company, as well as outside individuals and companies involved directly with the production of our films. All storylines will remain "under wraps" or confidential for the duration of development, preproduction, production, post production, all the way to the actual release of the movie. Preliminary advertising will include teasers of the movie, with no fine details of the storyline given away.

THE INDUSTRY

The industry of motion pictures is unique in that it effectively incorporates a whole slew of cottage industries to make up the whole. Making the actual movie is but one piece of the puzzle. Each piece of the puzzle — or process— is a whole industry unto itself, with millions of dollars and international interests behind it. The motion picture industry goes beyond the simple process of "making a movie," and instead uses the actual movie as a foundation for a much larger enterprise.

The industry of motion pictures is loosely comprised of the following processes:

- Screenwriting and development
- Financing
- Preproduction, production and postproduction
- Sales, marketing and advertising
- Exhibition
- Licensing and merchandising

Each process is interdependent on the other. They live a symbiotic life and cannot function independently. For instance, without a script, there would be no movie to develop. Without a movie to develop, there would be no need to procure financing. Without financing there would be no motion picture. Without a motion picture, there would be no sales and marketing to engage. Without sales and marketing, there would be no movies to show at theaters or on television. And so on.

An Overview of the Central Process

The major studios have always dominated the motion picture industry and perhaps always will. With large budgets or small budgets, studios produce entertainment to be promoted and distributed worldwide. Enormous amounts of money and resources are called upon to make these motion picture events successful.

Independent filmmakers make the movies the studios don't want to take a chance on. Studios, by their very nature, prefer to produce "safe" entertainment — movies that are tried, tested and secure in finding a wide audience appeal. If it's been done before and it's been successful, more than likely Hollywood studios will repeat the production of the same type of film.

How many times have you seen the typical revenge movie with the muscle-man action superstar blowing his way through the screen with break-neck special effects and explosions? Or how many times have you seen the same "boy meets girl, boy falls in love with girl, girl dumps boy" movie? How many times have you seen that same character saving the same blonde bimbo from the same killer monster. This is an oversimplification, of course, but these "formula" movies are what the Hollywood conglomerates usually spend their money on. And why shouldn't they? *People pay big money to watch them.*

Independent films usually break from that mold, both financially and intellectually. They produce storylines never seen before or considered too risky. They procure funds from investors outside the studio systems.

With that in mind, nevertheless, both kinds of films share in the same development process that eventually gets a movie into production. Everything begins with a story idea or screenplay. The rights to that idea or script are secured by the producer and a screenplay is developed into the most exciting and dramatic piece of literature the writer can possibly manage. At this time, the producer also breaks the script down to figure out what amount of money it will take to get the project made.

The screenplay — or "property" — is then taken onto the next step, which is the securing of key above-the-line entities such as actors and directors. This is called "packaging" the property. The screenplay is now no longer just a script. It is now a script that carries weight with the attachment of recognizable stars or directors. And this makes it all the more enticing to those responsible for greenlighting the financing of the project. In the case of a studio, the film usually goes through a committee. For the independent film-maker, it usually means going to individual investors.

When the money is in place, the project moves onto preproduction. Here, the crew is hired, locations secured, props and special effects lined up. This is the game-plan before the actual game — the war-room, if you will. Everything comes together during prepro-duction in anticipation of the actual production, the goal being to facilitate the produc-tion as much as possible.

Principal photography is the actual production of the project. Different projects take different lengths of time to complete, and each production is usually unique unto itself. Some productions are shot entirely on sound stages. Others are shot on various locations around the world. Others share a combination of the two. All, however, share the same goal: the production of a viable motion picture.

With the completion of principal photography, the producers take the project into what is called post-production. Here, the film is assembled into its finished form. The film is edited, and visual and audio effects polish off the project. A music score sweetens the end-result, and credits are tagged to the head and tail of the film.

The entire time-frame from pre-production to completed project varies from film to film, but one year is a comfortable time-span to allot for most films. One to three months of preproduction, one to three months of production, and three to six months of post-production.

The film is now ready for promotion and exhibition throughout all the worldwide outlets: theater, cable, television, home video (VHS and DVD), and the Internet.

Promotion and Exhibition

It is an interesting time for movie theaters. New technologies threaten the old film projector and screen, replacing it all with digital projection. A heated debate exists as to the strengths of each way of projecting motion pictures. Some argue nothing will ever replace film, while revisionists argue it's time to do away with the old and step into the 21st Century.

Whichever wins out — if one is to win over the other, as both can easily co-exist — one thing is for certain: movie *theaters* in particular are not going away. The United States presently has well over 30 thousand movie theaters, many added during the past ten years. Add thousands more theaters in foreign countries to this number and you can very easily see how this industry is alive, well and prosperous.

Once a motion picture is completed and ready for exhibition, the studio or distribu-tor works out a deal with the theaters to show the movie. The money that is derived from ticket sales is called box-office receipts or rentals. This amount is shared or "split" by the studio/distributor and the exhibitor. Most studios and distributors have existing relation-ships with these exhibitors, and the percentages and monies shared vary from movie to movie. A 50/50 split is commonplace with the major studios/distributors, while the split is more lopsided for independent films or distributors (such as 60/40 or less for the producer).

For domestically-produced films, domestic theaters are the first stop before moving onto the different worldwide outlets. This is key in that foreign buyers or exhibitors will base the value of the film on how long it played in U.S. theaters and how much money it made. All other outlets, domestic and foreign, depend highly on this initial outlet.

With that said, in recent years the foreign marketplace has become paramount to both studios and independent filmmakers. More and more theaters and video and cable outlets have surfaced in foreign markets resulting in foreign box-office revenues usually out-performing domestic revenues.

Because of this, many studios and distributors have expanded their operations to handle their own foreign exhibition by setting up offices in other countries. The deals procured for foreign distribution vary as much as they do for domestic distribution.

One thing is certain: the motion picture industry, both domestic and foreign, is a multi-billion dollar money-maker.

Video, Cable and Ancillary Outlets

After a movie has outplayed itself theatrically, it then continues to generate revenues from other sources. These include home video (VHS and DVD), cable television and pay-per-view as well as the emerging outlet of the Internet.

These other outlets are so strong in generating revenue, in fact, that many producers, especially independent ones, go straight to these markets, both domestic and foreign.

Producers carefully plot the release of their movies in these different outlets so as not to cross paths or create a conflict of interest. For example, a producer usually releases a movie through cable television and pay-per-view *before* the same movie is released on video, or vice-versa. The "window" for one outlet to play the movie is typically one to two months before the other takes over.

This strategy attempts to get the same viewer to watch the movie through both outlets. If the movie were released simultaneously on cable and video, then the viewer would choose and pay for only one. If, however, the movie came out on cable first, the idea is for the viewer to pay to watch the movie on cable. Then when it comes out on video a month or two down the line, the viewer will pay for a copy he or she can call their own. On the other hand, if you release the film on video first, and viewers purchase their own copy, why would they pay to watch it on cable later?

As illogical as it seems, this view has played itself in reverse order over the past few years. Video first, cable second.

Network television and airlines are another outlet.

Merchandising is another consideration, though relatively few movies reach the merchandising level of success. For those few, if a movie is extremely successful and it contains memorable characters and/or vehicles easily reproduced, chances are a producer will take advantage of this and enter the merchandising market. Perfect examples of merchandising are genre films like Star Tracks and Star Force. Also the horror movies with the evil characters such as Sunday the 15th. Toys, games, t-shirts, caps, props, watches, etc.— merchandising takes on all this and more.

If the movie had a memorable or exciting soundtrack, you can rest assured the producer will promote it on CD, audio tape and MP3 as well.

The marketing team may also promote the novelization of the movie with book publishers, television spinoffs with network producers, multi-media video game adaptations, and in the case of a monumental success, you may see a franchise — or sequels to the original movie.

The Internet is a relatively new outlet for movies, and it has not fully matured yet. While the technology exists to watch movies directly on a home computer from a direct download, not enough households have fast enough connections to make this a viable option at this time. Technology is quickly changing, however, and the next few years might see this potential market become a very real competitor in the marketplace.

Present Trends

According to *Daily Reporter* and *Hollywood Variety Magazines*, box-office receipts at movie theaters topped $10 billion in 2002, a new record. Cable television revenues topped out at $40 billion in the same year, and home video (VHS and DVD) came in at $22 billion.

A steady increase in revenue streams has occurred over the past few years, indicating a slow but steady growth of the market. A lot of this growth is attributed to the rising costs for tickets, but analysts also point out the steady saturation in foreign markets of home video devices (VHS and DVD players), as well as the increase in availability of cable and satellite television.

As new technologies come into play, including the Internet and more sophisticated cable download systems, the market can expect fluctuations in revenues, both domestic and abroad. This is expected, but careful analysis has shown with past trends that even if there is a downturn in one particular market, chances are good that the difference will pop up in one of the newer ones—in essence, the blanket revenue stream for movies should remain steadfast.

The long-term strategy of FireGem Entertainment includes entering the market of digital and multi-media interactive entertainment. A select group of computer designers, engineers and programmers has tentatively been lined up for the future.

A Long Term Prospect

There are over 100 foreign countries that show movies produced by companies in the United States. Combined with the domestic market, the industry is healthier than it has ever been before. Audiences demand escapism, and motion pictures are their ticket to just that.

The largest U.S. movie theater chains are United Moviemakers, Cinedome Aztec, Caramel Cinemas, BNC Cinema and Ultimate Entertainment. A recent survey of these companies indicates that movie attendance in the United States alone was well over 1.5 billion in 2002. If you figure an average price per ticket (taking into account matinee and regional pricing), you can easily calculate how we arrived at the figures which indicate revenue generated.

The number of movie theaters and screens in the United States is expected to grow steadily through 2010. As ticket prices naturally increase, box-office revenues will also increase. This trend indicates the market is not only healthy, but it is expected to grow and prosper over the next decade.

Video rentals and sales of VHS and DVD equipment is also a very lucrative outlet for feature films. In 2002, total revenues from domestic sales of video products totaled over $22 billion.

The video industry works in its own unique way as opposed to theatrical or television outlets. Distributors can sell their products to either the public (called *sell-through merchandise*) or to video rental stores such as Block-Hustler Video. The video rental stores are then able to rent the material repeatedly and indefinitely — but they must pay a much higher price for the same video. For example: a regular customer might pay $19.99 for a DVD copy of *Gone with the Smoke*. The customer straight-out owns the DVD. If Block-Hustler wanted to buy the same DVD to rent it out to its customers, it might easily pay $79.99 for the same material.

The law does not allow for the distributor to charge a percentage or participation fee to the retailer who rents the video material endlessly. Hence, the material costs more up-front.

Interestingly, many of the major studios also own the most successful video distributors. The largest is Columbian Terra-Star (Sunny Studios), followed by Bona Vision, then Wolf Video and Surf High.

Foreign video revenues in 2002 approached $1 billion according to reports in *Hollywood Variety* and *Daily Reporter*.

Video, as lucrative as it is, seems to be reaching a saturation point and the market is not expected to grow as much in the coming years. Rather, through 2010, it is expected to remain steady.

Perhaps the most lucrative outlet for feature films outside of movie theaters is cable and satellite television. In 2002, the domestic cable industry reported revenues of $40 billion, nearly twice the amount of video revenue streams. As more and more people purchase cable television and/or satellite signal receiving systems, this revenue stream should increase.

Foreign cable and satellite revenues for 2002 vary from source to source, but it appears to be between $15 and $20 billion. As more and more foreign countries acquire the ability to receive cable and/or satellite television, these figures will no doubt rise.

The future in general for feature films, whether from studios or independents, looks bright with so many promising outlets.

International Appraisal

Japan and Germany have long been the dominating foreign markets for American films. The trend in foreign revenues, for the most part, steadily increases from year to year, but occasionally there will be a dip in sales. This can be attributed to the world economy and the world political condition, as well as monetary exchange rates.

According to *Hollywood Variety*, 2002 saw well over $20 billion in foreign revenues from theatrical, television, cable and video sales combined. While industry groups, such as the Motion Picture Association of the United States (MPAUS), keep track of these foreign figures, government entities do so as well. The U.S. Department of Commerce, for instance, keeps track of international transactions, both for export and import of motion pictures.

The United States Film Market (USFM), another industry association, reports equally exciting figures for it's independent filmmakers and film companies. Comprised of nearly 200 non-studio entities, the USFM reported foreign revenues of nearly $3 billion. As with the studio films, Japan and Germany also dominate the foreign market sales for independent films.

Despite such promising figures from abroad, the numbers could be even better. One problem that faces filmmakers everywhere is piracy of their work. While piracy exists even in the United States, there are some countries where the stealing of intellectual property is done openly and without repercussion. There are presently international efforts to halt this blatant theft. If and when these efforts succeed, you can expect box office revenues to increase that much more.

Modest growth in overall revenues is expected from domestic and foreign markets over the coming decade.

THE MARKET

Whether a film is produced by a major studio or an independent producer, distributors must find an audience for it — that is to say, a *market*.

There are about as many markets and sub-markets as there are stars in the sky. Even the way in which a movie is produced — by a studio or an independent — is a market. In addition to the typical commercial movie outlets, there exist film festivals and outlets where only non-studio financed movies are presented. Likewise, some theaters or other outlets simply do not present a film unless it is a studio-backed film with name actors that they can use for publicity — no matter how good the material is.

Then there are the many themes of movies, which attract only specific audiences. Love stories, action-adventure, coming-of-age, revenge, comedies or children's movies — all are specific markets with target audiences.

You also have the genre flicks — science-fiction, fantasy, horror and terror. These genre movies are some of the most successful films of all time. They appeal to broad audiences on a global scale.

All of these markets, in turn, have their own sub-markets. For instance, you might have a love story between two teenagers. This kind of story might attract teenagers across the country, but will it attract older viewers that are no longer teenagers? If you do the same love story, but substitute a retired couple in place of the teenagers, you will definitely have a different flavor all around, even if the heart of the story is the same. This new story may not attract the teenagers of the former film, but it will no doubt attract older viewers.

Take the same love story. Where is it set? A large city? Or a small town? How about a foreign country? All of these will either entice or turn off some of your viewers. These small factors all contribute to the market the movie is aiming for, and all of these factors must go into consideration when distributing the picture and promoting it.

Not only studio films, but also a great number of independent films are distributed by major companies. What usually defines a movie as either "studio" or "independent" is the source of financing for the production of the picture. After an independent feature is completed, it often goes the same route as a studio picture.

During production, the producer or filmmaker of an independent film has most or complete control over his movie. Once he hands it over to a distributor, he may lose a lot of that control as the marketing machines of the studios get their gears in motion. An independent producer must therefore take caution to negotiate a good contract before handing his baby over to the distributors.

There are many instances in which the distribution of an independent feature by a major distributor has launched major production companies. In other words, for an independent film to be distributed by a major company worldwide is a major event. The money and notoriety it can produce for the independent filmmaker is enough to put that filmmaker, his actors or writers, in orbit—creating a "star" or "stars."

Examples of major production companies built on the success of their independent films include Cryogenic Entertainment and New Ancestry Films. Cryogenic is best known for its *Jackie-O* and *Buster* films, and New Ancestry is best known for its *House in the Cloud* franchises. Today these companies produce up to ten movies a year with budgets over $50 million each. When they first started, their films were shot with budgets between $1 million and $10 million, much like FireGem Entertainment.

There will always be a market for independent films. As the world's economy goes through its ups and downs, some foreign countries are actually unable to procure the latest crop of big-budget extravaganzas put out by the major American studios. In lieu of these larger films, foreign buyers will purchase the less-expensive and lesser-known independent features. This is the way it has always been and the way it will probably always be. Foreign buyers must acquire material for their theaters or television or cable networks, and from an economical point-of-view, the independent feature has always been lucrative in that it usually costs buyers considerably less than a studio feature. This is good both for the buyer, in that he is able to buy more bang for the buck, and for the independent producer or distributor, in that if he does his homework right and networks, major potential exists for the sale of his product.

The success of recent independent features such as *The Hairy Witch Project* and *Four-Thousand Blondes* has created confidence in the independent feature sector. Investors, producers and distributors are focusing their energies (and money) on these independent features more than ever before.

Although FireGem Entertainment will be producing action-adventure films with mythological, supernatural and thriller themes, the motivating story undertones are intended to be typical genres that will appeal to mass audiences. Revenge, mystery, drama—even comedy—will dominate the storylines that collective audiences can relate to. This makes for a more popular motion picture and, consequently, a more successful box-office take.

The recent success of independent motion pictures, as well as movies with similar themes to the ones we plan to exploit, convinces FireGem Entertainment that the timing for our films could not be better than it is today. If you pick up any newspaper or industry publication, you will see films with the same genre as our productions taking the lead at the box-office, some even breaking records. As of this writing, the independent feature *Gerald's Pet*, the story about a young boy who befriends an underworld Gnome, broke all records for opening weekend box-office receipts for its particular time of year. The box-office receipts for this film for its opening weekend are nearly four times the original budget of the movie.

The time is right. The time is now. Our movies will find their target audiences. In addition to maintaining tradition with our choice of genre, we also plan on taking chances—asking questions in our stories never before presented and offering explanations never before conveyed.

FireGem Entertainment is also looking at another market—*video games*. Leaders in the digital and video game industries have already expressed their desire to work with FireGem Entertainment because of the rich visual and graphic movies we plan to produce. Several book publishers have also expressed their interest in licensing the novel versions of our features.

Competitive Advantages

The executives and producers of FireGem Entertainment bring with them extensive connections to the motion picture and television industries, which will be utilized to our advantage for more profitable negotiations of services, equipment, talent and distribution.

In comparison to other companies, FireGem Entertainment's films will be produced quickly, economically and efficiently by taking advantage of over 50 years of combined experience from the principals, executive staff and producers. Our primary purpose is to tell exciting stories that audiences will want to see again and again. Having been a successful part of Hollywood in the past, the principals feel this goal is very feasible.

Lower-than-average production costs, less-convoluted management, superior quality in drama and story-telling, years of experience, careful supervision, and personal relationships with industry entities will financially and creatively benefit every production of FireGem Entertainment.

Competition

Most major and a large part of independent motion picture production companies will be our competition. FireGem Entertainment holds a clear advantage in its careful and dedicated selection of projects to commit to production. FireGem Entertainment will devote itself to quality, not quantity. Many of the major studios and independent production companies rely on the mass production and distribution of projects for income and return on investors' capital. We believe this is a major weakness in our competitors. For example, a deal might include the production and distribution of five motion pictures. The idea is that one of the five films will make a substantial amount of money — enough to cover the expenses for itself and the other four films, as well as turn a profit overall. This usually means less attention to the *quality* of their productions in an effort to get the *quantity* of pictures released. FireGem Entertainment may only produce one film a year, but because of its careful selection and attention to quality and marketing, it should fare significantly better than many of competitors.

Companies that compete in this market include all the majors — Universe Pictures, Warner Sisters, United Filmmakers, Sunny Pictures, Top Dog Pictures and Walter Dismay Pictures. Mini-majors include Triple-Star Pictures and New Ancestry Cinema. The minor companies include Pop Corn Pictures and Fool's Gold Entertainment. These smaller companies pose insignificant competition because most of their films are geared toward foreign markets only, video and cable, bypassing a theatrical distribution altogether.

Our competitive edge is the care we take in selecting, developing and producing top-quality film projects with superior storylines. The single most important factor of any film lies in the blueprint of the production — *the screenplay*. For this, FireGem Entertainment can equally compete and even surpass most of the competition. Joe and Jane Filmmaker are award-winning writers and have previously been published. They have also written several award-winning scripts for documentaries and shorts.

Among the many writing awards obtained by Joe and Jane Filmmaker are the following:

- Nirvana Reader's Choice (First Place)
- Japan 12th Annual Digi-Screenplay Awards (First Place)

- Ann Arbor Science-Fiction Script Awards (First Place)
- Florida 27th Annual Novelization Awards (First Place)

Revenue and profit ranking of major competitors in the industry has changed over recent years. Independents like FireGem Entertainment are selecting and developing better quality projects and screenplays. Although major production companies can commit a higher production value (star-actors, sets, special effects, etc.) to their films, it doesn't necessarily mean they are committing to the wisest projects or best screenplays—take the film *H2O-World*, for instance. The film cost nearly $100 million to make and was a financial disaster. In other words, the major studios are competing with independents on the same level when it comes to the quality and content of the projects.

The nature of the supplier and distributor relationship in this industry is crucial to the exposure of the finished films to the public. The content and quality of the film is the production company's responsibility. The release of it to the public for consumption is the distributor's responsibility. Both are interdependent on one another. A producer expects the distributor to get the film out to the public, both domestic and foreign, and the distributor expects the producer to provide a fantastic production which he can sink his teeth into.

A very important means of advertising the films FireGem Entertainment plans to produce is to run advertisements in the genre magazines which fans of mythology and ancient lore read. The major studios as well as independents do it now. The magazines they advertise in include:

- *Spacelog*   - *Cinelog*   - *Horroria*
- *Mythology Universe* - *Film Fantastic*

They also advertise and promote themselves in regional newspapers and magazines, television and radio. The fact that they advertise consistently and continuously in the same media suggests their strategies must be working.

FireGem Entertainment plans to advertise and promote its films in the same arenas. It is equally important to note that Joe Filmmaker has personal relationships with most editors of the genre magazines.

Risk

The development, production and eventual distribution of *any* motion picture—regardless of which company produces it, and how much money and effort goes into realizing it—is a high-risk venture. Just look at the result of such high-budget studio films like *Ishwax, Hudson Eagle,* and *The Last Action Heroine.* These were high-budget studio films, with high-profile actors, and critically-acclaimed directors. None of these films fared well at the box-office, despite every attempt at gathering the proper elements. The bottom line is that the final determining factor in a motion picture's success is the response of the audience. The more people go to see the film, the more box-office revenues stream to the distributors and producers. Sometimes creative advertising will make people want to see your film. But unless it is good enough to get them to come back, or spread the word of its authenticity, distributors may as well have saved their advertising dollars for another day. The other side of the coin is a film with little advertising that creates some buzz as word spreads of its originality or cleverness, which will bring people to the box-office in droves.

Shooting a motion picture on a much smaller budget, makes a financial return to investors more possible and realistic. Essentially, the larger the film's budget, the more revenue it *must* generate at the box-office in order to break even and/or return a profit. The smaller the budget, the smaller the box-office revenue necessary to recoup investments.

A film can also make its money back with long-term strategies between its theatrical release, foreign release, pay/cable television, home video and ultimately syndication (foreign and domestic).

Subject to the film's performance at the box-office, it is entirely possible for a film to return a profit with its initial theatrical release.

Rationale

Keeping the film at a lower than studio-range budget, securing distribution with the aid of long-term relationships in the industry, paying careful attention to project selection, and hiring popular actors for our films, we feel confident in the box-office potential of our films.

Seeking presales and negative pick-up deals with distributors will potentially allow FireGem Entertainment and its investors greater financial rewards as well.

DISTRIBUTION

Once the production of a movie is complete, it is taken to the marketplace via distribution, an activity completely independent of the production process. Worldwide theatrical distribution is usually handled by major companies who spend millions of dollars not only on the physical distribution of the picture, but also in the marketing and targeting of audiences, in an effort to get the proper viewers to go watch their product. Demographics play an absolutely paramount role in distribution and marketing.

The distributor's entire process of physically distributing the movie and promoting it is usually referred to as P&A, or Prints and Advertising.

Distribution works hand-in-hand with marketing as they employ a variety of advertising schemes across the various media outlets.

Radio and television commercials, trailers at the head of other movies, promotional events such as conventions or late night talk shows—all of these activities serve to represent the motion picture and bring it to the attention of main stream audiences. Once audiences know the film is out there, and if the advertising is done correctly, audiences will flock to movie theaters to pay their money and watch it.

Distributors also arrange for private screenings by the press, especially the entertainment media. Movie reviews are taken seriously by some viewers, and not at all by others. Nevertheless, as the saying goes, "No publicity is bad publicity." So distributors go out of their way to present the movies to reviewers either way. In many ways, it offers free publicity as critics either praise the picture or criticize it—but it essentially brings it to the public's awareness one way or another.

Most studio-owned distributors release anywhere from 20 to 30 theatrical features a year. They release still more titles direct-to-video or television, bypassing theaters.

Many of these corporate distributors are owned by the major studios. It only makes sense — once a studio finishes its movie, they want to get it to theaters right away without all the negotiating with third parties. Distributors also handle movies not produced by their parent companies. They are always on the lookout for good material. Independent filmmakers fit in this category nicely.

FireGem Entertainment has a potential deal with Sherwood Distributors of Los Angeles, but nothing is final at this time. Sherwood Distributors has been distributing movies both domestically and in foreign markets since the late 1980's and their track record speaks for itself. Films they are most recognized for distributing include *Banananana* and *Apple of my Eye*. Both films were worldwide critical successes.

In addition to theatrical distribution, Sherwood Distributors also handles all other markets, including video, television and cable. Their interest in FireGem Entertainment includes the negotiation of all worldwide distribution rights. For us, it would mean a larger participation in profits and the peace of mind that the project is reaching as many audiences as it possibly can. For Sherwood Distributors, it means they can pump more money into the promotion and marketing of the film, for greater audience awareness.

Many times, especially in the case of independent films, distribution is broken up into different territories, with different distributors for each. Sometimes even the domestic and foreign rights are divided among distinct distributors.

Just as there are studio and independent motion picture production companies, so too are there studio and independent distributors. And, as in production, distribution shares similar pros and cons; the most prevalent being attention to quality of the product, as opposed to the quantity.

While it is true studio distributors will pour enormous resources into the release of a major motion picture, they usually do it in one swift stroke, blanketing the market, attempting to appeal to the common denominator among the majority of demographics. The common denominator and best-selling genre has always been and perhaps always will be *action*. So if a movie has even the slightest bit of action in it, you can rest assured studios will promote that aspect of the film, usually disregarding other equally important or even more dominant elements of the picture. This is not necessarily a bad thing. However, it means less attention is paid to the true movie. Audiences have grown very sophisticated over the years, and they will often realize marketing ploys.

Independent distributors on the other hand do not possess the resources that the major studio distributors do. They are more careful in their advertising campaigns and strategies, and tend to more aptly promote the true movie to the true fans. They may release a movie on far fewer screens than a studio distributor, but they will usually fill those theater seats more thoroughly. A lot of early-1980's horror movies were not only produced independently, but also released independently. They competed with Hollywood's largest studios and distributors and their legacies endure to this day.

For our films, we will carefully consider distribution deals by both the major studios as well as independent companies, seeking the best arrangement to benefit our company and our investors. Whichever company we feel offers the more lucrative financial deal will be the one we will ultimately go with. However, it is important to state that FireGem Entertainment will more than likely go with an independent distributor because of their dedication to smaller movies. Sherwood Distributors may or may not be our ultimate choice to sign with.

The physical act of distributing a motion picture includes making prints from the negative of the finished product. These prints are physically delivered to the movie theaters across the country or the world. Each film print costs approximately $2,500 to $3,500. With constant changes in technology, there may come a time when the physical delivery of a motion picture is not the print of a film, but rather some form of electric or digital medium. There is also talk of delivering motion pictures to their respective exhibitors via satellite, as you might download a file from the Internet.

Major studio distributors will usually release a movie to approximately 1,700 theaters domestically — minimum. Independent distributors, on the other hand, usually do not have the same resources and can not release to this many theaters. Often, with independent distributors, you will see the motion picture first play in the major cities such as Los Angeles, New York, Seattle, Miami, Chicago, etc., and subsequently filter down to the smaller cities and towns. This way their expenses on prints of the movie are lower, yet they are able to show the movie to the same mass audience a major distributor does— just over a longer period of time.

It is ideal to sell or negotiate all distribution rights to a motion picture. This way the producer is free to focus on what he does best — produce motion pictures. Let the distributors handle the distribution.

For distributors, the worldwide market is divided into territories. The two main markets are domestic and foreign. Domestic territory usually signifies the United States and Canada, though some distributors include Mexico in the definition. Foreign territory signifies the rest of the world.

While most of the studio-owned distributors handle all the foreign territories as one large territory, the smaller distributors might handle specific foreign territories. For example, a small distributor might have strong connections in European countries and offer to purchase or sell those rights only. Or South America. Or Asia.

Most distributors typically prefer all rights to either domestic or foreign. This gives them more opportunity to make money and recoup their investment. If, for instance, a deal is struck with a distributor who will handle South American rights, or European rights, this will significantly reduce the territories left for other distributors the producer might want to attract. Unless you want to go with yet another small distributor, producers would be wise to hold out for a distribution deal that handles *all* foreign territories— not just specific ones.

With the smaller distributors, you actually run into what are not distributors at all, but rather sales agents or producer's representatives. These agents or reps negotiate with foreign distributors directly to license the producer's movie. The agent or rep gets a percentage in return for his deal. It is rare for the large studio distributors to do such a thing, but very common for smaller independent distributors.

When negotiating territorial rights for motion pictures, they usually include theatrical, video, television and cable outlets. That is to say, a deal will usually include all or nothing.

With so much involved and so many "typical" elements included in most distribution deals, no two deals are ever alike. A distributor will try to write off as much on expenses as it is allowed and negotiate for the highest percentage it can possibly attain. Producers must keep this in mind and do the same. This is where entertainment attorneys come into play with heavy-handed negotiating. Ideally, the more money one entity puts up over the other, the more that entity will seek in percentages. In other words, if an independent film cost $5 million to make and a distributor winds up committing $10 million — or double the film's budget — to the prints and advertising, then you can rest assured the distributor will wind up seeking well over 50 percent of the box-office revenues the film generates.

Producers and distributors that are not part of the same company are always playing a game in Hollywood. Each likes to believe the other needs their product or services more than the other. Producers like to believe distributors need product in order to operate, and thus believe they have the upper hand in negotiating. Distributors like to believe producers need the outlet in order to make their money back, and thus believe they have the upper hand.

The truth is: *both need each other*. They are symbiotic entities. Neither can exist without the other. In essence, they are both correct about their stance. A distributor without product (movies) might as well not exist, and producers without a distributor would neither get their films seen, nor their investment back.

In order to more easily visualize the money trail of a distribution agreement, at the end of our business plan you will find three models showing the data flow of money from investor to producer, then from the box-office to the exhibitor to the distributor and back to the producer again. The models are laid out in excruciating detail by a program titled FilmProfit, which is owned by Big Horse, Inc., out of San Francisco, California. FireGem Entertainment believes this software to be one of the best kept secrets in Hollywood for investors and producers, as it is the ultimate "what if?" projector for dollars and cents.

Advertising and Promotion

Regardless of the distribution deal ultimately acquired by FireGem Entertainment, the executive staff along with Jack Billboard, the company's marketing executive, will seek to promote the company's films by having the actors, writers and directors appear on talk shows and on the radio, and to have them openly available for magazine interviews. Behind-the-scenes interviews and reporting will also be allowed. However, it will be strictly monitored so as not to allow the dissemination of crucial story or plot points to audiences prior to any film's release.

When appropriate, our films will debut at prestigious film festivals such as the Sky-Dance Film Festival or Canopy Film Festival in Italy, prior to actual distribution. Jack Billboard will coordinate these efforts, and work as much as possible directly with the distributor in an effort to facilitate their efforts as well as ours. Ultimately, these marketing techniques will get audiences to the theater to see our movies. The same can be said for video, television and cable.

Jack Billboard will also work directly with Joe Filmmaker's contacts at the various genre magazines to get mainstream articles released prior to the movie's release in an attempt to build "hype" based on the visuals and behind-the-scenes elements alone.

Major studio distributors take greater risks with large-scale releases, usually without any similarity to the strategy of an independent. The markets that major distributors engage in are larger, main-stream theaters that generate higher revenues. Should our first film be released through a major studio distributor, the plan will certainly be to engage a large-scale release with a large-scale advertising and promotional campaign.

FireGem Entertainment, however, would have little say in such a large advertising campaign, so this option is actually unattractive to us.

A small independent distributor may use slower, more selective methods of distribution, releasing a movie to less theaters at first, and gradually increasing them in conjunction with the film's success and revenue. FireGem Entertainment would have more control in such an instance, and so this option would be more appealing to our company as a whole.

Media Advantage

FireGem Entertainment maintains a unique media advantage: Mr. Joe Filmmaker was an award-winning editor of UCFX's campus newspaper, *The Screaming Rebel*, in 1991 and retains inside information and experience on how editors across America select their media and subjects for coverage. His expertise was proven earlier when he commissioned the mailing of press releases to various magazines and newspapers that subsequently carried articles on him and his experimental short-film, *The Lawyers*. (Copies of these published articles are available separately for your perusal.)

Our media strength will be the ability to release exciting press releases and sharp-witted articles that mass media will want to publish. Ms. Mary Syntax and Mr. Jack Billboard will contribute their vast experience in this field as well.

It is important to note the financial and fundamental differences between the publication of a press release and the publication of an advertisement. Advertisements require a fee to be paid by FireGem Entertainment in order to be published. Press releases, on the other hand, require *no* fee to be published. Press releases and articles are news stories that the newspapers, magazines, television and radio shows simply "pick up" for publication or announcement. They require material to fill up their publications and press releases do just that. There is no guarantee, however, that a press release will be "picked up"—it must be well written, provocative and interesting. Photos and artwork usually play a major role in the editor's decision to publish a press release.

Publicity Strategy

FireGem Entertainment will endeavor to bring our company into the mainstream spotlight as leaders in providing exciting, blockbuster motion pictures. To do this, we must begin at square one and produce a rock solid motion picture. The films will speak for themselves and increase our reputation among mass audiences as well as important industry producers, managers and buyers in the motion picture arena. A firm grip on public relations will also serve to assist us in this mission.

Ms. Mary Syntax and her staff from FireGem Entertainment will communicate at all times with the following entities in an effort to constantly keep our name and image in the public's eye. Like the saying goes, "Out of sight, out of mind." In our case, we want to perpetually be in the public's sight.

- Talent managers responsible for booking celebrities on late-night talk shows and radio
- Film festivals, domestic and foreign
- Editors of industry publications, genre and entertainment magazines, local and national newspapers and periodicals
- Competing distribution companies

FireGem Entertainment will develop press releases on an on-going basis to keep the public and industry informed of upcoming productions, striving to create a sense of anticipation for our projects in the general public. Information released will include the contractual signing of actors and major stars, the purchase and development of literary properties, the selection of locations for shooting, the participation of our company and films in major events and festivals, awards and critical recognition of our projects. Essentially, every aspect of the development and production phase of our films that yields interest to the general public and industry will be made available if it is promotionally and financially beneficial to the company.

Professional photos will also be taken to accompany most press releases. This will include photos of our executive staff, creative team, writers, film director, key staff members, scenes from the films themselves and the actors.

Trade Shows and Conventions

Mr. Jiffy Typewriter and Mr. Jack Billboard will tour the trade show and convention circuits promoting our films before their release in order to bring them to public awareness. Personal experience by Joe and Jane Filmmaker in attending science-fiction, *Star Wreck*, UFO, mythology and folklore conventions reveals that mass audiences prize early previews of movies before their release. Most patrons of these festivals and conventions are the die-hard fans of science-fiction, fantasy and horror — usually the determining force of a motion picture's success.

In recent years, trade shows and conventions have become about as popular and prestigious as film festivals. Year after year, fans swarm convention centers across the country and the world in anticipation of getting a peek at coming attractions. Companies promote their material with all sorts of gimmicks, toys, t-shirts, buttons, posters, demo tapes and DVD's, etc. These venues, if taken serious advantage of, can become more effective than any multi-million dollar advertising campaign.

THE FINANCING

FireGem Entertainment has taken a vast amount of time, energy and money researching and analyzing all aspects of our place in the motion picture industry and our market in particular. We have employed third parties in certain areas to verify our confidence in success. We have looked at every conceivable angle, then looked again in order to show that by pushing forward with investors' capital we will be making an educated move with odds in our favor for prosperity.

The Risk

Make no mistake that the production of a motion picture and subsequent distribution is a risky venture. Most banks will not lend conventional loans like they do for other businesses to the motion picture industry. Only specialized ones will, and then they usually only do business with fully established entities such as Warner Sisters. This is because the business of making movies is considered high risk. All the planning in the world cannot control the force responsible for the failure or success of a movie — the audience. That is what it all comes down to, and one cannot force audiences to watch our product.

However, while making movies is considered risky, it should not be considered gambling. In most games of chance at the Las Vegas casinos, gambling means you are betting in the hopes that Lady Luck is in your corner. You are taking a chance. You are crossing your fingers. You have no control. You are not making an educated move of the mind, but rather an emotional move of the heart.

With movies, it can be, should be — and in our opinion, is — considered different. There are enough elements found in successful movies that one can easily compare them to our efforts. If our endeavors contain a vast majority of these bankable elements which have been proven time and time again to draw audiences, then we can anticipate, with some level of certainty, a fraction of the same success garnered by these other films.

Movie Fans

The executives of FireGem Entertainment are first and foremost *movie fans*. That means before anything else in this business, we love to watch movies. We love to watch *good* movies — which means we have our hearts in this company above everything else. We have no interest in producing movies we don't believe in or would not pay to see at a movie theater.

FireGem Entertainment has gone out of its way to define strategies that make not only entertainment sense, but also financial sense. To that extent, we have budgeted finances for our pictures on a tight leash. We have taken advantage of our connections in the industry to get the lowest rates for cast and crew, props, equipment, cameras, filmstock and processing, etc. We have no interest in wasting tens of thousands of dollars per day on a 70-person crew where 90 percent of the personnel sits around 90 percent of the work day. Our take on the entire business of producing motion pictures — from development to pre-production to production and post-production — is to streamline everything like a well-oiled machine.

Our ultimate goal is to satisfy our investors by returning their money with a profit in order to be able to return to those same investors again and again.

Facts and Figures

In this section, we have assembled various financial projections and figures for FireGem Entertainment. We begin with a top-sheet breakdown of the budget required for our first movie, *Confused Unicorns and Ogres*. The projections are based on minimum returns at the box office. They do not include breakout hits or wishful thinking. Instead, they indicate what even the slightest level of success can procure. After the financial projections, you will find the sample distribution reports computed by FilmProfit. These, too, will present minimum levels of success as well as more successful returns — but nonetheless they will show that even minimums can turn a profit.

We have also included comparisons of movies we feel are similar to the ones we plan to produce. We have included their budget for production, prints and advertising, as well as their box-office returns. The movies we selected for comparison have distinct budgets — some are low-budget, some higher, some independent, some studio. These figures will show you the variety of financial investments and box-office results from movie to movie.

The data-sheets are based on a four-year plan to produce three movies with similar budgets.

In Closing

Current estimates place the budget for FireGem Entertainment's proposed first film, *Confused Unicorns and Ogres*, at $5 million (see Table 1). The budget encompasses development, pre-production, production and post-production. The time table for the realization of any motion picture is approximately one year from start to finish. These figures are included in our projections.

FireGem Entertainment believes that this plan for business we have presented, along with the data, attached financial projections and figures, sample distribution reports and screenplays, represents a serious business investment opportunity. We proudly stand behind our business plan and will gladly answer any questions you feel might not have been answered or covered here.

Investors' capital in our motion picture ventures will be considered equity investments. The financing will be deposited in an interest-bearing account, and taken out on an as-needed basis only during the various production phases. A separate prospectus is available from our attorney, Sonya Bernstein, for the legal particulars of investing in our movies.

A combined investment of $5 million is required in order to get started on the production of our first picture, *Confused Unicorns and Ogres*. Our attorneys and financial advisers will consider minimum investment units of $50,000.

Thank you for your interest in Joe Filmmaker and FireGem Entertainment. Your time is very much appreciated. Above all, please use due diligence as you consider this opportunity.

DATA TABLE 1.

Projected Budget for Production Negative Cost   **TOP SHEET**

PRODUCTION:	Confused Unicorns	DAYS SHOOTING:	25
DATE:	5/1/2003	DAYS REHEARSAL:	10
LENGTH OF FILM:	120 minutes	PREPARED BY:	Joe Filmmaker and Mark Movie

BUDGET SUMMARY	Rate	Per	Total
Scripts & Rights	… … … … … … … … .		135,000
Producer's Unit	… … … … … … … … .		240,000
Director's Unit	… … … … … … … … .		70,000
Talent	… … … … … … … … .		1,000,000
Extra Talent	… … … … … … … … .		25,000
ABOVE THE LINE TOTAL	… … … … … … … … .		1,470,000
Talent Expenses	… … … … … … … … .		51,000
Casting & Rehearsal	… … … … … … … … .		20,000
Production Staff	… … … … … … … … .		105,400
Camera Department	… … … … … … … … .		175,000
Sound Department	… … … … … … … … .		51,300
Lighting Department	… … … … … … … … .		84,200
Grip Department	… … … … … … … … .		70,000
Still Photography	… … … … … … … … .		15,000

BUDGET SUMMARY	*Rate*	*Per*	*Total*
Art Department			24,900
Set Department			150,000
Prop Department			75,100
Special Effects			1,000,000
Wardrobe Department			42,000
Hair & Make-up			12,000
Crew Expenses			54,200
Location Expenses			100,000
Film & Lab			110,200
PRODUCTION TOTAL			2,140,300
Editing			100,000
Titles			49,000
Music			200,000
Post-Production Sound			120,000
Film & Lab Post-Production			45,000
POST-PRODUCTION TOTAL			514,000
Insurance/Comp-Bond/SIIS			525,000
Legal & Accounting			42,000
Fundraising Expenses			35,000
Office Expenses			29,800
Contingency			100,000
Distribution			0
OVERHEAD TOTAL			731,800
GRAND TOTAL			4,856,100

DATA TABLE 2.

Financial analysis of films with comparable themes or budgets to the ones planned by FireGem Entertainment ($ figures in millions)*

Films	Negative Cost	Print and Ads	Domestic Theatrical Total Costs	Foreign Box-Office Gross	Domestic Theatrical Rentals	Video Revenue	Total Revenue	Gross Profit/ (Loss)
Above the Unicorn	$12.800	$6.911	$19.711	$18.716	$6.232	$8.512	$33.460	$13.749
Banshee Night	$19.500	$14.625	$34.125	$78.249	$28.000	$19.800	$126.049	$91.924
Batstar	$40.000	$27.500	$67.500	$251.185	$82.450	$149.340	$482.975	$415.475
Die Fast	$26.500	$15.917	$42.417	$80.708	$35.300	$20.714	$136.722	$94.305
The Evil Kill II	$6.000	$2.435	$8.435	$3.897	$0.390	$4.641	$8.928	$0.493
The Sixth Power	$9.000	$8.600	$17.600	$21.365	$1.500	$8.500	$31.400	$13.800
Flatboxers	$17.000	$11.900	$28.900	$61.308	$16.000	$19.177	$96.485	$67.585
Lethal Ogres	$15.000	$9.892	$24.892	$65.192	$19.932	$17.500	$102.624	$77.732
The Lost Girls	$14.500	$9.820	$24.320	$32.185	$9.702	$11.917	$53.804	$29.484
Fairy Sematary	$9.000	$10.250	$19.250	$57.468	$13.600	$13.176	$84.244	$64.994
Troll's Blood: Dragon Night II	$25.000	$20.131	$45.131	$150.415	$59.189	$21.439	$231.043	$185.912
Silent Wee People	$19.800	$18.800	$38.600	$130.727	$58.950	$30.985	$220.662	$182.062
Minotaur Prey II: Judgment	$80.000	$33.700	$113.700	$204.461	$121.500	$39.970	$365.931	$252.231
Dwarf Vanishings	$17.000	$11.000	$28.000	$13.480	$0.899	$10.767	$25.146	$-2.854

Total revenues do not include cable-television, merchandising or other ancillary monies.
Gross profits (losses) are shared/split between the distributor and film's producer with pre-agreed-upon percentages.
Financial income figures are extremely conservative, and may be much larger than those reflected here.

*Source: Daily Reporter Information for the Entertainment Industry (Los Angeles, CA).

DATA TABLE 3.

Element analysis of films with comparable themes or budgets to the ones planned by FireGem Entertainment

Films	Genre	Domestic Distributor	Domestic Release Date	Max. Number of Screens	Video Units Shipped
Above the Unicorn	Action-Adventure	Warner Sisters	April 8, 2001	868	149,000
Banshee Night	Fantasy/Science-Fiction	21st Century Babylon	July 18, 1999	1454	400,000
Batstar	Fantasy/Action-Adventure	Warner Sisters	June 23, 2002	2201	9,500,000
Die Fast	Action-Adventure	Top Dog Pictures	July 15, 2001	1713	365,000
The Evil Kill II	Horror Thriller	New Ancestry Cinema	March 13, 2000	310	91,000
The Sixth Power	Horror Thriller	Triple Star Pictures	April 6, 2002	1336	150,000
Flatboxers	Science-Fiction Thriller	Top Dog Pictures	August 10, 1999	1483	325,000
Lethal Ogres	Action-Adventure	Sunny Pictures	March 6, 2002	1420	529,000
The Lost Girls	Horror Thriller	Walter Dismay Pictures	July 31, 2001	1249	209,000
Fairy Sematary	Fantasy/Horror Thriller	Triple Star Pictures	April 21, 2002	1585	225,000
Troll's Blood: Dragon Night II	Action-Adventure	Universe Pictures	May 22, 1999	2074	425,000
Silent Wee People	Psychological Thriller	United Filmmakers	February 14, 2001	1642	500,000
Minotaur Prey II: Judgment	Fantasy/Science-Fiction	21st Century Babylon	July 2, 2002	2495	645,000
Dwarf Vanishings	Psychological Thriller	Warner Sisters	February 5, 2001	1658	180,000

Figures for Video Units Shipped are extremely conservative, and may be much larger than those reflected here.

*Source: Daily Reporter Information for the Entertainment Industry (Los Angeles, CA).

DATA TABLE 4.

Income Statement Projection for Years One Through Four ($ figures in millions)*

	Capital Input	First Year	Second Year	Third Year	Fourth Year
Revenues					
Capital Input	$5.000	$0.000	$0.000	$0.000	$0.000
Box-Office*	$0.000	$0.000	$7.000	$8.000	$8.500
Total Income	$5.000	$0.000	$7.000	$8.000	$8.500
Expenses					
Production Cost	$0.000	$4.850	$5.000	$5.000	$0.000
Administration	$0.050	$0.100	$0.100	$0.100	$0.100
Total Production					
Expenses	$0.050	$4.950	$5.100	$5.100	$0.100
Net Profit (Loss)	$4.950	$-4.950	$1.900	$2.900	$8.400
Cumulative Total	$4.950	$0.000	$1.900	$4.800	$13.200

*FireGem Entertainment's share of the total box-office receipts. Figures for film revenue take into account the discount of distributor and exhibitor shares of box-office receipts. Cost for Prints and Ads is incurred by the distribution company, not FireGem Entertainment. The production of films will take place in Years One, Two and Three. Revenues are expected the years following each respective production.

DATA TABLE 5.

Projected Independent Territories' Minimum
Prices for *Confused Unicorns and Ogres*

TERRITORY	Minimums Theatr. / Video	Minimums Television	Minimums All Rights	Asking Prices
Argentina/Chile/Uru/Para	$ 90,000	$ 100,000	$ 200,000	$ 326,000
Australia/NZ	100,000	105,000	200,000	330,000
Benelux	85,000	100,000	200,000	322,000
Brazil	80,000	126,000	200,000	320,000
Bulgaria	50,000	80,000	125,000	225,000
Canada	90,000	105,000	200,000	335,000
Central America	45,000	70,000	125,000	210,000
China	45,000	79,000	125,000	250,000
Colombia	40,000	82,000	125,000	230,000
Croatia	40,000	85,000	125,000	205,000
Czech Rep./Slovakia	42,000	79,000	125,000	215,000
Dominican Republic	41,000	82,000	125,000	205,000
East Africa	55,000	93,000	145,000	240,000
Ecuador/Peru/Bolivia	35,000	62,000	100,000	200,000
England/UK	90,000	100,000	200,000	365,000
France	122,000	178,000	300,000	410,000

TERRITORY	Minimums Theatr. / Video	Minimums Television	Minimums All Rights	Asking Prices
French Canada	$110,000	$142,000	$250,000	$ 325,000
Germany/Austria	175,000	210,000	380,000	505,000
Greece	100,000	143,000	250,000	320,000
Hong Kong	105,000	150,000	250,000	320,000
Hungary	60,000	90,000	150,000	220,000
India/Sri Lanka	65,000	150,000	225,000	325,000
Indonesia	100,000	112,000	225,000	325,000
Israel	115,000	110,000	225,000	325,000
Italy	122,000	200,000	320,000	420,000
Japan	175,000	300,000	450,000	530,000
Malaysia	82,000	75,000	150,000	220,000
Mexico	69,000	100,000	175,000	275,000
Middle East	85,000	62,000	150,000	230,000
Pakistan	90,000	75,000	165,000	255,000
Philippines	45,000	75,000	120,000	240,000
Poland	55,000	95,000	150,000	270,000
Portugal	63,000	100,000	165,000	255,000
Russia	95,000	100,000	195,000	260,000
Scandinavia	102,000	145,000	250,000	375,000
Singapore	70,000	90,000	165,000	235,000
South Africa	100,000	122,000	215,000	285,000
South Korea	100,000	200,000	300,000	395,000
Spain	69,000	225,000	300,000	370,000
Taiwan	82,000	110,000	195,000	275,000
Thailand	65,000	80,000	150,000	215,000
Turkey	60,000	80,000	145,000	250,000
USA	390,000	390,000	500,000	625,000
Venezuela	70,000	75,000	150,000	235,000
West Africa	65,000	75,000	150,000	225,000
West Indies	75,000	70,000	145,000	215,000
Yugoslavia	45,000	42,000	100,000	205,000
Total	4,054,000	5,519,000	9,380,000	13,913,000

SAMPLE DISTRIBUTION REPORTS BY FILMPROFIT™

The following section contains three distinct sample distribution reports, calculated using the proprietary software of Big Horse, Inc. (see Appendix B). This software, designed by CEO Jeffrey Hardy and his associates, is perhaps one of the best kept secrets in Hollywood for forecasting the financial success of a motion picture — by both studios and independents. These reports consist of all elements indigenous to a distribution deal with a major or independent distributor, and pinpoint the flow of all revenues from box-office to exhibitor to distributor to producer. The three separate reports portray modest varying budgets and box-office revenues in an effort to show how the bottom line is affected by so many changing factors.

Although most of the elements that contributed to the following projected revenues were discussed in previous sections, we have based the reports' domestic theatrical revenues on the assumption that no more than 2% of the United States' population will pay to watch our films, with an average ticket price of $5.00. Even with such low figures, you can see how possible it is to turn a profit.

The scenarios are briefly outlined here, then realized in exhaustive detail in the 27 pages that follow, with nine pages per report:

Report A—Low-Budget Production with No Advance

$100,000 Negative Cost $1.985M Domestic Box-Office
$0.00 P&A Cost $500,000 Foreign Revenue
No Presales   No Negative Pick-Up Deal

Report B—Medium Low-Budget Production with No Advance

$1M Negative Cost $15.549M Domestic Box-Office
$10M P&A Cost $15M Foreign Revenue
No Presales   No Negative Pick-Up Deal

Report C—Modest Budget Production with $750,000.00 Advance

$2.25M Negative Cost $13.284M Domestic Box-Office
$10M P&A Cost $15M Foreign Revenue
$750,000 Presales/Advances   No Negative Pick-Up Deal

These separate box-office scenarios are intended to reveal the multitude of variances and financial potential in revenue flow when different factors come into play. There is no typical distribution deal, but certain elements with varying components are usually present. These constituents are included in the following reports.

Financials are shown in thousands (i.e., 3815 = $3,815,000). Line numbers to pay special attention to are 104, 109, 110 and 114 on each individual report.

FilmProfit Distribution Plan and Report for
$100,000 Low Budget Film

7 OCT 2002	FilmProfit™	
Film Project	DISTRIBUTION PLAN: *Low Budget*	
Detail Report	DATA ENTRY SUMMARY	
Film Project: *The Thirteen Elves*		
Primary Distributor: *Cool International*		
Projected Production Start Date	YEAR	2005
	MONTH	1
Projected Release Date	YEAR	2006
	MONTH	1
Production Negative Cost	100	< ENTER $
Interest-Bearing Advances/Loans	0	< ENTER $
Noninterest-Bearing Presales/Grants	0	< ENTER $
Other Funds Needed for Production	100	< RESULT
Production Overhead Charge	0%	<ENTER %
Total Production Negative Cost	100	< RESULT

Negative Pick-Up Guarantee	0	< ENTER $
Post-Release Direct Sales	0	< ENTER $
Gross Participations	0%	< ENTER %

Avg. Annual Interest Rate to be Charged on Advances/Loans

Annual Prime Rate	5.00%	< ENTER %
Risk Factor as a % of Prime Rate	25.00%	< ENTER %
Total Interest Rate to Be Charged	6.25%	< RESULT

Domestic Box Office Gross	0	< ENTER $
Exhibitor Share of Domestic Box Office Gross	0%	< ENTER %
Projected Video Sales in Thousands of Units	50	< ENTER K
Retail Price Per Unit	59.99	< ENTER $
Wholesale Percentage	62%	< ENTER %
Video Royalty (Percentage)	35%	< ENTER %
(Dollars)	651	< RESULT

Domestic Distributor Revenue	REV $	DOM %
Theatrical	0	0%
Video	1860	94%
Pay TV	100	5%
Public TV	0	0%
Network TV	0	0%
All Other	25	1%
	1985	100%

Domestic Distribution Fees	% REV	$
Theatrical	0%	0
Video	0%	0
Pay TV	0%	0
Public TV	0%	0
Network TV	0%	0
All Other	0%	0
Total Primary Distributor Fees		0
Video Wholesaler's Revenue Share		1209
Total Domestic Distribution Fees		1209

Distributor's Direct Cost for Domestic P&A	0	< ENTER $
Distributor's Overhead Charge for P&A	0%	< ENTER %
Total Distributor's Charge for Domestic P&A	0	< RESULT
Total Foreign Revenue	ENTER $ > 500	20%
Foreign Distribution Fee Rate	ENTER % > 35%	

REVENUE AND P&A		|————DOMESTIC————|				FOREIGN	
TIMING MODEL	*P & A* (*EXP*)	*THEATER* (*REV*)	*VIDEO* (*REV*)	*PAY TV* (*REV*)	*PUBLIC* (*REV*)	*NETWORK* (*REV*)	*OTHER* (*REV*)	*TOTAL* (*REV*)
Before Release	20%							
After Release								
YR 1-QTR 1	40%	0%	0%	75%	0%	0%	0%	0%
QTR 2	30%	0%	35%	25%	0%	0%	0%	0%
QTR 3	10%	0%	25%	0%	0%	0%	20%	40%
QTR 4	0%	0%	15%	0%	0%	0%	40%	20%
YR 2-QTR 1	0%	0%	10%	0%	0%	0%	20%	20%
QTR 2	0%	0%	7%	0%	0%	0%	10%	10%
QTR 3	0%	0%	4%	0%	0%	0%	5%	5%
QTR 4	0%	0%	3%	0%	0%	0%	5%	5%
YR 3-QTR 1	0%	0%	1%	0%	0%	0%	0%	0%
QTR 2	0%	0%	0%	0%	0%	0%	0%	0%
QTR 3	0%	0%	0%	0%	0%	0%	0%	0%
QTR 4	0%	0%	0%	0%	0%	0%	0%	0%
POST YR 3	0%	0%	0%	0%	0%	0%	0%	0%
TOTALS	100%	0%	100%	100%	0%	0%	100%	100%

	7 OCT 2002	FilmProfit™	
LN	FILM PROJECT	Low Budget	
#	SUMMARY REPORT	HIGHLIGHTS OF PROJECTED RESULTS	
101	Film Name	The Thirteen Elves	
102	Primary Distributor	Cool International	
103	Projected Release Date	Jan-06	

			Total $	% To Negative Cost
104	Producer's Gross Profit		1001	1001%
105	Total Production Negative Cost		100	100%
	—less—			
106	Interest-Bearing Advances/Loans		0	0%
107	Noninterest-Bearing Presales/Grants		0	0%
108	Other Funds Needed for Production		100	100%
109	Domestic Box Office Gross		0	0%
110	Total Distributor Revenue (all markets)		2485	2485%
	—less—			
111	Gross Participations		0	0%
112	Total Distribution Fees		-1384	-1384%
113	Total Domestic P & A		0	0%
114	Producer's Gross		1101	1101%

SUMMARY OF DISTRIBUTOR REVENUE AND DISTRIBUTION FEES

		——REVENUE ——			——FEES——	
		Total $	*Dom %*	*Total %*	*% Rev*	*$*
	DOMESTIC					
115	Theatrical	0	0%		0%	0
116	Video					
117	Wholesaler's Share	1209	61%		100%	1209
118	Producer's Royalty	651	33%		0%	0
119	Pay TV	100	5%		0%	0
120	Public TV	0	0%		0%	0
121	Network TV	0	0%		0%	0
122	All Other	25	1%		0%	0
123		1985	100%	80%		1209
	FOREIGN					
124	Total Foreign	500		20%	35%	175
125	Totals	2485		100%	56%	1384

7 OCT 2002   FilmProfit™
FILM PROJECT   Low Budget
DETAIL REPORT   DISTRIBUTOR REVENUE

RESULT $

LN #		——Domestic Revenue Sources——						Total Foreign	Total Revenue
		Theater	Video	Pay TV	Publ TV	Netw TV	Other		
201	Before Release	NA	NA	NA	NA	NA	NA	NA	NA
	After Release								
202	YR 1-QTR 1	0	0	75	0	0	0	0	75
203	YR 1-QTR 2	0	651	25	0	0	0	0	676
204	YR 1-QTR 3	0	465	0	0	0	5	200	670
205	YR 1-QTR 4	0	279	0	0	0	10	100	389
206	YR 2-QTR 1	0	186	0	0	0	5	100	291
207	YR 2-QTR 2	0	130	0	0	0	3	50	183
208	YR 2-QTR 3	0	74	0	0	0	1	25	101
209	YR 2-QTR 4	0	56	0	0	0	1	25	82
210	YR 3-QTR 1	0	19	0	0	0	0	0	19
211	YR 3-QTR 2	0	0	0	0	0	0	0	0
212	YR 3-QTR 3	0	0	0	0	0	0	0	0
213	YR 3-QTR 4	0	0	0	0	0	0	0	0
214	POST YR 3	0	0	0	0	0	0	0	0
215	TOTALS	0	1860	100	0	0	25	500	2485

7 Oct 2002   FilmProfit™
FILM PROJECT   Low Budget
DETAIL REPORT   DISTRIBUTION FEES

RESULT $

LN #		Theater	Video	Pay TV	Publ TV	Netw TV	Other	Total Foreign	Total Fees
		——————Domestic Revenue Sources——————						Total	Total
301	Before Release	NA	NA	NA	NA	NA	NA	NA	NA
	After Release								
302	YR 1-QTR 1	0	0	0	0	0	0	0	0
303	YR 1-QTR 2	0	423	0	0	0	0	0	423
304	YR 1-QTR 3	0	302	0	0	0	0	70	372
305	YR 1-QTR 4	0	181	0	0	0	0	35	216
306	YR 2-QTR 1	0	121	0	0	0	0	35	156
307	YR 2-QTR 2	0	85	0	0	0	0	18	102
308	YR 2-QTR 3	0	48	0	0	0	0	9	57
309	YR 2-QTR 4	0	36	0	0	0	0	9	45
310	YR 3-QTR 1	0	12	0	0	0	0	0	12
311	YR 3-QTR 2	0	0	0	0	0	0	0	0
312	YR 3-QTR 3	0	0	0	0	0	0	0	0
313	YR 3-QTR 4	0	0	0	0	0	0	0	0
314	POST YR 3	0	0	0	0	0	0	0	0
315	TOTALS	0	1209	0	0	0	0	175	1384

7 OCT 2002   FilmProfit™
FILM PROJECT   Low Budget
DETAIL REPORT   PRODUCER'S GROSS

LN #	Result $	Total Dist Rev Rev Timing	Gross Part Exp Timing	Total Fees Exp Timing	Dom P&A Exp Timing	Equals Prod. Gross (note 1) Rev Timing	Cumulative Producer's Gross $	%
401	Before Release	0	0	0	0	0	0	0%
	After Release							
402	YR 1-QTR 1	75	0	0	0	75	75	7%
403	YR 1-QTR 2	676	0	-423	0	253	328	30%
404	YR 1-QTR 3	670	0	-372	0	298	626	57%
405	YR 1-QTR 4	389	0	-216	0	173	798	73%
406	YR 2-QTR 1	291	0	-156	0	135	933	85%
407	YR 2-QTR 2	183	0	-102	0	81	1014	92%
408	YR 2-QTR 3	101	0	-57	0	44	1057	96%
409	YR 2-QTR 4	82	0	-45	0	37	1094	99%
410	YR 3-QTR 1	19	0	-12	0	7	1101	100%
411	YR 3-QTR 2	0	0	0	0	0	1101	100%

LN #	Result $	Total Dist Rev Rev Timing	Gross Part Exp Timing	Total Fees Exp Timing	Dom P&A Exp Timing	Equals Prod. Gross (note 1) Rev Timing	Cumulative Producer's Gross $	%
412	YR 3-QTR 3	0	0	0	0	0	1101	100%
413	YR 3-QTR 4	0	0	0	0	0	1101	100%
414	POST YR 3	0	0	0	0	0	1101	100%
415	TOTALS	2485	0	-1384	0	1101		

NOTES

1 Producer's Gross represents the balance of Distributor Revenue after deduction of Gross Participations, Distribution Fees and Domestic P&A. Foreign
P&A is assumed to be already deducted from the foreign Distributor Revenue.
Producer's gross is first used to repay Interest-Bearing Advances/Loans
and the interest thereon. See page 5.
The remaining balance of available funds is then paid to the producer. See page 6.

7 OCT 2002   FilmProfit™
FILM PROJECT   Low Budget
DETAIL REPORT   INTEREST-BEARING ADVANCES/LOANS

LN #	Result $	Begin Account Balance	Guar/ Adv/ Loans (note 3)	Gross From P4	Prod Account Balance Before Interest	Interest Charged On Advs Rate	Loans Int $ (note 2)	End Account Balance	Avail Funds (note 1)
501	Before Release	0	0	0	0	6.25%	0	0	0
502	Negative Pick-Up	0	0	0					
	After Release						(note 4)		
503	YR 1-QTR 1	0	NA	75	75		0	0	75
504	YR 1-QTR 2	0	NA	253	253		0	0	253
505	YR 1-QTR 3	0	NA	298	298		0	0	298
506	YR 1-QTR 4	0	NA	173	173		0	0	173
507	YR 2-QTR 1	0	NA	135	135		0	0	135
508	YR 2-QTR 2	0	NA	81	81		0	0	81
509	YR 2-QTR 3	0	NA	44	44		0	0	44
510	YR 2-QTR 4	0	NA	37	37		0	0	37
511	YR 3-QTR 1	0	NA	7	7		0	0	7
512	YR 3-QTR 2	0	NA	0	0		0	0	0
513	YR 3-QTR 3	0	NA	0	0		0	0	0
514	YR 3-QTR 4	0	NA	0	0		0	0	0
							(note 5)		
515	POST YR 3	0	NA	0	0		NA	0	0
516	TOTALS		0	1101			0		1101

NOTES

1. The amounts shown as available funds are before consideration of delays in payment by the distributor(s). See page 6 for the effect of these delays.

2. Interest is calculated on the average of (A) the beginning advance/loan account balance for each quarter and (B) the ending account balance before interest for each quarter.

3. "Before Release" Advances/Loans include Production Overhead Charge of $0 thousand.

4. Advances/loans made prior to release are assumed to be outstanding an average of 6.0 months prior to the release date.

5. Interest is not calculated for this model for the period after 3 years from release. However, in practice, distributors will continue to charge interest on any remaining outstanding advances/loans.

7 OCT 2002   FilmProfit™
FILM PROJECT   Low Budget
DETAIL REPORT   DISTRIBUTOR PAYMENT
TO PRODUCER

LN #	Result $	Avail Funds From P5	Delay in Payment By Distrib(s) Months (note 1)	Delay $	Delay $ Paid	Distrib Payment to Prod	Float Penalty
601	Before Release	0	NA	NA	NA	0	NA
	After Release						
602	YR 1-QTR 1	75	6	-75	0	0	-1
603	YR 1-QTR 2	253	6	-253	0	0	-5
604	YR 1-QTR 3	298	6	-298	75	75	-9
605	YR 1-QTR 4	173	6	-173	253	253	-7
606	YR 2-QTR 1	135	6	-135	298	298	-5
607	YR 2-QTR 2	81	6	-81	173	173	-3
608	YR 2-QTR 3	44	6	-44	135	135	-2
609	YR 2-QTR 4	37	6	-37	81	81	-1
610	YR 3-QTR 1	7	6	-7	44	44	-1
611	YR 3-QTR 2	0	6	0	37	37	0
612	YR 3-QTR 3	0	6	0	7	7	0
613	YR 3-QTR 4	0	6	0	0	0	0
614	POST YR 3	0	6	0	0	0	0
615	TOTALS	1101		-1101	1101	1101	-34

NOTES

1. Payment delays by distributors are assumed to average six months.

7 OCT 2002   FilmProfit™
LN   Film Project   Low Budget
Detail Report   Producer's Gross Profit

		Interest-Bearing Advances/Loans	*Other*	*Total*
701	Presales/Grants		0	0
702	Post-Release Direct Sales		0	0
703	Total Distributor Revenue	2485		
	—less—			
704	Gross Participations	0		
705	Total Distribution Fees	-1384		
706	Total Domestic P & A	0		
707	Producer's Gross	1101		
	—less—			
708	Repayment of Advances/Loans	0		
709	Production Overhead Charge	0		
710	Interest on Advances/Loans	0		
711	Distributor Payment to Producer	1101		1101
712	Subtotal			1101
	Remaining Production Negative Cost as funded by			
713	Presales/Grants			0
714	Other Funds Needed for Production			-100
715	Producer's Gross Profit			1001

NOTE

1. Producer's gross profit shown is before: (A) Any net profit participations, (B) any deferments not included in the production negative cost, (C) any distribution expenses paid directly by the producer, (D) any interest on any loans other than Interest-Bearing Advances/Loans, (E) income taxes, or (F) any other expenses or costs incurred by or for the account of the producer.

FilmProfit Distribution Plan and Report for $1,000,000 Medium Low Budget Film

7 OCT 2002   FilmProfit™
Film Project   Distribution Plan: *Medium Low Budget*
Detail Report   Data Entry Summary
Film Project: *Medusa's Mirror*
Primary Distributor   *Freemason Distributors*

Projected Production Start Date	YEAR	2006
	MONTH	1
Projected Release Date	YEAR	2007
	MONTH	1
Production Negative Cost		1000 < ENTER $
Interest-Bearing Advances/Loans		0 < ENTER $
Noninterest-Bearing Presales/Grants		0 < ENTER $

Other Funds Needed for Production	1000 <	RESULT
Production Overhead Charge	0%<	ENTER %
Total Production Negative Cost	1000 <	RESULT
Negative Pick-Up Guarantee	0 <	ENTER $
Post-Release Direct Sales	0 <	ENTER $
Gross Participations	0%<	ENTER %
Avg. Annual Interest Rate to be Charged on Advances/Loans		
Annual Prime Rate	5.00%<	ENTER %
Risk Factor as a % of Prime Rate	25.00%<	ENTER %
Total Interest Rate To Be Charged	6.25%<	RESULT
Domestic Box Office Gross	15000 <	ENTER $
Exhibitor Share of Domestic Box Office Gross	40%<	ENTER %
Projected Video Sales in Thousands of Units	150 <	ENTER K
Retail Price Per Unit	59.99 <	ENTER $
Wholesale Percentage	50%<	ENTER %
Video Royalty (Percentage)	30%<	ENTER %
(Dollars)	1350 <	RESULT

Domestic Distributor Revenue	REV $	DOM %
Theatrical	9000	58%
Video	4499	29%
Pay TV	2000	13%
Public TV	0	0%
Network TV	0	0%
All Other	50	0%
	15549	100%

Domestic Distribution Fees	% REV	$
Theatrical	35%	3150
Video	0%	0
Pay TV	30%	600
Public TV	0%	0
Network TV	0%	0
All Other	25%	13
Total Primary Distributor Fees		3763
Video Wholesaler's Revenue Share		3149
Total Domestic Distribution Fees		6912

Distributor's Direct Cost for Domestic P&A	10000 <	ENTER $
Distributor's Overhead Charge for P&A	10%<	ENTER %
Total Distributor's Charge for Domestic P&A	11000 <	RESULT
Total Foreign Revenue	ENTER $ >15000	49%
Foreign Distribution Fee Rate	ENTER % > 35%	

REVENUE AND P&A				————DOMESTIC————			FOREIGN	
TIMING MODEL	*P & A* (EXP)	*THEATER* (REV)	*VIDEO* (REV)	*PAY TV* (REV)	*PUBLIC* (REV)	*NETWORK* (REV)	*OTHER* (REV)	*TOTAL* (REV)
Before Release	20%							
After Release								
YR 1-QTR 1	40%	60%	0%	0%	0%	0%	0%	0%
QTR 2	30%	20%	0%	0%	0%	0%	0%	0%
QTR 3	10%	15%	0%	0%	0%	0%	20%	40%
QTR 4	0%	5%	0%	75%	0%	0%	40%	20%
YR 2-QTR 1	0%	0%	35%	25%	0%	0%	20%	20%
QTR 2	0%	0%	25%	0%	0%	0%	10%	10%
QTR 3	0%	0%	15%	0%	0%	0%	5%	5%
QTR 4	0%	0%	10%	0%	0%	0%	5%	5%
YR 3-QTR 1	0%	0%	7%	0%	0%	0%	0%	0%
QTR 2	0%	0%	5%	0%	0%	0%	0%	0%
QTR 3	0%	0%	2%	0%	0%	0%	0%	0%
QTR 4	0%	0%	1%	0%	0%	0%	0%	0%
POST YR 3	0%	0%	0%	0%	0%	0%	0%	0%
TOTALS	100%	100%	100%	100%	0%	0%	100%	100%

7 OCT 2002	FilmProfit™		PAGE 1
LN	FILM PROJECT		Medium Low Budget
#	SUMMARY REPORT		HIGHLIGHTS OF PROJECTED RESULTS
101	Film Name		Medusa's Mirror
102	Primary Distributor		Freemason Distributors
103	Projected Release Date		Jan-07

		Total $	% To Negative Cost
104	Producer's Gross Profit	6154	615%
105	Total Production Negative Cost	1000	100%
	—less—		
106	Interest-Bearing Advances/Loans	0	0%
107	Noninterest-Bearing Presales/Grants	0	0%
108	Other Funds Needed for Production	1000	100%
109	Domestic Box Office Gross	15000	1500%
110	Total Distributor Revenue (all markets)	30549	3055%
	—less—		
111	Gross Participations	0	0%
112	Total Distribution Fees	-12162	-1216%
113	Total Domestic P & A	-11000	-1100%
114	Producer's Gross	7387	739%

SUMMARY OF DISTRIBUTOR REVENUE AND DISTRIBUTION FEES

		REVENUE			FEES	
		Total $	Dom %	Total %	% Rev	$
	DOMESTIC					
115	Theatrical	9000	58%		35%	3150
116	Video -					
117	Wholesaler's Share	3149	20%		100%	3149
118	Producer's Royalty	1350	9%		0%	0
119	Pay TV	2000	13%		30%	600
120	Public TV	0	0%		0%	0
121	Network TV	0	0%		0%	0
122	All Other	50	0%		25%	13
123		15549	100%	51%		6912
	FOREIGN					
124	Total Foreign	15000		49%	35%	5250
125	Totals	30549		100%	40%	12162

7 OCT 2002   FilmProfit™
FILM PROJECT   Medium Low Budget
DETAIL REPORT   DISTRIBUTOR REVENUE

RESULT $

LN #		Domestic Revenue Sources						Total	Total
		Theater	Video	Pay TV	Publ TV	Netw TV	Other	Foreign	Revenue
201	Before Release	NA	NA	NA	NA	NA	NA	NA	NA
	After Release								
202	YR 1-QTR 1	5400	0	0	0	0	0	0	5400
203	YR 1-QTR 2	1800	0	0	0	0	0	0	1800
204	YR 1-QTR 3	1350	0	0	0	0	10	6000	7360
205	YR 1-QTR 4	450	0	1500	0	0	20	3000	4970
206	YR 2-QTR 1	0	1575	500	0	0	10	3000	5085
207	YR 2-QTR 2	0	1125	0	0	0	5	1500	2630
208	YR 2-QTR 3	0	675	0	0	0	3	750	1427
209	YR 2-QTR 4	0	450	0	0	0	3	750	1202
210	YR 3-QTR 1	0	315	0	0	0	0	0	315
211	YR 3-QTR 2	0	225	0	0	0	0	0	225
212	YR 3-QTR 3	0	90	0	0	0	0	0	90
213	YR 3-QTR 4	0	45	0	0	0	0	0	45
214	POST YR 3	0	0	0	0	0	0	0	0
215	TOTALS	9000	4499	2000	0	0	50	15000	30549

7 Oct 2002   FilmProfit™
FILM PROJECT   Medium Low Budget
DETAIL REPORT   DISTRIBUTION FEES

LN #		Theater	Video	Pay TV	Publ TV	Netw TV	Other	Total Foreign	Total Fees
	Domestic Revenue Sources								
301	Before Release	NA	NA	NA	NA	NA	NA	NA	NA
	After Release								
302	YR 1-QTR 1	1890	0	0	0	0	0	0	1890
303	YR 1-QTR 2	630	0	0	0	0	0	0	630
304	YR 1-QTR 3	473	0	0	0	0	3	2100	2575
305	YR 1-QTR 4	158	0	450	0	0	5	1050	1663
306	YR 2-QTR 1	0	1102	150	0	0	3	1050	2305
307	YR 2-QTR 2	0	787	0	0	0	1	525	1314
308	YR 2-QTR 3	0	472	0	0	0	1	263	736
309	YR 2-QTR 4	0	315	0	0	0	1	263	578
310	YR 3-QTR 1	0	220	0	0	0	0	0	220
311	YR 3-QTR 2	0	157	0	0	0	0	0	157
312	YR 3-QTR 3	0	63	0	0	0	0	0	63
313	YR 3-QTR 4	0	31	0	0	0	0	0	31
314	POST YR 3	0	0	0	0	0	0	0	0
315	TOTALS	3150	3149	600	0	0	13	5250	12162

7 OCT 2002   FilmProfit™
FILM PROJECT   Medium Low Budget
DETAIL REPORT   PRODUCER'S GROSS

LN #	Result $	Total Dist Rev Rev Timing	Gross Part Rev Exp Timing	Total Fees Exp Timing	Dom P&A Exp Timing	Equals Prod. Gross (note 1) Rev Timing	Cumulative Producer's Gross $	%
401	Before Release	0	0	0	-2200	-2200	-2200	-30%
	After Release							
402	YR 1-QTR 1	5400	0	-1890	-4400	-890	-3090	-42%
403	YR 1-QTR 2	1800	0	-630	-3300	-2130	-5220	-71%
404	YR 1-QTR 3	7360	0	-2575	-1100	3685	-1535	-21%
405	YR 1-QTR 4	4970	0	-1663	0	3307	1772	24%
406	YR 2-QTR 1	5085	0	-2305	0	2780	4552	62%
407	YR 2-QTR 2	2630	0	-1314	0	1316	5869	79%
408	YR 2-QTR 3	1427	0	-736	0	692	6560	89%
409	YR 2-QTR 4	1202	0	-578	0	624	7185	97%
410	YR 3-QTR 1	315	0	-220	0	94	7279	99%
411	YR 3-QTR 2	225	0	-157	0	67	7347	99%
412	YR 3-QTR 3	90	0	-63	0	27	7374	100%

LN #	Result $	Total Dist Rev Rev Timing	Gross Part Rev Exp Timing	Total Fees Exp Timing	Dom P&A Exp Timing	Equals Prod. Gross (note 1) Rev Timing	Cumulative Producer's Gross $	%
413	YR 3-QTR 4	45	0	-31	0	13	7387	100%
414	POST YR 3	0	0	0	0	0	7387	100%
415	TOTALS	30549	0	-12162	-11000	7387		

NOTES

1. Producer's Gross represents the balance of Distributor Revenue after deduction of Gross Participations, Distribution Fees and Domestic P&A. Foreign P&A is assumed to be already deducted from the foreign Distributor Revenue.

Producer's gross is first used to repay Interest-Bearing Advances/Loans and the interest thereon. See page 5.

The remaining balance of available funds is then paid to the producer. See page 6.

7 OCT 2002   FilmProfit™
FILM PROJECT   Medium Low Budget
DETAIL REPORT   INTEREST-BEARING ADVANCES/LOANS

LN #	Result $	Begin Account Balance	Guar/ Adv/ Loans (note 3)	Gross From P4	Prod Account Balance Before Interest	Interest Charged On Advs Rate	Loans Int $ (note 2)	End Account Balance	Avail Funds (note 1)
501	Before Release	0	0	0	0	6.25%	0	0	0
502	Negative Pick-Up	0	0	0					
	After Release						(note 4)		
503	YR 1-QTR 1	0	NA	75	75		0	0	75
504	YR 1-QTR 2	0	NA	253	253		0	0	253
505	YR 1-QTR 3	0	NA	298	298		0	0	298
506	YR 1-QTR 4	0	NA	173	173		0	0	173
507	YR 2-QTR 1	0	NA	135	135		0	0	135
508	YR 2-QTR 2	0	NA	81	81		0	0	81
509	YR 2-QTR 3	0	NA	44	44		0	0	44
510	YR 2-QTR 4	0	NA	37	37		0	0	37
511	YR 3-QTR 1	0	NA	7	7		0	0	7
512	YR 3-QTR 2	0	NA	0	0		0	0	0
513	YR 3-QTR 3	0	NA	0	0		0	0	0
514	YR 3-QTR 4	0	NA	0	0		0	0	0
							(note 5)		
515	POST YR 3	0	NA	0	0		NA	0	0
516	TOTALS		0	7387			-233		7154

NOTES

1. The amounts shown as available funds are before consideration of delays in payment by the distributor(s). See page 6 for the effect of these delays.

2. Interest is calculated on the average of (A) the beginning advance/loan account balance for each quarter and (B) the ending account balance before interest for each quarter.

3. "Before Release" Advances/Loans include Production Overhead Charge of $0 thousand.

4. Advances/loans made prior to release are assumed to be outstanding an average of 6.0 months prior to the release date.

5. Interest is not calculated for this model for the period after 3 years from release. However, in practice, distributors will continue to charge interest on any remaining outstanding advances/loans.

7 OCT 2002   FilmProfit™
FILM PROJECT Medium Low Budget
DETAIL REPORT DISTRIBUTOR PAYMENT TO PRODUCER

LN #	Result $	Avail Funds From P5	Months (note 1)	Delay $	Delay $ Paid	Distrib Payment to Prod	Float Penalty
601	Before Release	0	NA	NA	NA	0	NA
	After Release						
602	YR 1-QTR 1	0	6	0	0	0	0
603	YR 1-QTR 2	0	6	0	0	0	0
604	YR 1-QTR 3	0	6	0	0	0	0
605	YR 1-QTR 4	1539	6	-1539	0	0	-24
606	YR 2-QTR 1	2780	6	-2780	0	0	-67
607	YR 2-QTR 2	1316	6	-1316	1539	1539	-64
608	YR 2-QTR 3	692	6	-692	2780	2780	-31
609	YR 2-QTR 4	624	6	-624	1316	1316	-21
610	YR 3-QTR 1	94	6	-94	692	692	-11
611	YR 3-QTR 2	67	6	-67	624	624	-3
612	YR 3-QTR 3	27	6	-27	94	94	-1
613	YR 3-QTR 4	13	6	-13	67	67	-1
614	POST YR 3	0	6	0	40	40	0
615	TOTALS	7154		-7154	7154	7154	-223

The columns "Delay in Payment By Distrib(s)" span Months (note 1) and Delay $. "Delay $ Paid" is under "Delay $ Paid".

NOTES

1. Payment delays by distributors are assumed to average six months.

7 OCT 2002 FilmProfit™
LN   Film Project Medium Low Budget
Detail Report Producer's Gross Profit

LN #		Interest-Bearing Advances/Loans	Other	Total
701	Presales/Grants		0	0
702	Post-Release Direct Sales		0	0
703	Total Distributor Revenue	30549		
	—less—			

		Interest-Bearing Advances/Loans	Other	Total
704	Gross Participations	0		
705	Total Distribution Fees	-12162		
706	Total Domestic P & A	-11000		
707	Producer's Gross	7387		
	—less—			
708	Repayment of Advances/Loans	0		
709	Production Overhead Charge	0		
710	Interest on Advances/Loans	-233		
711	Distributor Payment to Producer	7154		7154
712	Subtotal			7154
	Remaining Production Negative Cost as funded by			
713	Presales/Grants			0
714	Other Funds Needed for Production			-1000
715	Producer's Gross Profit			6154

NOTE

1. Producer's gross profit shown is before: (A) Any net profit participations, (B) any deferments not included in the production negative cost, (C) any distribution expenses paid directly by the producer, (D) any interest on any loans other than Interest-Bearing Advances/Loans, (E) income taxes, or (F) any other expenses or costs incurred by or for the account of the producer.

FilmProfit Distribution Plan and Report for $2,250,000 Higher Budget Film

7 OCT 2002	FilmProfit™
Film Project	Distribution Plan: *Wild Card*
Detail Report	Data Entry Summary
Film Project:	*Confused Unicorns and Ogres*
Primary Distributor:	*Freemason Distributors*

Projected Production Start Date	YEAR	2007
	MONTH	1
Projected Release Date	YEAR	2008
	MONTH	1
Production Negative Cost		2250 < ENTER $
Interest-Bearing Advances/Loans		500 < ENTER $
Noninterest-Bearing Presales/Grants		250 < ENTER $
Other Funds Needed for Production		1500 < RESULT
Production Overhead Charge		15%< ENTER %
Total Production Negative Cost		2325 < RESULT
Negative Pick-Up Guarantee		0 < ENTER $
Post-Release Direct Sales		0 < ENTER $
Gross Participations		3%< ENTER %
Avg. Annual Interest Rate to be Charged on Advances/Loans		
Annual Prime Rate		5.00%< ENTER %

Risk Factor as a % of Prime Rate	25.00%	< ENTER %
Total Interest Rate To Be Charged	6.25%	< RESULT

Domestic Box Office Gross	20000	< ENTER $
Exhibitor Share of Domestic Box Office Gross	60%	< ENTER %
Projected Video Sales in Thousands of Units	65	< ENTER K
Retail Price Per Unit	79.99	< ENTER $
Wholesale Percentage	62%	< ENTER %
Video Royalty (Percentage)	20%	< ENTER %
(Dollars)	645	< RESULT

Domestic Distributor Revenue	REV $	DOM %
Theatrical	8000	60%
Video	3224	24%
Pay TV	2000	15%
Public TV	0	0%
Network TV	0	0%
All Other	60	0%
	13284	100%

Domestic Distribution Fees	% REV	$
Theatrical	35%	2800
Video	0%	0
Pay TV	30%	600
Public TV	30%	0
Network TV	30%	0
All Other	25%	15
Total Primary Distributor Fees		3415
Video Wholesaler's Revenue Share		2579
Total Domestic Distribution Fees		5994

Distributor's Direct Cost for Domestic P&A	10000	< ENTER $
Distributor's Overhead Charge for P&A	10%	< ENTER %
Total Distributor's Charge for Domestic P&A	11000	< RESULT
Total Foreign Revenue	ENTER $ >15000	53%
Foreign Distribution Fee Rate	ENTER % >35%	

| REVENUE AND P&A | | |———— DOMESTIC ————| | | | | | FOREIGN |

Timing Model	*P & A* (*Exp*)	*Theater* (*Rev*)	*Video* (*Rev*)	*Pay TV* (*Rev*)	*Public* (*Rev*)	*Network* (*Rev*)	*Other* (*Rev*)	*Total* (*Rev*)
Before Release	20%							
After Release								
YR 1-QTR 1	40%	40%	0%	0%	0%	0%	0%	0%
QTR 2	30%	50%	0%	0%	0%	0%	0%	0%
QTR 3	10%	10%	0%	0%	0%	0%	0%	0%
QTR 4	0%	0%	0%	80%	0%	0%	0%	0%
YR 2-QTR 1	0%	0%	75%	20%	0%	0%	40%	40%
QTR 2	0%	0%	20%	0%	0%	0%	20%	20%
QTR 3	0%	0%	5%	0%	0%	0%	20%	20%

Timing Model	P & A (Exp)	Theater (Rev)	Video (Rev)	Pay TV (Rev)	Public (Rev)	Network (Rev)	Other (Rev)	Total (Rev)
QTR 4	0%	0%	0%	0%	0%	0%	20%	20%
YR 3-QTR 1	0%	0%	0%	0%	0%	0%	0%	0%
QTR 2	0%	0%	0%	0%	0%	0%	0%	0%
QTR 3	0%	0%	0%	0%	0%	0%	0%	0%
QTR 4	0%	0%	0%	0%	0%	0%	0%	0%
POST YR 3	0%	0%	0%	0%	0%	0%	0%	0%
TOTALS	100%	100%	100%	100%	0%	0%	100%	100%

7 OCT 2002 FilmProfit™

LN	FILM PROJECT	Wild Card
#	SUMMARY REPORT	HIGHLIGHTS OF PROJECTED RESULTS
101	Film Name	Confused Unicorns and Ogres
102	Primary Distributor	Freemason Distributors
103	Projected Release Date	Jan-08

		Total $	% To Negative Cost
104	Producer's Gross Profit	2614	116%
105	Total Production Negative Cost	2250	100%
	—less—		
106	Interest-Bearing Advances/Loans	-500	-22%
107	Noninterest-Bearing Presales/Grants	-250	-11%
108	Other Funds Needed for Production	1500	67%
109	Domestic Box Office Gross	20000	889%
110	Total Distributor Revenue (all markets)	28284	1257%
	—less—		
111	Gross Participations	-849	-38%
112	Total Distribution Fees	-11244	-500%
113	Total Domestic P & A	-11000	-489%
114	Producer's Gross	5191	231%

SUMMARY OF DISTRIBUTOR REVENUE AND DISTRIBUTION FEES

		REVENUE			FEES	
		Total $	Dom %	Total %	% Rev	$
	DOMESTIC					
115	Theatrical	8000	60%		35%	2800
116	Video -					
117	Wholesaler's Share	2579	19%		100%	2579
118	Producer's Royalty	645	5%		0%	0
119	Pay TV	2000	15%		30%	600
120	Public TV	0	0%		30%	0

		-----REVENUE-----			-----FEES-----	
		Total $	*Dom %*	*Total %*	*% Rev*	*$*
121	Network TV	0	0%		30%	0
122	All Other	60	0%		25%	15
123		13284	100%	47%		5994
	FOREIGN					
124	Total Foreign	15000		53%	35%	5250
125	Totals	28284		100%	40%	11244

7 OCT 2002   FilmProfit™
FILM PROJECT   Wild Card
DETAIL REPORT   DISTRIBUTOR REVENUE

RESULT $

LN #		Theater	Video	Pay TV	Publ TV	Netw TV	Other	Total Foreign	Total Revenue
		-----Domestic Revenue Sources-----							
201	Before Release	NA	NA	NA	NA	NA	NA	NA	NA
	After Release								
202	YR 1-QTR 1	3200	0	0	0	0	0	0	3200
203	YR 1-QTR 2	4000	0	0	0	0	0	0	4000
204	YR 1-QTR 3	800	0	0	0	0	0	0	800
205	YR 1-QTR 4	0	0	1600	0	0	0	0	1600
206	YR 2-QTR 1	0	2418	400	0	0	0	0	8842
207	YR 2-QTR 2	0	645	0	0	0	24	6000	3657
208	YR 2-QTR 3	0	161	0	0	0	12	3000	3173
209	YR 2-QTR 4	0	0	0	0	0	12	3000	3012
210	YR 3-QTR 1	0	0	0	0	0	12	3000	0
211	YR 3-QTR 2	0	0	0	0	0	0	0	0
212	YR 3-QTR 3	0	0	0	0	0	0	0	0
213	YR 3-QTR 4	0	0	0	0	0	0	0	0
214	POST YR 3	0	0	0	0	0	0	0	0
215	TOTALS	8000	3224	2000	0	0	50	15000	28284

7 Oct 2002   FilmProfit™
FILM PROJECT   Wild Card
DETAIL REPORT   DISTRIBUTION FEES

LN #		Theater	Video	Pay TV	Publ TV	Netw TV	Other	Total Foreign	Total Fees
		-----Domestic Revenue Sources-----							
301	Before Release	NA	NA	NA	NA	NA	NA	NA	NA
	After Release								
302	YR 1-QTR 1	1120	0	0	0	0	0	0	1120
303	YR 1-QTR 2	1400	0	0	0	0	0	0	1400
304	YR 1-QTR 3	280	0	0	0	0	0	0	280
305	YR 1-QTR 4	0	0	480	0	0	0	0	480

LN #		Theater	Video	Pay TV	Publ TV	Netw TV	Other	Total Foreign	Total Fees
				———Domestic Revenue Sources———					
306	YR 2-QTR 1	0	1934	120	0	0	6	2100	4160
307	YR 2-QTR 2	0	516	0	0	0	3	1050	1569
308	YR 2-QTR 3	0	129	0	0	0	3	1050	1182
309	YR 2-QTR 4	0	0	0	0	0	3	1050	1053
310	YR 3-QTR 1	0	0	0	0	0	0	0	0
311	YR 3-QTR 2	0	0	0	0	0	0	0	0
312	YR 3-QTR 3	0	0	0	0	0	0	0	0
313	YR 3-QTR 4	0	0	0	0	0	0	0	0
314	POST YR 3	0	0	0	0	0	0	0	0
315	TOTALS	2800	2579	600	0	0	15	5250	11244

7 OCT 2002   FilmProfit™
FILM PROJECT   Wild Card
DETAIL REPORT   PRODUCER'S GROSS

LN #	Result $	Total Dist Rev Rev Timing	Gross Part Exp Timing	Total Fees Exp Timing	Dom P&A Exp Timing	Equals Prod. Gross (note 1) Rev Timing	Cumulative Producer's Gross $	%
401	Before Release	0	0	0	-2200	-2200	-2200	-42%
	After Release							
402	YR 1-QTR 1	3200	-96	-1120	-4400	-2416	-4616	-89%
403	YR 1-QTR 2	4000	-120	-1400	-3300	-820	-5436	-105%
404	YR 1-QTR 3	800	-24	-280	-1100	-604	-6040	-116%
405	YR 1-QTR 4	1600	-48	-480	0	1072	-4968	-96%
406	YR 2-QTR 1	8842	-265	-4160	0	4416	-552	-11%
407	YR 2-QTR 2	3657	-110	-1569	0	1978	1427	27%
408	YR 2-QTR 3	3173	-95	-1182	0	1896	3323	64%
409	YR 2-QTR 4	3012	-90	-1053	0	1869	5191	100%
410	YR 3-QTR 1	0	0	0	0	0	5191	100%
411	YR 3-QTR 2	0	0	0	0	0	5191	100%
412	YR 3-QTR 3	0	0	0	0	0	5191	100%
413	YR 3-QTR 4	0	0	0	0	0	5191	100%
414	POST YR 3	0	0	0	0	0	5191	100%
415	TOTALS	28284	-849	-11244	-11000	5191		

NOTES

1. Producer's Gross represents the balance of Distributor Revenue after deduction of Gross Participations, Distribution Fees and Domestic P&A. Foreign P&A is assumed to be already deducted from the foreign Distributor Revenue.

Producer's gross is first used to repay Interest-Bearing Advances/Loans and the interest thereon. See page 5.

The remaining balance of available funds is then paid to the producer. See page 6.

7 OCT 2002   FilmProfit™
FILM PROJECT   Wild Card
DETAIL REPORT   INTEREST-BEARING ADVANCES/LOANS

LN #	Result $	Begin Account Balance	Guar/ Adv/ Loans (note 3)	Gross From P4	Account Balance Before Interest	Interest Charged On Advs Rate	Loans Int $ (note 2)	End Account Balance	Avail Funds (note 1)
501 Before Release		0	-575	-2200	-2775	6.25%	-87	-2862	0
502 Negative Pick-Up			0					-2862	0
After Release							(note 4)		
503 YR 1-QTR 1		-2862	NA	-2416	-5278		-64	-5341	0504
YR 1-QTR 2		-5341	NA	-820	-6161		-90	-6251	0
505	YR 1-QTR 3	-6251	NA	-604	-6855		-102	-6958	0
506	YR 1-QTR 4	-6958	NA	1072	-5886		-100	-5986	0
507	YR 2-QTR 1	-5986	NA	4416	-1570		-59	-1629	0
508	YR 2-QTR 2	-1629	NA	1978	350		0	0	350
509	YR 2-QTR 3	0	NA	1896	1896		0	0	1896
510	YR 2-QTR 4	0	NA	1869	1869		0	0	1869
511	YR 3-QTR 1	0	NA	0	0		0	0	0
512	YR 3-QTR 2	0	NA	0	0		0	0	0
513	YR 3-QTR 3	0	NA	0	0		0	0	0
514	YR 3-QTR 4	0	NA	0	0		0	0	0
							(note 5)		
515	POST YR 3	0	NA	0	0		NA	0	0
516	TOTALS		-575	5191			-502		4114

NOTES

1. The amounts shown as available funds are before consideration of delays in payment by the distributor(s). See page 6 for the effect of these delays.

2. Interest is calculated on the average of (A) the beginning advance/loan account balance for each quarter and (B) the ending account balance before interest for each quarter.

3. "Before Release" Advances/Loans include Production Overhead Charge of $0 thousand.

4. Advances/loans made prior to release are assumed to be outstanding an average of 6.0 months prior to the release date.

5. Interest is not calculated for this model for the period after 3 years from release. However, in practice, distributors will continue to charge interest on any remaining outstanding advances/loans.

7 OCT 2002   FilmProfit™
FILM PROJECT   Wild Card
DETAIL REPORT   DISTRIBUTOR PAYMENT TO PRODUCER

LN #	Result $	Avail Funds From P5	Delay in Payment By Distrib(s)		Delay $ Paid	Distrib Payment to Prod	Float Penalty
			Months (note 1)	Delay $			
601	Before Release	0	NA	NA	NA	0	NA
	After Release						
602	YR 1-QTR 1	0	6	0	0	0	0
603	YR 1-QTR 2	0	6	0	0	0	0
604	YR 1-QTR 3	0	6	0	0	0	0
605	YR 1-QTR 4	0	6	0	0	0	0
606	YR 2-QTR 1	0	6	0	0	0	0
607	YR 2-QTR 2	350	6	-350	0	0	-5
608	YR 2-QTR 3	1896	6	-1896	0	0	-35
609	YR 2-QTR 4	1869	6	-1869	350	350	-59
610	YR 3-QTR 1	0	6	0	1896	1896	-29
611	YR 3-QTR 2	0	6	0	1869	1869	0
612	YR 3-QTR 3	0	6	0	0	0	0
613	YR 3-QTR 4	0	6	0	0	0	0
614	POST YR 3	0	6	0	0	0	0
615	TOTALS	4114		-4114	4114	4114	-129

NOTES

1. Payment delays by distributors are assumed to average six months.

7 OCT 2002   FilmProfit™
LN   Film Project   Wild Card
Detail Report   Producer's Gross Profit

		Interest-Bearing Advances/Loans	Other	Total
701	Presales/Grants		250	250
702	Post-Release Direct Sales		0	0
703	Total Distributor Revenue	28284		
	—less—			
704	Gross Participations	-849		
705	Total Distribution Fees	-11244		
706	Total Domestic P & A	-11000		
707	Producer's Gross	5191		
	—less—			
708	Repayment of Advances/Loans	-500		
709	Production Overhead Charge	-75		
710	Interest on Advances/Loans	-502		
711	Distributor Payment to Producer	4114		4114

712	Subtotal	4364
	Remaining Production Negative Cost as funded by	
713	Presales/Grants	-250
714	Other Funds Needed for Production	-1500
715	Producer's Gross Profit	2614

NOTE

1. Producer's gross profit shown is before: (A) Any net profit participations, (B) any deferments not included in the production negative cost, (C) any distribution expenses paid directly by the producer, (D) any interest on any loans other than Interest-Bearing Advances/Loans, (E) income taxes, or (F) any other expenses or costs incurred by or for the account of the producer.

Appendix B
Resources

The following resources were put together to further assist you as you assemble your business plan. These resources were meticulously researched and selected by the author to appear in this section. The author and publisher of this book, however, do not necessarily endorse any of the entities or organizations listed below. The information presented here is included for your information and reference only. The information appears in no particular order:

TO CONTACT THE AUTHOR:

Gabriel Campisi
Starlight Pictures
1725 S. Rainbow Blvd.
Suite 2 — Box 186
Las Vegas, NV 89102
E-mail: gabe@gabrielcampisi.com
Website: www.gabrielcampisi.com

TO CONTACT THE PEOPLE IN THIS BOOK:

Fred Olen Ray
Retromedia Entertainment
6260 Laurel Canyon Blvd.
Suite 201
North Hollywood, CA 91606
E-mail: olenray@aol.com
Website: www.aipfilm.com

Jeffrey Hardy
Big Horse, Inc.
Media Project Strategists
1067 Market Street, Suite 1020
San Francisco, CA 94103 USA
E-mail: info@bighorse.com
Website: www.bighorse.com

Kevin J. Lindenmuth
Brimstone Productions
7900 State Street
Brighton, MI 48116
E-mail: brimstoneprod@aol.com
Website: www.lindenmuth.com

Ron Ford
Fat Free Films
P.O. Box 56Cusick, WA 99119
E-mail: fordius@aol.com
Website: www.geocities.com/ron_ford_page
(temporary)

Ted V. Mikels
TVM Global Entertainment, Ltd.
3230 W. Hacienda Ave.
Suite 307
Las Vegas, NV 89118
E-mail: tvmstudios@aol.com
Website: www.tedvmikels.com

Ed Hansen
Atomic Hollywood
P.O. Box 661510
Arcadia, CA 91006
E-mail: atomic@loop.com

Philip R. Cable
AAA American Entertainment
415 N. Akers Street

Suite 100
Visalia, CA 93291
E-mail: philipcable@aol.com

David Michael Latt and David Rimawi
The Asylum
6671 Sunset Blvd.
Bldg. 1593
Hollywood, CA 90028
E-mail: asylumthe@aol.com
Website: www.theasylum.cc

Mark Pacella
Ace Storyboards on Demand
E-mail: mark@markpacella.com
Website: www.acestoryboards.com

ENTERTAINMENT AND FINANCE ATTORNEYS:

The attorneys listed here are at the top of their field and should be able to assist you in just about any capacity related to film investments and legal issues.

Loeb & Loeb Entertainment
  Law Attorneys
This firm has multiple addresses:
10100 Santa Monica Boulevard
Suite 2200
Los Angeles, CA 90067-4164
Phone: 310-282-2000Fax: 310-282-2200

1000 Wilshire Boulevard
Suite 1800
Los Angeles, CA 90017-2475
Phone: 213-688-3400Fax: 213-688-3460

345 Park Avenue
New York, NY 10154-0037
Phone: 212-407-4000
Fax: 212-407-4990

1906 Acklen Avenue
Nashville, TN 37212-3740
Phone: 615-749-8300
Fax: 615-749-8308
E-mail: info@www.loeb.com
Website: www.loeb.com

Rutter Hobbs & Davidoff, Incorporated
1900 Avenue of the Stars, Suite 2700
Los Angeles, California 90067-4301
Phone: 310-286-1700
Fax: 310-286-1728
E-mail: info@rutterhobbs.com
Website: www.rutterhobbs.com

Gibson, Dunn & Crutcher, LLP
This firm has multiple addresses:
333 South Grand Avenue
Los Angeles, CA 90071-3197
Phone: 213-229-7000
Fax: 213-229-7520

2029 Century Park East
Los Angeles, CA 90067-3026
Phone: 310-552-8500
Fax: 310-551-8741
E-mail: info@gdclaw.com
Website: www.gdclaw.com

Also has offices in New York; Washington, D.C.; Dallas; Denver; San Francisco; Palo Alto; Orange County; Paris; London; and Munich.

Baker & Hostetler
This firm has multiple addresses:
333 South Grand Avenue, Suite 1800
Los Angeles, CA 90071-1523
Phone: 213-975-1600
Fax: 213-975-1740
600 Anton Boulevard, Suite 650
Costa Mesa, CA 92626-7221

Phone: 714-754-6600
Fax: 714-754-6611
E-mail: info@bakerlaw.com
Website: www.bakerlaw.com
Also has offices in Cincinnati; Cleveland; Columbus; Denver; Houston; New York; Orlando; Washington, D.C.; with affiliates in Juarez, Mexico and Sao Paulo, Brazil.

GOVERNMENT:

Small Business Administration (SBA)
Headquarters Office
409 Third Street, SW
Washington, DC 20416
Phone: 1-800-U-ASK-SBA
E-mail: answerdesk@sba.gov
Website: www.sba.gov

The Federal Securities and Exchange Commission (SEC)
There are twelve offices located across the country. Contact the headquarters below for the office nearest you.
SEC Headquarters
450 Fifth Street, NW
Washington, DC 20549
Phone: 202-942-7040
E-mail: help@sec.gov
Website: www.sec.gov

BUSINESS STRUCTURE ASSISTANCE:

Bizfilings
8025 Excelsior Drive
Suite 200
Madison, WI 53717
Phone: 1-800-981-7183 or 608-827-5300
Fax: 608-827-5501
Email: info@bizfilings.com
Website: www.bizfilings.com

My Corporation Business Services, Inc.
30141 Agoura Road
Suite 205

Agoura Hills, California 91301
Phone: 1-888-692-6771 or 818-879-9079
Fax: 818-879-8005
customersupport@mycorporation.com
Website: www.mycorporation.com

FindLaw
2440 W El Camino Real Third Floor
Mountain View, CA 94040
Phone: 650-210-1900Fax: 650-210-1996
E-mail: bizdev@findlaw.com
Website: www.findlaw.com

MOTION PICTURE DATA:

Independent Feature Project (IFP)
The Source for Independent Filmmakers
This firm has multiple addresses:
Dawn Hudson, Executive Director
8750 Wilshire Boulevard, Second Floor
Beverly Hills, CA. 90211
Phone: 310-432-1200
Fax: 310-432-1203

Michelle Byrd, Executive Director
104 West 29th Street, 12th Floor
New York, NY 10001-5310
Phone: 212-465-8200
Fax: 212-465-8525
E-mail: info@ifp.org
Website: www.ifp.org
Also has offices in Chicago, Miami, Minneapolis — St. Paul and Seattle.

The Association of Independent Video and Filmmakers (AIVF)
304 Hudson Street, 6th Floor
New York, NY 10013
Phone: 212-807-1400
Fax: 212-463-8519
E-mail: *info@aivf.org*
Website: *www.aivf.org*

American Film Institute (AFI)
This firm has multiple addresses:
2021 North Western Avenue
Los Angeles, CA 90027
Phone: 323-856-7600
Fax: 323-467-4578

The John F. Kennedy Center for the Performing Arts
Washington, D.C. 20566
Phone: 202-833-2348
Fax: 202-659-1970
E-mail: *info@afi.com*
Website: *www.afi.com*

American Film Market (AFM)
12242 Wilshire Blvd.

VENTURE CAPITAL FIRMS:

Second Venture Corporation
3 Truman Ct, Suite 100
Norwalk, CT 06854
Phone: 413-622-0077
E-mail: *info@fundingpost.com*
Website: *www.fundingpost.com*

National Venture Capital Association (NVCA)
1655 North Fort Myer Drive Suite 850
Arlington, VA 22209
Phone: 703-524-2549

MAGAZINES & PUBLICATIONS:

MovieMaker Magazine
2265 Westwood Blvd.
Suite 479

Los Angeles, CA 90025
Phone: 310-446-1000
Fax: 310-446-1600
E-mail: *www.afma.com*
Website: *info@afma.com*

Academy of Motion Picture Arts and Sciences (AMPAS)
Academy of Motion Picture Arts and Sciences Academy Foundation
8949 Wilshire Boulevard
Beverly Hills, California 90211
Phone: 310-247-3000
Fax: 310-859-9351
E-mail: *ampas@oscars.org*
Website: *www.oscars.org*

Movie Magic Software
Entertainment Partners
2835 N. Naomi Street
Burbank, CA 91504
Phone: 818-955-6299
Fax: 818-845-6507
E-mail: *csupport@entertainment partners.com*
Website: *www.entertainmentpartners.com*

Fax:703-524-3940
E-mail: *lturner@nvca.org*
Website: *www.nvca.org*

vFinance, Inc.
World Headquarters
3010 North Military Trail Suite 300
Boca Raton, FL 33431
Phone: 561-981-1017
E-mail: *info@vfinance.com*
Website: *www.vfinance.com*

Los Angeles, CA 90064
Phone: 310-234-9234
Fax: 310-234-9293

E-mail: info@moviemaker.com
Website: www.moviemaker.com
Filmmaker Magazine
501 Fifth Avenue
Suite 1714
New York, NY 10017
Phone: 212-983-3150
Fax: 212-973-0318
E-mail: info@filmmakermagazine.com
Website: www.filmmakermagazine.com
The Independent Film and Video Monthly
c/o AIVF304 Hudson Street, 6th Floor
New York, NY 10013
Phone: 212-807-1400
Fax: 212-463-8519
E-mail: info@aivf.org
Website: www.aivf.org

Hollywood Reporter
5055 Wilshire Blvd.
Los Angeles, CA 90036-4396
Phone: 323-525-2000
Fax: 323-525-2377
E-mail: info@hollywoodreporter.com
Website: www.hollywoodreporter.com

Daily Variety Magazine
5700 Wilshire Blvd.

Suite 120
Los Angeles, CA 90036
Phone: 323-857-6600
Fax: 323-932-0393
E-mail: varietycomments@reedbusiness.com
Website: www.variety.com

Hollywood Creative Directory
IFILM Publishing
1024 N. Orange Dr.
Hollywood, CA 90038
E-mail: hcdcustomerservice@ifilm.com
Website: www.hcdonline.com

Video Business
This firm has multiple addresses:
5700 Wilshire Blvd. Suite 120
Los Angeles, CA 90036-5804
Phone: 323-857-6600
Fax: 323-965-2419

360 Park Avenue South
New York, NY 10010
Phone: 646-746-6692
Fax: 646-746-6959
E-mail: info@reedbusiness.com
Website: www.videobusiness.com

WEBSITE MISCELLANEOUS:

Business Nation
www.businessnation.com

Entrepreneur: Solutions for Growing Businesses
www.entrepreneur.com

IndieFilms
www.indiefilms.com

The Industry
www.theindustry.la

IndieClub
www.indieclub.com

Yahoo Box Office Reports
dir.yahoo.com/entertainment/movies_and_film/box_office_reports

The Numbers: Box Office Data
www.the-numbers.com

RECOMMENDED READING:

You should be able to find these publications at most mainstream book stores and Internet booksellers such as barnesandnoble.com and amazon.com:

Bagley, Constance E., and Craig E. Dauchy. The Entrepreneur's Guide to Business Law. 2d edition. Howard W. Sams, 2002.

Bartlett, Joseph W., and Peter Economy. *Raising Capital for Dummies.* For Dummies, 2002.

Cones, John W. *43 Ways to Finance Your Feature Film: A Comprehensive Analysis of Film Finance.* Updated edition. Southern Illinois University Press, 1998.

Crouch, Holmes F. *Profits, Taxes, and LLCs.* All Year Tax Guides, 2002.

Daniels, Bill, David Leedy and Steven D. Sills. *Movie Money: Understanding Hollywood's (Creative) Accounting Practices.* Silman-James, 1998.

Dealmaking in the Film and Television Industry: From Negotiations through Final Contracts. 2nd edition, expanded and updated. Silman-James, 2002.

Drucker, Peter F. *Concept of the Corporation.* Reprint edition. Transaction, 2001.

Erickson, Gunnar; Mark Halloran and Harris Tulchin. *The Independent Film Producer's Survival Guide: A Business and Legal SourceBook.* Schirmer, 2002.

Garon, Jon M. *The Independent Filmmaker's Law and Business Guide: Financing, Shooting and Distributing Independent and Digital Films.* Chicago Review, 2000.

Gladstone, David, and Laura Gladstone. *Venture Capital Handbook: An Entrepreneur's Guide to Raising Venture Capital. Revised and Updated Edition.* Prentice Hall, 2001.

Hamilton, Robert W. *Cases and Materials on Corporations, Including Partnerships and Limited Liability Companies.* West Wadsworth, 2003.

Landau, Camille and Tiare White. *What They Don't Teach You at Film School: 161 Strategies for Making Your Own Movie No Matter What.* Hyperion, 2000.

Lee, John J. *Producer's Business Handbook.* Focal, 2000.

Levy, Frederick. *Hollywood 101: The Film Industry.* Renaissance, 2000.

Litwak, Mark. *Contracts for the Film and Television Industry: 62 Useful Contracts for Producers That Cover All Areas of Film and Television Production.* 2d expanded edition. Silman-James, 1999.

Merritt, Greg. *Film Production: The Complete Uncensored Guide to Filmmaking.* Lone Eagle, 1998.

Moore, Schuyler M. *The Biz: The Basic Business, Legal, and Financial Aspects of the Film Industry.* Silman-Jones, 2003.

Peacock, Richard Beck. *The Art of Movie Making: Script to Screen.* Prentice Hall, 2000.

Sitarz, Daniel and Dan Sitarz. *Small Business Accounting Simplified.* 3rd edition. Nova, 2002.

Weise, Michael. *The Independent Film and Videomaker's Guide.* 2d edition. Michael Weise Productions, 1998.